"Tosh Berman's sweet and affecting memoir provides an intimate glimpse of his father, Wallace, and the exciting, seat-of-the-pants LA art scene of the 1960s, and it also speaks to the hearts of current and former lonely teenagers everywhere." —**Luc Sante**, author of *The Other Paris*

"This book is like a fascinating series of autobiographical post-cards that could be subtitled *Growing Up Semina*. As the son of artist Wallace Berman, Tosh presents fly-on-the-wall impressions of his parents' coterie in the '60s and '70s—a grouping that included such luminaries as Dennis Hopper, Brian Jones, Toni Basil, and Andy Warhol. His memoir give us a glimpse into the 'other' Los Angeles—a bohemia that thrived in the '60s and '70s in numerous enclaves such as Topanga Canyon, Venice Beach, and West Hollywood. This is the story of a kid growing up inside of art world history, retelling his upbringing warts and all. A well-written, fast-moving book that is candid, funny, often disturbing, and never dull." —**Gillian McCain**, co-author of *Please Kill Me: The Uncensored Oral History of Punk*

"As the son of artist Wallace Berman, Tosh Berman had a front row seat for the beat parade of the '50s, and the hippie extravaganza of the '60s. It was an exotic, star-studded childhood, but having groovy parents doesn't insulate one from the challenge of forging one's own identity in the world. Berman's successful effort to do that provides the heart and soul of this movingly candid chronicle of growing up bohemian." —**Kristine McKenna**, co-author of *Room to Dream* by David Lynch

"Through the prism of Tosh Berman, only child, born 1954 to Wallace and Shirley, who personified the wild heart of 20th-century West Coast art, we are offered a truly intimate invitation into a magic world of outliers, visionaries and shooting stars. *TOSH* recounts a life 'lived like a good book on a bookshelf,' a memoir resonant with discovery, passion, music, art, sex, celebrity, ego, desire, and dignity. All told with a son's love for his father, a continuing light into the creative life." —**Thurston Moore**, musician & writer

"This book is sublime: vertiginous, melancholy, highly amusing!" —**Johan Kugelberg**, Boo-Hooray

"One could not wish for a better guide into the subterranean and bohemian worlds of the California art/Beat scene than Tosh Berman, only scion of the great Wallace. Tosh has a sly wit and an informed eye, he is both erudite and neurotic, and often hilarious. *TOSH*, the book, is packed with keen observations and unique anecdotal factoids that could only come from a true insider. It's a must for anyone who cares about California counter-culture and the raggedy-ass drumbeat of the Beat Generation." —**John Taylor**, Duran Duran

"Tosh Berman is one of the most valuable writers, much less people, the earth has upon it. This book is exquisite. I can't think of another word. What it says, how it says it, what it is." —**Dennis Cooper**, author of *The Marbled Swarm*

"I first met Tosh Berman when he was assigned to sit next to me in 5th grade. We rode the Topanga school bus together for many years and even drove with each other to our high school graduation. But the overlap doesn't end there. Our parents frequented many of the same movie theaters, clubs, and galleries. Neither of our mothers drove, either. Both of our families had the celebrities of the day passing through our houses. I witnessed much of what Tosh saw and writes about, and I can say that *TOSH: Growing up in Wallace Berman's World* captures the times, places, and people with accuracy, sensitivity, humor, and, at times, great sadness. This is a beautifully written memoir, and I highly recommend it to those who are interested in the Sixties, Topanga Canyon, the Southern California art scene, and for those who wonder what it might mean to grow up as the son of one of our most acclaimed artists." —**Lisa See**, author of *The Tea Girl of Hummingbird Lane*

"Reading *TOSH*, I felt like I was lying on a couch, completely relaxed and engrossed, while Tosh Berman sat in a chair beside me and told me his amazing life story. And at the end, I was very moved and wanted to cry. The effect that *TOSH*—the book and the man—had on me was that feeling I get when exposed to great art: a mix of sadness and wonder, which seem to be the two faces of the human heart. Wonderment at the beauty around us—the world, its people—and the sadness that nothing lasts, that all must perish. But this is our journey on planet earth: to be brave and feel both things at once, and it's great art, like this book, that reminds us to do so." —**Jonathan Ames**, author of *You Were Never Really Here*

"What compels about Tosh Berman's gorgeously written memoir is the proximity of the quotidian and the familiar to the extraordinary, the shocking even, and the enviably glamorous. He recounts a coming of age in which the unexpected laces the ordinary as surely at it does in *Alice in Wonderland*—only for Tosh, growing up, a cast of artists, nutcases, iconoclasts, stars, and extremists of all kinds provide the distraction and disruption once supplied by the White Rabbit or Cheshire Cat. Add to this his exemplary taste in, and understanding of, a particular pop sensibility—TV, music, Warhol, and comic books. That then heady and head-spinning world, soundtrack to a sentimental education, that was for the young romantics of the mid-twentieth century what clouds and peaks were to those of mid-nineteenth. Brava, Tosh Berman!" —**Michael Bracewell**, writer

"If the first movie your father takes you to as a child is . . . *And God Created Woman*, you can be sure of two things. First, that your father is an extraordinary person. Second, that you are destined to lead an extraordinarily interesting life. Both of these suppositions are made evident in Tosh Berman's vivid and loving memoir, *TOSH: Growing Up in Wallace Berman's World*. What a world!" —**Ron Mael**, Sparks

"Reading *TOSH* is like meeting your idols, one at a time, for a quiet chat. Everyone is disarmed, and it feels like you've been in the same room with them for about ten hours, or so. Dennis Hopper is unconstrained and friendly, Toni Basil is bubbly, and Brian Jones has just stopped by to say hello. Topanga, as a place is remote—filled with pockets of escapism, winding landscapes of tumult and ennui. Tosh's world is both expansive and crystalline, he traces the edges of his world, and Wallace's world. We get to come and go with Tosh as he navigates his place in and around the tangle of the time." —**Soo Kim**, artist, Professor at Otis College of Art and Design

"Sexually giddy, clairvoyant, messianic—Wallace Berman's socially astute photo-collages were vital bread and butter for several generations of artists. The Wallace B bloodline, from which Tosh sprouted, is a verdant gene pool. For artists-readers, *TOSH*, the memoir, is a luscious document of Los Angeles in the last four decades of the 20th century. Every page is filled with juicy history. Such surprises include a teenaged Sammy Davis Jr. sleepover, a pet alligator, Mae West, Allen Ginsberg, and dozens of remarkable side characters. Bask in Tosh Berman's honesty and gentle style. He is a one-of-a-kind gem." —**Benjamin Weissman**, artist & writer

TOSH

Growing Up in Wallace Berman's World

TOSH BERMAN

City Lights Books | San Fransisco

Cover and book design by Linda Ronan

Library of Congress Cataloging-in-Publication Data
Names: Berman, Tosh, 1954- author.
Title: Tosh : growing up in Wallace Berman's world / Tosh Berman.
Description: San Francisco : City Lights Books, [2018]
Identifiers: LCCN 2018046540 (print) | LCCN 2018051961 (ebook) | ISBN
    9780872867642 | ISBN 9780872867604
Subjects: LCSH: Berman, Tosh, 1954- | Authors, American—20th
    century—Biography. | Children of artists—United States--Biography. |
    Berman, Wallace, 1926-1976--Family. | Berman, Wallace, 1926-1976—Friends
    and associates.
Classification: LCC PS3602.E75882 (ebook) | LCC PS3602.E75882 Z46 2018
    (print) | DDC 818/.603 [B] —dc23
LC record available at https://lccn.loc.gov/2018046540

City Lights Books are published at the City Lights Bookstore
261 Columbus Avenue, San Francisco, CA 94133
www.citylights.com

contents

preface
by **Amber Tamblyn**

For as long as I can remember, my parents' Los Angeles apartment has harbored a collection of iconic art. Their home is stuffed with the rusted, burned, patina-patterned works of art from some of the greatest American visual artists of the 20th century. In their office, a variety of wild works cover the walls: the George Herms piece made of mangled white wire, glued to a water-stained plank of wood; the Bruce Conner mélange of black ink prints, popping off the white paper like a bevy of baby Rorschachs; my father's own vibrant assemblages of electrified planets orbiting a blackened, blizzard sky. There are the fine photographs of Dennis Hopper and the fine arts of Dean Stockwell. On the glass book shelves are the books of poetry by Michael McClure and Jack Hirschman's handbound chapbooks. And beneath it all, in a silver frame, a photo of a man sits on a wooden table as if the art above him were thought bubbles. The man has long hair and a long beard and looks straight out at you, his hand placed on a rock with a letter from the Kabbalah emblazoned on its surface. His gaze is gentle, his eyes as soft as a baby's palm. This man is Wallace Berman.

I was very young the first time I ever asked about the man in the silver frame. Who was he? A guru? A hippie? A friend? An artist? A father? A visionary? A revolutionary? It turns out he was all of these things plus one more: a victim of a drunk driver. When I first asked my dad about his friend Wallace, his eyes softened and he made the kind of physical closure one does with a well of untapped pain: He clasped his hands across his chest, crossed his bony dancer legs, and looked down to the floor. "Wallace," he said, "was everything."

To my father, Wallace was a brother. Wallace was a mentor to an entire world in which my father and other artists like him lived. In 1976, at the age of 50, Wallace was killed by a drunk driver in Topanga Canyon, a moment that permanently broke my father's heart. My father once told me the story of the night he ran into Wallace's killer at a local Topanga bar. And while that's a story for my father to tell someday, it bears noting here that he applied what Wallace had taught him that night, in a testament to Wallace's spirit: Cut your enemies down with love.

Wallace was a purveyor of love, a seeker of love, and a maker of love. Love was in his marrow, and poets, filmmakers, painters, and dancers flocked to him. He was the frontman of the era's as-semblage art movement, and his work has been revered, admired, and even copied by some of the most legendary artists of our time.

Of course, next to almost every heterosexual male artist who devotes himself to his work is a damn good woman who keeps the fires lit. Wallace's wife Shirley Berman, a dancer and the subject of many of his pieces, is an incredible woman whose impact on Wallace was huge. If artists lived inside the world that was Wallace Berman, then Shirley was the sun around which he orbited. Shirley, the daughter of a traveling circus dancer, is a beacon of feminism in my view, as are most women who lived through the masculinity of that era. As Tosh writes so beautifully in this book, "At best, women were expected to be the backup in case the male fell apart." These words still ring true for many women today.

One of the most stunning works of art Wallace and Shirley Berman made was their son, Tosh. While reading *Tosh*, I found such a tender kinship to his journey, one that parallels my own in many ways. We were both born and raised in Los Angeles, surrounded by a strong family structure and a similar mixture of eclectics and eccentrics from around the world. Tosh and I grew up around junk artists, Beat poets, and musicians who would some day become rock 'n' roll legends, everyone from Ed Ruscha to Neil Young. Through his father, Tosh was introduced to a world most could only hope to experience, and through my father's connection to that legacy, so too was I.

I have much to thank Wallace and Shirley Berman for, as their mentorship and friendship with my father led to my own mentor and friend, the poet and activist Jack Hirschman. I was fortunate to grow up hearing Jack read his poems many times in my parents' living room, and he became a powerful mentor for me. He inspired and urged me to write, nurturing my poetic and political voice from an early age, even publishing my very first poem when I was 11 years old. My work and life as a poet has run parallel to my work and life as an actress for over two decades, and the former very much informs the latter. I have my dad to thank for my relationship with Jack, who came to us from the world of Wallace Berman. I am forever grateful for that man in the silver frame, even though I never got to meet him.

After you read this compelling, glorious journey of growing up wild, free, and radical amongst some of the most fascinating people in America, you'll be grateful for Wallace too.

A Note
on **Wallace Berman**

February 18, 1926 – February 18, 1976

My father Wallace Berman was an artist. Or, I should say, he *is* an artist; though his body is not here anymore, his art is very much part of this world. He's considered the father of the California art assemblage movement, but he also was one of the first artists to work with a photocopier, specifically a Verifax, which was a wet-chemical-process copy machine for office workers. Wallace got a hold of one and eventually modified it to make art. It became his brush, canvas, and camera all in one. He's also known for his art and literature journal *Semina*, which was handmade, individually numbered and signed, and only given out to friends or people he admired. He was a pioneer of DIY publishing, without a thought of financial profit or concern for the art market. He also never left the medium of sculptures, making works on rock and boulders. He was a charismatic figure in the arts landscape from the 1950s until his early death in 1976. I've never believed it was a coincidence that he's one of the faces on the cover of *Sgt. Pepper's Lonely Hearts Club Band* (1967), or that he appears in the background of Dennis Hopper's *Easy Rider* (1969), or his appearance in Andy Warhol's *Tarzan and Jane Regained . . . Sort Of* (1964). Wallace never gave interviews to the press, nor did he like talking about his art. He did art, and only did art. He was a family man, but that doesn't adequately express who he was. It's my hope that this memoir will reveal not only yours truly, but also the presence of Wallace as a father, the Batman to my Robin, as well as the constant misery and disappointment of him not being here. But we do have his art, and he does live in my book.

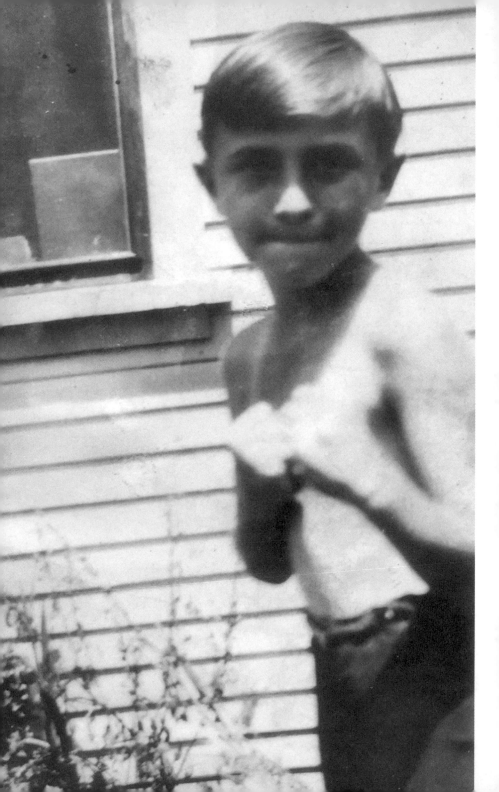

Wallace / chapter 1

My mother, Shirley Morand, first saw her future husband—my father—driving a convertible, with a cat wrapped around his neck, somewhere on the streets of Hollywood. Wallace Berman, at that time, never left the house without his cat. The 19th-century French writer Gérard de Nerval had a pet lobster named "Thibault," and he would take it out for evening walks through Paris, attached to a silk leash. Wallace, in his fashion, was returning to the eminent, artistic, eccentric personalities of 19th- and 20th-century Paris. Without a doubt, he made backward glances to the artists he greatly admired and their peculiar habits. I learned style through both parents, due to their knowledge of such dandies of the past and present, as well as the art and literature that dwell in that world of provocateurs and visionaries. I understood the importance of the past as a reference for the ideal life, and I inherited a passion for artists and poets who didn't belong in the world, who had to invent a landscape in which they could live and do their art. I learned that from Wallace, due to his numerous homages to the artistic set that lived before him.

At the time of my mom's first sighting of Wallace with his cat, he cut quite a striking figure that screamed "Los Angeles dandy."

Wallace Berman as a child

A man who had an understanding of the criminal street life, he knew that the results of such a life had to be fine clothing, which to him meant zoot suits. It was World War Two, the height of the zoot suit craze, and there was, in fact, a law on the books that forbade the zoot suit, owing to the excess fabric in making the outfit; all surplus material was expected to be sent to the government for the war effort. What could attract a criminal-minded youth more than wearing such clothing at the height of war?

My father's family had come from another part of the world. His mother Anna and his grandmother were Russian Jews. They settled in Staten Island, New York, where his father was an owner of a candy store. According to speculation, the store was a front, either for a speakeasy or for bootlegging. My grandfather seemed to have too much money just for owning a neighborhood candy store. In the only picture I've seen of Wallace's father, he's wearing tennis clothes—long white pants, tight white shirt—with a racket in his hand. My mom also told me that she used to own a photograph of Wallace's mother and father in a large car with a chauffeur. When he died, which I think was from the aftereffects of tuberculosis, he only left two books for Wallace, a collection of tales by Oscar Wilde and T.E. Lawrence's *Seven Pillars of Wisdom* (1926). After his death, the family, which by then included Anna's brother Harry, relocated to Boyle Heights, Los Angeles.

At the time, Boyle Heights was a community of Japanese Americans, Latinos, and Jews. Much of the neighborhood's population changed after the 1950s, when the freeways were built. The Berman clan eventually moved to another Jewish neighborhood, in Fairfax, which is very close to Hollywood. Around this time Wallace had a best friend by the name of Sammy Davis, Junior. My grandmother Anna said to me that her heart began to race one morning when she went into Wallace's bedroom and saw Sammy asleep in the bed. At first, she thought Wallace had turned black, but he was sleeping by the bedside on the floor,

WALLACE BERMAN /
Anna Berman, Wallace's mom, 1958, Larkspur

giving Sammy his bed. I remember my dad telling me how he and Sammy went to the Hollywood Palladium on Sunset Boulevard to see Glenn Miller and his big band and weren't allowed to go in because of Sammy's skin color. Wallace never told me how they initially met, but I presume they first laid eyes on each other on Central Avenue, in one of the jazz or dance clubs of the 1940s. They totally lost touch with each other after their teenage years, but right before Wallace died, he saw Sammy at the dentist.

Wallace popped his head into the office and said hello. My dad told me that Sammy—dental tools still in his mouth—nearly perished in the chair. Wallace said a quick "Hello, how are you?" and then got out of there.

During his late teens, in the middle of the '40s, Wallace underwent a series of failures. First, he got kicked out of Fairfax High School for gambling. Then he enlisted and got kicked out of the Navy due to a nervous breakdown. Then he went to Chouinard Art School, and was kicked out of there for reasons unknown. Be they cause or effect of these failures, my father's taste for the outsider's life and distaste for mainstream American life were firmly established. It's been hinted to me that my dad was involved in the criminal world as a teenager, though I've never heard any stories of his actual criminal activity. But he clearly never felt comfortable in the "straight" world. The nine-to-five schedule wasn't for him. He had no problem with people who preferred that life, but for him, there was another world out there that was so much more attractive, the world that existed in the night. The key to that world was, at first, criminal activity, but that led to his beloved pursuits of jazz, poetry, and the visual arts.

Wallace discovered the world of books at the Los Angeles Downtown Library on Fifth Street and Flower. This library was probably where he discovered the poetry of Rimbaud, Baudelaire, and perhaps the early surrealist writers. For sure, he became acquainted with the visual world in the library's art department. At the time, in Los Angeles, there weren't any huge contemporary art collections. So his initial exposure, specifically to art made in the past, came from books. The very first painting that I was conscious of as a child was Henri Fantin-Latour's *Coin de Table* (1872), a portrait of Verlaine and Rimbaud among other poets of their time. My mom and dad had a print of this painting on the wall in our house in Beverly Glen. I looked at this work, not knowing anything, really, except who Rimbaud was—even though, of course, as a child, I never read him. My father taught me his name as soon as I began to form words on my own.

But Wallace also kept an eye on American popular culture. Ever since he was a kid, he had a love for Alex Raymond's comic strip *Flash Gordon*. The comic was published in the newspapers beginning in 1934, the year of my mom's birth. He was fascinated by Raymond's drawings, and the design of the strip inspired him to emulate Raymond's skill, matching it with his love for jazz and surrealist culture. He was also a fan of the *Flash Gordon* film serials that came out of the 1930s, starring Buster Crabbe as Flash. To Wallace, both media were equal, and the serials pretty much followed the pictorial sense of Raymond's vision in the comic strip. My dad later used images from the serials in his film *Aleph* (1966) and in the Verifax collages, and I think for him, *Flash Gordon* followed a natural progression from the comic strip to the big screen to his artwork.

He also appreciated the design and costumes in the *Flash* films; in a way, they were not that different from those of a Diaghilev ballet. Both the *Flash Gordon* serials and the Ballets Russes were highly in tune with my dad's sense of aesthetics, for my dad without a doubt appreciated the art of dance. There are images of the dance world in his artwork, and he loved ballet. Or, I should point out, he loved the *images* of the ballet. I don't recall him ever going to, or showing interest in actually attending, a dance recital. But I was raised with a variety of portraits of Vaslav Nijinsky in the family home. He never commented to me about his love for Nijinsky or the ballet. Many people would have sat you down and talked about why they liked a particular artist or entertainer, but not Wallace. His reasons were in his head, and he often showed his love for these artists in his artwork. I believe he felt that his art alone explained everything.

Wallace was also a huge admirer of Nijinsky's diary, the disjointed writings of a man who lost the plot, but nevertheless left a large shadow of genius on its pages. Nijinsky being part of the Ballets Russes (the company started and controlled by Sergei Diaghilev with the help of Picasso, Erik Satie, and Jean Cocteau, among others) also held a tremendous appeal for Wallace. The dance world is a vast spectacle. For a sharp-minded borderline street thug like my dad, that world must have seemed impossible to attain, but reasonable to imagine. And while he never attended a ballet, Wallace was heavily into swing dancing. It was a portal through which to make progress in another culture, and he was never afraid to step through that entrance to see what was on the other side. One of the many pleasures of big band jazz was the dancing and the whole world within the dance club. Dancing also led to his discovery of numerous musicians who were part of the big bands, and in turn became part of the be-bop movement in jazz. That world never left my father's aesthetic. As much as he took in contemporary music, he never tired of the late '40s to early '60s experimentation in sound, fury, and beauty known as be-bop.

The earliest artwork that exists to my knowledge by "Wally Berman" is the cover for Dial Records' compilation *Be-Bop Jazz* (1947), renowned as the first appearance of Charlie Parker on a 78 rpm recording. It's a highly collectible record on two fronts: one, if you're a Charlie Parker fan, this is the holy grail of his recordings; and two, it was the first appearance of Wallace's artwork for public consumption. The label head, Ross Russell, had a record store in Los Angeles that specialized in be-bop, called Tempo Music, which was located at 5946 Hollywood Boulevard. Besides the Downtown Library, this was the crucial location for Wallace. The record store was devoted exclusively to be-bop, and I imagine every great musician had been through its doors. Due to my father's hanging out at the store, Russell hired him to draw the artwork for the cover. Wallace also went to the original recording session with Charlie Parker on March 28, 1946. He saw Parker as one of the great artists of his time, yet he never conveyed his thoughts on the session, or what it

WALLACE BERMAN /
Untitled (*Be-Bop Jazz* Yellow Cover), 1948

was like to be in the presence of Parker, or his favorite singer at the time, Billie Holiday. He told me that he delivered food or perhaps some pot for her, but I can't remember which. Perhaps both?

The drawing had been made when he was a teenager, but Wallace was 20 when he selected it for the cover of *Be-Bop Jazz*. He also designed the original logo for the Dial label. Jazz has traditionally been an important element in the world of the arts, and Wallace was only one of many who felt its seductive pull. There was just an incredible amount of communication between the visual arts and the music. Around the same time that my dad was hanging out at Tempo Records, Boris Vian in France was in the process of opening the world of American jazz to the French public through his writing and his activity as an A&R man for various French labels. Although they never met, they clearly belong to the same generation of artists and writers who were drawn to jazz. Wallace had one foot in the jazz culture of his time, and the other in the fine arts. The jazz world called out to my father, and he embraced the sounds and culture with open heart and arms.

Loree Foxx / chapter 2

Wallace had had a very prominent girlfriend before my mom, and that was Loree Foxx, a born criminal who stole not only from people she didn't know but also from anyone in her social circle and their families. She snatched objects like people breathe air. It came totally natural to her. Loree saw the world as a playground of thieving fun. She had the ability not to care if she was robbing from the rich or the poor, or even from pals. I have heard from my uncle, who became her boyfriend after Wallace, that Loree would start off her day by looking through fashion magazine ads, marking off each outfit and accessory she wanted. By that evening, her apartment would be filled with the clothing that she desired. Loree also had a knack for finding additional talented people who would allow themselves to become part of her gang of thieves. In her world, she was very much Fagin. Her mother had a thing for circus elephant objects: elephants in or on crystal snowballs, drawings, etchings, that type of stuff. Loree and her gang stole a circus elephant ride for kids that was parked in front of the entrance of a supermarket, and she gave it to her mom as a gift, which was highly unusual, since she never bestowed gifts. A reporter noticed the oversize kiddie ride in her mom's yard and did a story on it. I'm sure Loree left the neighborhood for a moment or two till everything cleared up regarding the elephant ride scandal.

SEMINA TWO

Like my father with his cat, Loree had her version of Nerval's lobster, keeping a pet alligator by her side. The reptile probably made her look like the prototype of a James Bond villain. At night, she would take her alligator out with a leash attached to its mouth and torso. My father agreed to keep an eye on the alligator from time to time when Loree's living space was compromised. He placed the alligator in his mom's bathtub. Anna, my grandmother, would scream whenever she had to use the bathroom. Every time she went in, the alligator made snapping sounds with its jaws, though she was perfectly safe, as long as she didn't join the beast in the bathtub.

Wallace and Loree were the king and queen of the swing dance world in Los Angeles. My uncle Donald told me that my dad and Loree dominated the dance floor. Wallace was very much a zoot-suited jazz obsessive who danced extremely well. This makes perfect sense given his lifelong love for music—why not dance, as well? After Wallace's death, my mom found his dance trophies at Grandma Anna's house. I'm sure they weren't of value to anyone because otherwise Loree would have stolen them and sold them off.

Wallace once played craps with another gambler in some vacant alley, and Loree was right beside him. The other player, who was losing and sore about it, was anxious to check the dice my dad was using. Loree immediately took the dice out of Wallace's hands and threw them away, which, in turn, meant that my father got beaten to a pulp by the other gambler. Sadly, Loree was mistaken about the dice. They were not loaded.

I remember Loree from when I was a child. I remember thinking at the time, "Was she that bad?" She was neither here nor there for me, nor did I pick up on any troublesome vibrations from her. But alas, I think I was just small enough to fly under her radar. Loree was fascinating because she sounded to me like pure evil, yet she was very close to my parents and, of course, my uncle. Oddly enough, as far as I know, Donald only ever had one serious relationship with a woman, and it was with the queen of crime. I grew up in an environment where people were not judged for their weaknesses or faults. I never heard my father say a harsh word towards anyone. There never were any snap judgments, like "So and so is evil," or "So and so is no good," or any view of someone on a subjective level. All were accepted, or not. I hardly ever heard my parents condemn anyone for anything. Loree would break into the homes of her friends to steal without giving a second thought to the morality of it all. It never crossed her mind, or my parents' or their friends'.

Loree once broke into our house in Beverly Glen to steal my mother's passport, but once she found it, she realized it was a family document with my name attached to it, and therefore she couldn't use it for her devilish purposes. When Loree and Donald settled in New York City, my mom visited them and stayed for a whole summer in their apartment. Shirley wrote to her new boyfriend Wallace on a regular basis, and she let Loree mail out the letters for her. Loree opened the correspondence, destroyed it, and wrote her version of the letters to Wallace, signed Shirley. As you might gather, she was, among her many talents, an expert forger. She almost ruined their relationship, but Wallace and Shirley figured out the trouble. Oddly enough, my parents never had a harsh word for Loree. They accepted her fully. She was a criminal and not to be trusted. On the other hand, she was a swell gal.

Nevertheless, Wallace and Shirley did eventually end their friendship with Loree, because they just couldn't trust her in any form or fashion. It wasn't because she stole from them so much as they realized any of their friends could have become a victim of her criminal schemes. This meant my mom's brother also didn't

WALLACE BERMAN /
Loree Foxx, 1955

talk to my parents for a while. Donald and Loree relocated to the desert near Palm Springs, where I presume she robbed all the Palm Springs ladies as much as possible. Their house was a farm, and since Loree had a taste for exotic pets, she had not only the alligator but all sorts of wild birds, as well as two lions. One Christmas, at my grandparents' home in Topanga Canyon, Donald brought one of the lions with him. The doorbell rang, I opened the front door, and this lion jumped upon me. The giant cat had no teeth, but it did pull me around the living room like I was a rag doll.

I was terrified, but the grown-ups around me just watched the action in front of them and were all highly amused.

Unhappily, though perhaps fortunately for some, Loree died in a prison cell in 1972 while having an asthma attack. Throughout her life, Loree suffered from asthma. The guards gave her medicine that she was allergic to, and she died right there on the spot, in her cell. Her niece Suzy, also a friend of my parents (and featured on the cover of *Semina* 2), went to the jail unit to identify the body. She went not out of courtesy, love, or family duty, but out of fear that Loree might be still alive and faking her death. But alas, Loree Foxx, artist, ex-girlfriend to my father and Uncle Donald, and master thief, was sincerely dead.

Shirley / *chapter 3*

My mother is the daughter of Roudolph and Martha Morand. My grandmother, born Martha Jensen, came from Hamburg, Germany. My most vivid memory of her is as a butcher at the Hollywood Ranch Market on Vine Street. It always struck me as a weird occupation for a woman, but there was something very practical about her ability to cut up a side of meat. Of our family, she impressed me as the most hands-on. Way before America and her career as a butcher, she had been a teenage cabaret performer in Hamburg. No wonder I weep whenever I hear Lotte Lenya sing the cabaret theater songs by her husband Kurt Weill and Bertolt Brecht, even though I don't know my grandmother's repertoire. She left the German port town sometime in the 1920s to become part of a traveling circus called 101 Ranch Wild West Show.

Martha's traveling circus took her from Oklahoma to Cuba and then to California, where she quit to escape her first marriage to a cowboy trick rider by the name of Hank Durnell. Durnell was a stunt rider for the famous Tom Mix. Mix is legendary now as one of the first great cowboy movie stars. His horse "Tony" was as famous as he was. Mix and Tony were a big part of the 101 Ranch Wild West Show, which over the years also featured the talents of Buffalo Bill Cody, as well as the great Will Rogers. Martha and Durnell had a child by the name of Marcela, but the marriage ran aground when Durnell's drinking got out of hand. Martha left the circus, and she eventually married Roudolph Morand, better known to his family and friends as "Dodo."

At the time they met, Dodo resembled a young Cary Grant and was an iceman serving customers in the Hollywood area. He supplied ice to Mae West, who once gave him a car. This seems like an excessive gift for an iceman's service, but, as I say, he was quite handsome. As a tot, I knew him to be entirely lovable, but he apparently had a temper and a touch of cruelty. For me, he was the perfect grandfather. When I knew him, he kept odd hours because he was a security guard for Howard Hughes's plane. Since he worked the nightshift, he saw Hughes many times. Howard was very responsive to my grandfather. Dodo watched over the H-4 Hercules, better known as *The Spruce Goose*, which was Hughes's huge plane made of birch wood. Commissioned by the government in 1942 during the Second World War, the plane was a failure, even though Hughes worked on it obsessively and went way over budget and time; he was still struggling with it up to 1947, well after the war's end. Hughes kept the plane in a giant hangar until his death in 1976. My granddad once told me he was in the hangar in the middle of the night when Hughes came in unannounced. He wanted to fire up the plane to see how it was running. Hughes asked my grandfather to go to the right wing to see if the engine was working properly. The wingspan is 320 feet long. Once Dodo reached the precise spot, he signaled Hughes to start the motor. Instead of turning on the right side engine, he turned on the left. My grandfather told me that this was typical of Hughes's sense of humor.

I have an early memory of my mom's parents living very close to the Chinese Theater on Hollywood Boulevard. They eventually moved to Topanga and lived in the Fernwood section of that haunted canyon. Like our house on Crater Lane in Beverly Glen, their house was a shack, but still a very comfortable two-story cabin with a newly built swimming pool and bar. I loved playing

Martha, Tosh's maternal
grandmother

in the wet bar area, because it seemed so grown up, and there was something aesthetically pleasing about having an outdoor bar with stools and water faucets. I never saw a water faucet in a backyard before, so to me, that was a complete novelty. Also, the whole area smelled like a forest. A lot of trees brought a fresh scent as the year went on, and their house was a perfect location for Christmas Day and family gatherings. I was never big on nature unless it was a controlled environment. But having a bar, three or four bar stools, and a swimming pool seemed to me like a divine version of nature.

Wallace would often play an extended version of gin rummy with Martha, who like my father had a great love for card games. Also like my dad, she was a very experienced player and quite competitive. Her manner in the game was serious, even when she played with me. My grandmother had a determined look on her face whenever she was playing, and when she won (which was often), she would give a charming, brief smile all of a sudden. Martha played to win, and not to pass the time. She and Wallace got along extremely well. Famously, there's supposed to be tension between the son-in-law and the wife's parents, but I never heard or saw any bad vibes between Wallace and my mother's parents. Like my parents and my uncle, they were totally accepting of almost any social group, and very undemanding but supportive people.

My mom went to Hollywood High School with David Nelson of *Ozzie & Harriet*, the big brother of Ricky, and with Carol Burnett. Shirley and Uncle Don were truly part of the romantic Hollywood neighborhood years. Somewhere on their block lived the Robert Mitchum family with its various kids. There were plenty of children in her community, and in some ways, it must have been like a 1940s Hollywood family film. Unlike in the movies, however, my grandfather checked out of the household to live with another woman. He eventually came back to the family, after being with a pair of women (separately, as far as I know) named Virginia and Georgia. When he reappeared, my uncle asked if he'd run out of states.

As a child, until she was a teenager, my mom was interested in expressing herself through dance. She studied ballet under Michel Panaieff, who was the principal dancer for the Belgrade Opera and a member of the original Ballets Russes. He eventually settled in Los Angeles during the Second World War. Panaieff opened a dance studio in Hollywood, where my mother, through a large window facing Hollywood Boulevard, saw the first two major loves in her life. One was a boy name Fergie, who saw her dancing through the front window, and the second, some time after Fergie, was my dad, looking through that same window. Eventually, she landed on her foot the wrong way, which caused permanent damage to her ankle. She could walk easily but couldn't dance anymore. The injury was a major disappointment, and it seems to have been a goodbye to having a creative life under her name. I don't believe she had a Plan B, and the marriage angle was a natural progression to exiting the family home.

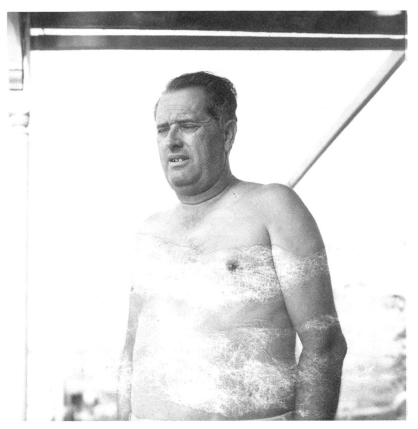

Roudoulph Morand ("Dodo"), Tosh's maternal grandfather

I can't speak for Fergie because I never met him, but Wallace—although very gentle, and even an artistic genius (as he was in life, as well)—was very much an American male of that era. He required a woman who would support his one-way route to art-life and not put restrictions on his time and his need for attention. If I'd been her, I wouldn't have married him, which might seem to be an odd thing for the offspring of that relationship to say. But the women of that era had a bad deal in terms of gender equality. It was almost an act of cruelty in that one could see a window of opportunity opening up for them. But the counterculture itself was no better than the previous generation. At best, women were expected to be the backup in case the male fell apart. In the world of the beats, if you were a woman, and not an artist or writer, you tended to be treated as an individual who supported the male author/artist. You were supposed to keep the home intact, as well as clean up after the artist, and cook the meals. And, God forbid, if you had a child, you pretty much had to take care of that as well, due to the artist or writer spending long hours in the studio focusing on his art, and preoccupied with the thought of the female as Muse. Every artist needed one to encourage the work. Of course, it was the worst kind of horseshit, because it was a power play; it gave the female credit for something she didn't do and therefore served as a safe ground culturally to both praise and condemn the woman. But if the work didn't happen, whose fault was it? The Muse's?

As a child, I never picked up on any of this, but as an adult, I can now clearly see the horror that was the hippie and beat dream, which was geared towards the male. There were more opportunities for those who knew how to carry out the hustle. In the scene in those days, there were basically two types of women. There were wild ones like Loree, who embraced the criminal life, and who were chemically/naturally insane. Then there was my mom: sweet, obviously smart, terrific instincts in supporting a family, and, without a doubt, one of the most beautiful women at that time. Lucky for me, she was the greatest mother. I lived like a good book on a bookshelf. On one end was my mom and the other was my father, both holding me in place between their loving arms.

But being married to Wallace wasn't easy. For instance, my mother had been keeping a diary, and Wallace made her stop. My dad was either afraid how he would turn out or that his private life would be exposed, but I can't imagine how cruel that is, to stop my mom from keeping a journal. The proper husband should always support the wife doing whatever she wants to do. Surely one would think that "love" could only go so far. But I believe that it was very clear that Wallace wanted to be the househusband, working on the artwork and taking care of my basic needs, while his wife got a salary of some sort—in other words, very much the street mentality of a hustler and pimp.

It pains me that my mom wasn't allowed to keep a journal of the years she spent with my dad. Not simply because he's a known artist, but because there's very little literature from the beat era from a female point of view. Carolyn Cassady wrote a book about her relationship with Jack Kerouac and Neal Cassady, and there's Diana di Prima's memoir of being a writer during that era, but there aren't a lot of books from those crucial countercultural years written by women. To this day, I can never forgive Wallace for not allowing my mom to keep up her journal.

But though it was a selfish act on his part, I think he believed he was doing what was right for his wife and son. The gray areas where one lives were important for Wallace. I don't think it was intellectual, but more of an emotional response to how he saw the world between his life and the life outside his environment. Looking back, I often wonder why Wallace had such a desire to maintain his privacy. I suspect he had a profound distrust of the outside world. Somewhere down the path to becoming an artist, he'd had to reject parts of the straight world that he couldn't see eye-to-eye with, and the post-war years in America were harsh for that particular type of individual. Someone like my dad, who felt very much part of the black American underworld of jazz and street culture, just couldn't accept the mainstream. I suspect he felt that the straight world was out to destroy him and his chosen lifestyle. But this was the code that my father belonged to, and it wasn't like he had other choices in his life. He couldn't do anything else except be Wallace Berman: brilliant, iconic, magnetic, and a pain in the butt. In theory, genius is great, but God forbid anyone has to share the artist's world, because it is often frustrating for one who isn't allowed to get off the ride.

My mom is likely the most captivating person I know. She is perceived as deadly quiet, but she witnessed the most enchanting aspects of midcentury bohemian culture. Like Wallace, she attracted attention, obviously because of her looks, but also due to her aura; she has that "it" quality that you can't learn or acquire. You have to be born with "it," and that's very much part of Shirley's character as well. My parents didn't learn to be who they are; they simply were born with unique characteristics, almost like royalty. If Wallace had the knack to choose the right place and time, so did my mom, in her own fashion. Both were quiet. My mom was even more reserved, but like my dad, she has great instincts, and I would never doubt her opinion or position on something. She tends to react emotionally, which I think is good. Ten minutes later, she allows the emotion to pass, and then usually gives great advice. Wallace was also a man of emotional torrents. There was a quietness about him, but he never was shy in conveying an opinion, and he had a way of looking at something, whether it was mere entertainment or a serious work of art, that separated the bullshit from the package designed to make the shit not smell. Both of my parents were very honest.

By the end of the '50s, my mom had become an iconic figure and a muse of sorts, not only for my father, but also for photographers such as the very heterosexual Charles Brittin, and the very homosexual Edmund Teske. The ironic thing is, she doesn't like to have her picture taken. Wallace for sure hated to be photographed by someone else, but Shirley's attitude to the camera is that it's a machine that is bumping into her intimate space, and therefore her stance is one of not caring how or by whom or why the photo is made. Probably the most iconic image of my mom is the cover for *Semina* 4. She stares right into the

WALLACE BERMAN /
Shirley Berman, Beverly Glen, 1959

camera with a mixture of anger, defiance, and not giving a fuck. All three attitudes at the same time in front of a camera are very attractive, hence the portrait's iconic status. She told me many years later she was suffering from a migraine when that photo was taken. My dad took it, of course, and he should get some of the credit, but I feel it is my mom's personality that makes her such a great subject as a model for her three photographers. She's beautiful, but it's not her beauty alone that carries the image. Her attitude is part of the package, and it is quite remarkable even in this day and age to see someone so cool and willing to take the circumstances with that stance.

My mother was 19 when she gave birth to me. My father was 28, almost a decade older. This is a huge age difference between an adult who'd been around the block a few times and a teenager who was getting over her disappointment due to the end of her dancing career. For a man, marrying a very young wife is perhaps less of a risk than marrying someone the same age, who knows the bullshit of life. Shirley was just a teenager and her options restricted by the partnership of society and married life. She met my dad shortly after the cat-around-the-neck sighting. It made quite an impression on her. She must have been fated to meet Wallace face to face. Jean Cocteau's *Blood of a Poet* (1930) was the attraction that led both of them to stand in line at the Coronet Theater. My uncle escorted my mom to the film, and he introduced her to Wallace, who was a regular customer at the Coronet Theater film series.

In the early 1950s, the Coronet Theater was showing "underground" or, more accurately, "art" films. Wallace must have taken it as a good sign to meet the very young Shirley Morand at what was a vital art house theater. The Coronet was the kind of place that screened experimental films with D.W. Griffith in attendance. Hollywood always was and still is in a certain sense a classless society, due the ability of people to make up their individual identities there. Concerning cinema, there has historically been a bridge between the experimental film and mainstream Hollywood. Many filmmakers had their start in underground cinema, then eventually began to make narratives for a wider audience. Cinemagoers are people who want to explore the world via the inside of the movie theater, and most, if not all, like to travel without a passport between the two film cultures. With this in mind, the Coronet seems like a perfect spot for two people to come together and eventually alter the world, through Wallace's art and, I would argue quite passionately, my birth on this planet, as well.

Uncle Donald discovered my dad through curiosity about the world outside family life. Drawn towards figures who participated in the nightlife, Don obviously would have to be in contact with Wallace, who by all accounts was the main conduit between the art world and the street life of narcotics, jazz music, and swing dancing. By the time of their meeting, my father had had enough of the hustle of the gambling world and was looking forward to the life of an aesthete. He required a partner in crime who totally supported his quest for all things that were compelling in the world. Everyone agreed that Wallace finding Shirley was a magnificent thing.

WALLACE BERMAN /
Fuck Nationalism, 1950s

Tosh / chapter 4

My grandmother Anna got the house and property at 1548 Crater Lane in Beverly Glen—a canyon area between Coldwater on the Valley side, and Sunset Boulevard on the other side—through a subscription to a magazine. The house was an additional gift if one subscribed to that particular publication. Eventually, she just signed the house over to my mom, because Wallace refused to have anything in his name. The only legitimate card he had with his name on it, just because he couldn't get around it, was his driver's license—but beyond that, nothing. My dad tried to remain invisible. One would think he was on the run from the law, but I don't believe that was the case.

Wallace did not like to participate in the world unless he chose to. He never voted, either; his politics were more left than anything else, but I think if he hadn't been killed, he would have become a social libertarian. In a work Wallace once made, he wrote "FUCK NATIONALISM." That pretty much expressed his genuine political desire. Wallace was a man not happy to be contained by either borders or laws. I was never encouraged to participate in society, because he himself had no interest in it. Wallace craved anonymity like it was air. If he could have disappeared at will, he would have done so. My dad always had an enduring respect for someone like Houdini, the "escape artist," who fled from chains and jail cells. As a child, he saw Houdini newsreels and I'm sure they had a strong hold on him. And though I wasn't aware of it as a child, Wallace made the role of being an artist into a performance of some sort.

I was born on Wednesday, August 25, 1954, around 12:10 a.m. It was a hot, stinky, sweaty night, the type of weather I hate with an intense passion. My mother must have hated it even more. I read somewhere that giving birth is painful, but afterward one forgets about the pain. The world my parents provided for me was not too bad at all. From the moment I was born until now, I've lived the life of a pampered prince. I share my date of birth with Elvis Costello, who I like to imagine was born at the exact same time I was. I often examine his image on the Internet to compare my aging to his. I also share my birthday with Sean Connery, British novelist Martin Amis, Richard Greene (who starred in the British TV show *The Adventures of Robin Hood* [1955–59], a show of great importance to me in childhood), Tim Burton, Ivan the Terrible (who I only know through the Eisenstein film), Van Johnson, Ruby Keeler (of *42nd Street* [1933]), Leonard Bernstein (whose *West Side Story* [1961] had a profound effect on me), Yasuzo Masumura (who's my favorite Japanese film director), and Ludwig II (who had great taste in interior design).

To be born is genuinely an amazing thing, even though birth happens constantly. I've always felt honored to be a member of the Berman/Morand family, if not the larger collective known as the human race. I learned all my social skills from my parents. I didn't have that many close childhood friends. I did play games with others, but I never felt close to my fellow tots. I am an only child, and I am very comfortable in my skin, as well as being by myself. The only intimate friends I had were objects, which have a great importance for me. I remember as a baby being more interested in the packaging of the toy than the toy itself. My mother has told me that she and Wallace would buy gifts for me, and I would always spend more time with the box the gift came in than the gift itself. I got bored with objects that were manufactured specifically for one thing. So a box or even gift wrapping became more appealing to me. A box, for instance, could be a secret hideout or an additional room in the house. I always liked the world under the table, the chair, or in the box, because I am highly sensitive to a restricted space. It is something that pleases me greatly, as well as being incredibly scary under certain circumstances. As a baby or small child, the restricted area gave me a certain amount of comfort.

The name "Tosh" is from "Antosha." It's a Russian male name. Wallace, during his brief stint in the Navy, met an Antosha, my only knowledge of whom is that he was a huge jazz fan or music collector. He had a record shop in the San Francisco Bay Area that just focused on jazz. I've asked my mom about him. She never met him, but her understanding is that Wallace felt very close to him. I'm not sure if my dad met him in the Navy proper, or if Antosha was in the hospital Wallace was sent to after having a nervous breakdown. This breakdown was caused by the daily naval exercise of blowing up schools of dolphins. It seems dolphins read on the radar as possible enemy submarines, so when in doubt, blow them up. Wallace couldn't handle this daily slaughter. I was named after Antosha, but my legal name as it appears on my birth certificate is simply Tosh.

My first memory ever is seeing a bloody face outside my bedroom window staring at me. The memory of that horrific image takes place at the Beverly Glen house. Not only was this my first home, but we came back here after living in San Francisco. As a baby and a child, I felt like all roads led to our home. It seemed to me, even as a child, that our house was the scene of a nonstop party that lasted from one Saturday night to the next. I have very little memory of the family being there alone. It seems to me someone else was always in that house.

The night I saw the bloody face, a party was taking place in the living room. I was in a crib facing the window, which was near the backdoor entrance and exit from the living room. Ramblin' Jack Elliott seemed to have wandered out of the party, tripped by my bedroom window, and helped himself up by grasping the window ledge. All innocent enough, but for a baby seeing such a sight as a drunk man with blood on his face, it was a bit much. The fact that this is my earliest memory doesn't say a lot for my fragile psyche. I must have been somewhere between six months and a year old, and the horror of that moment is tattooed in my DNA.

I've never officially met Jack, but he's clearly the first monster in my life. I remember once my mom told me that when she was five, my uncle Donald would tease her that someone was outside the window looking in. There was a curtain covering the window, and as my uncle was cruelly reciting all of this, he threw open the curtain, only to expose a face looking inside the room from the second-floor windowsill. It was apparently a burglar, who was surprised by my uncle's sudden removal of the curtain. Donald fainted, my mom screamed, and the robber fell off the windowsill.

Our small house on Crater Lane had its share of visitors, living and breathing ones as well as spiritual ones. My mother told me that she had a loom in the living room; once in the middle of the night, she heard the sound of the loom weaving yarn. When she woke up, she noticed a pattern designed on the yarn on the loom where there hadn't been one before. That morning my parents moved the loom to the storage room underneath the house. Also, I remember guests at our home commenting during one party that they saw an old woman sitting in a rocking chair in our yard outside. According to my parents, they didn't know this lady, nor had they ever seen her on the premises. The house for sure had a vibe, but I always thought it was my over-the-top imagination that brought out the creepy stuff in our home. Maybe it was, but still, one can never know what happened on the land at Crater Lane.

Although I never witnessed it, there were stories of a spirit or two haunting our local eatery, Four Oaks, up the street from

WALLACE BERMAN /
Anna & Tosh Berman, 1955

Crater Lane on Beverly Glen Boulevard. A headless ghost with a yellow cape had reportedly been seen around the restaurant; according to legend, he had been murdered by a jealous husband after being caught in bed with the man's wife. Another ghost was also visible in Four Oaks, who, unlike the headless gentleman, seemed cruel and threatening. It's been suggested that perhaps he's the husband who committed the murder of the headless man with the yellow cape. Many people, mostly women, have pointed out that the headless ghost was a comforting spirit. Some women in the Glen have commented that the spirit's presence could be felt in their beds. The other ghost who was stuck in the Four Oaks structure was mean-spirited and destructive; once, a small fire started in the restaurant kitchen, and no one could figure out how else the blaze could have gotten started, except by the ghost.

There was another story about a friend of my parents bringing along an additional guest (everyone brought an additional guest to our house) whom he had just met for the first time at a nearby bus stop. This particular guest had an abnormal speech pattern; he mostly spoke in Middle English. It was like he was dropped on this planet in the wrong year, expecting the 15th century instead of 1950s Beverly Glen. (Maybe he got the 5s mixed up?) As the evening wore on, the company began to suspect that he was an alien visiting us.

Nevertheless, my parents found him perfectly charming, as he was amazed at the function of a corkscrew and other earthly objects. In the early hours of the morning, my parents' friend dropped him off at a street corner in Westwood but felt guilty right away about leaving him at dawn at a deserted bus stop. He immediately went back to the bus stop, but the mysterious visitor had disappeared. There was no sign of a bus or anyone walking on an early Sunday morning. He looked all over the neighborhood. But the guest had apparently transported himself back to his spaceship to give a detailed report on the advanced technology of the corkscrew and the living habits of the bohemian set. After fifty-some years, there's liable to be a monument to the corkscrew on some hilltop on Mars. Hopefully, in my lifetime, I'll be in a position to visit this memorial.

Beverly Glen / *chapter 5*

Midcentury America is very much my childhood era, but the style of that era had little to do with either my life or my parents'. Early in their marriage, before I was born, Wallace worked in a furniture restoration factory, where he went out of his way to damage perfectly beautiful tables by whipping them, to give them that old, slightly damaged appearance. Wallace made our household furniture, which was quite simple, practical, and I think beautiful. As far as I know he never took another job anywhere. During my lifetime I know he was offered a job at UCLA, but he turned it down because the job was to teach a master's class in photography and he was afraid someone would ask him how to put the film in a camera. My mother used to load his camera for him. Wallace also hinted to me in a very hush-hush tone that he had a second job as a bartender in Topanga Canyon, but I never believed him. I can't imagine him taking orders for beer or wine. It wasn't in his character. On top of that, I rarely saw him leave the house for more than a couple of hours. My understanding is that he didn't have a "feel" for work. He wasn't against it, nor was he for it. It just didn't exist in his world.

Shirley had to cope with bringing in the weekly paycheck by working at various jobs: as a model for illustrated ads for Bullocks Department Store, the sessions for which took place in the beautiful art deco building on Wilshire in the Miracle Mile district,

and as a shop girl at various boutiques in Beverly Hills. My mom pretty much had to bring the bacon home, as well as take care of the dishes and cooking. I remember being excited when she came back from work. Even as a baby, I missed her feminine touch in the household. Also, at a very young age, I was aware of the quality of the food when she was around.

Whenever we had guests, which was all the time in those years in Beverly Glen, she would have to serve the drinks and snacks, and make everyone feel comfortable. In the earliest years of my life, I have no memory of my parents being apart, except during my mom's nine-to-five work schedule. Even with her salary, which wasn't enough for a family of three, my dad had to kick in some dough. I knew he would play cards for food money. He had an innate ability to raise funds out of nowhere when the curtain was about to drop. But throughout my life, except during our time in San Francisco, my parents always owned the homes that they lived in, though strangely enough they never *purchased*

Tosh Berman with Alice from *Alice's Adventures in Wonderland*, 1963,
Beverly Glen

one. Yet my parents owned both of our houses in the Los Angeles area outright, or rather, my mom did. While Wallace craved anonymity, I think for him owning a home was the only way to move forward or have some financial control over his life and the family.

Almost immediately after my parents moved in, the Beverly Glen house became Ground Zero for the L.A. boho lifestyle. To me, at my age, it wasn't exceptional, but I now realize how extraordinary were those who came to visit my parents at this address. The entranceway was a dirt path with poison oak on the side of the hill. I have an active memory of falling into the poison oak and suffering greatly for a night or two. I can still feel the sticky paste of the medicinal cream all over my chest, arms, and legs. The worst part of it was being told by my mom not to touch or scratch my body. Apparently, I learned a form of Zen early on. If one could avoid the oak, which took some skill because it reached

WALLACE BERMAN /
1548 Crater Lane, Beverly Glen, 1956

far into the pathway, then one would reach the front entrance of the house, which went directly into the kitchen. That room was small but long. Next to the kitchen table was a life-size cardboard cutout of Alice from *Alice's Adventures in Wonderland* (1865), as illustrated by John Tenniel.

The front room was a combination of my dad's studio, our living room, and my parents' bedroom. There were no chairs in this room, just a floor-level table made by Wallace where we ate our meals. We had to sit on the floor or the bed, which became a couch during the daytime. The left side of the room was the studio, and my dad had a sturdy workbench that was attached to the wall. We also had a turntable with one large speaker. Records and their sleeves were stacked by the speaker or by the wall underneath the table. My dad had a stool, and that was it.

I had a private room for myself, your basic bedroom, but the bathroom was attached, so anyone who wished to use the single toilet had to go through my room. Also, across from the bathtub, there was a window facing the front entrance that led into the kitchen. If I took a bath at certain times, I might come across a visitor; the window had no curtains. To this day, I keep a very private inner life because I was accustomed to having my living space invaded by others. Living in small quarters with adults, one needs to make up a world that is suitable and invisible.

The house was on stilts facing Beverly Glen Boulevard. I had the feeling of floating above the land. I have no memory of this, but Diane di Prima claimed in her memoir *Recollections of My Life as a Woman* (2001) that she saw my father remove all of the furniture from the living room and put it outside in the yard. He then drilled a hole in the floor and brought in a water hose to wash the floorboards, so that all the water and the dirt ran down the hill. I don't know if this is true, but it does fit my father's character.

CHARLES BRITTIN / *Wallace Berman's "Cross," Ferus Gallery, 1957*

Ferus / chapter 6

I never knew a time when Wallace was not an artist. I still have strong memories of him working on the left side of the living room in Beverly Glen. The smell of parchment paintings is still in my nostrils. I often think of my dad's artworks in more of a textural context than a visual one. The smell of the parchment paintings (painted Hebrew characters) was a mixture of chemicals and glue, much like his later Verifax art. As a two-year-old, I was never told not to touch something, so I remember touching the paintings and feeling the layers of paint and glue over the work itself.

Wallace's workspace in the Beverly Glen House always appeared calm and organized, but not in an obsessive manner. It must have been difficult for him to work, since people came by all the time. The compactness of the house appears to have pleased my mom and dad. All the homes I lived in, except in San Francisco, were tiny; even the Topanga Canyon house, which had a significant amount of property around it, was a small structure. But the Beverly Glen house, in all its glory, was just a shack on stilts.

One of the many people who came to the house was Walter Hopps. I knew Walter all my life, from a distance. He struck me as a nice person, but to a kid, his personality was cold. I never felt any warmth towards him, but I assume he must have shared many things with Wallace. Both had wives named Shirley, for one, and Walter was a jazzer, like my dad. Indeed, as a teenager, he even saw my dad dance in a South Central nightclub and commented that Wallace had a presence from the very beginning. They approached art from the same angle; even though Walter went to school, he was very much a street-smart guy who knew art. Most people at that time who were into art, I think, were either wealthy or very well educated. Walter didn't learn art. He knew it by instinct. Walter was fortunate to hang out with the art collector and former modernist poet Walter Conrad Arensberg, who was a friend as well as a collector of Marcel Duchamp's art. To this day, I don't know if my dad ever met Arensberg, but what he had in common with Walter Hopps was a love of street culture and art. Also Walter had a Clark Kent vibe about him, not just because he wore black-rimmed glasses. There was something very mysterious about his presence, and how he carried himself. Even as a child, I thought he was eccentric and hiding that fact by wearing suits and ties.

Along with the artist Ed Kienholz, Walter started the Ferus Gallery, where Wallace had his first solo gallery show in 1957. It's unclear what exactly happened, but the police were called and informed that the show contained obscene works. The police came by and shut it down. There was a daylong trial, my father was convicted of exhibiting pornography, and he had to serve jail time. Luckily, his good friend Dean Stockwell bailed him out of jail. It seems that Ed and Walter were cheerful enough that they got some sort of publicity, and if my father rotted in a jail cell—then what the hell! The Ferus Gallery would go on to become a major force in Los Angeles art culture, under the direction of Irving Blum, who took over curatorial duties from Ed and Walter and later gave Andy Warhol his first solo exhibition. There's some controversy over whether Wallace was dropped from the gallery when Irving took over, or just left when he was convicted of the obscenity charge. But whatever Irving's intentions, Wallace for sure was not going to do another exhibition at Ferus.

The irony of it all is that there was only one artwork in the exhibition that was very sexually graphic. This was a close-up image of a penis in a vagina and was hard to miss, but somehow the vice squad did. Instead, they chose to bust my father for an image that wasn't by him, but rather by Marjorie Cameron, a drawing that was part of and within his assemblage. Wallace's arrest might have been seen as a joke to some, but he took it very seriously and was deeply offended to be in that position. He was disappointed that mainstream culture would want to incarcerate him. He never mentioned what became of the artwork from that show. Most of it disappeared. Some claim that a worker at the Ferus Gallery, not knowing it was art, threw it away, and some, like me, feel that Walter and Ed knew a lot more about what happened to it. One artwork from the show was later discovered in Walter's personal collection.

Wallace never had any harsh feelings towards Walter or Ed, but I suspect Ed didn't like Wallace. I've heard rumors to the effect that Ed was jealous of a woman's attention to my dad, or perhaps he was simply jealous of Wallace's art, but I do believe Ed himself was the one who called the cops on the show. He probably didn't think Wallace would get arrested; more likely he just wanted to create some publicity, which he did. But due to this experience, Wallace never had another solo commercial gallery exhibition in his lifetime. Wallace soured on the very idea of becoming a "professional" in the art world, and it was at this time he made the decision to move us to San Francisco.

WALLACE BERMAN /
Cameron, 1962

Cameron / chapter 7

The artist behind the "obscene" drawing for which my dad was arrested, Marjorie Cameron—better known to her friends and fans simply as Cameron—might be one of the most fascinating women to emerge in the 20th century, for various reasons. She was married to the rocket scientist Jack Parsons, a principal founder of the Jet Propulsion Laboratory and a well-known occultist, and she became his widow in 1952 when he accidentally blew himself up in his lab at their Pasadena home. My mom told me a bit about him. Without a doubt, he was a wild one. He and Cameron must have been a standout couple in an era when things were hush-hush. Their circle included fellow rocket scientists and various science fiction writers, including L. Ron Hubbard, later founder of Scientology. Some have claimed that Hubbard went through Parsons's trash to come up with the seeds or concept of Scientology. It's clear that from someone's trash, another can find gold if he or she knows what to look for.

Cameron herself was very much a free-spirited individual. She was a witch, yes, but to define her by that one category would be a huge mistake. As a child and as an adult, I never once had a discussion with her about her specific interest in magick, though the occult arts were obviously a subject she had a deep interest in. Cameron, according to my mom, compartmentalized her social life to a certain degree. She first met my dad and mom at her house that she shared with Jack. It was an afternoon party, and Cameron was drawn to Wallace and Shirley because they were the only artists at this specific party. Everyone else was a rocket scientist or in some other science field. Parsons was always friendly to my mom and dad, but it was Cameron who was drawn to my parents, and without her presence, I don't think they would have entered the world of Jack Parsons. My mom has commented to me how handsome Jack was, in the movie star mode of handsomeness. My parents had dinner over at their house, and Shirley mentioned that Jack would make a dramatic entrance into the room. It was more his style than anything else. He knew his presence made an impression on people.

Through Cameron, Wallace and Shirley met actor and raconteur Samson de Brier, who invited them to his Hollywood house to attend his big Halloween party, the theme of which was "Come as Your Madness." My dad dressed up as Alice B. Toklas, Gertrude Stein's better half. That particular party was the inspiration for Kenneth Anger's *Inauguration of the Pleasure Dome* (1954). Cameron played the Scarlet Woman in the film, and Anaïs Nin starred as Astarte, with her head in a birdcage, which I believe was her costume for the original Halloween party. Joan Whitney, a close friend of my parents, played Aphrodite.

Samson was a total mystery to me as a kid, and now he's even more so. Others have commented that his colorful stories about his life may not have been true, but to this day I believe what he said. Very much an iconic fixture in Hollywood, Samson had a house that was full of either treasures or junk, depending on one's point of view. Always flamboyant, Samson, in my memory, was surrounded by women who appeared to have no trouble worshipping him. He was one of those figures that could stand perfectly still, not do anything, and yet attract attention from the right people. My parents were very fond of him, and he also caught the attention of Hollywood stars curious about the other side of

WALLACE BERMAN /
Samson de Brier

life. Everyone from James Dean to Marlon Brando was believed to have spent some time at his pad on Barton Avenue. Anger shot *Inauguration of the Pleasure Dome* there. One presumes that the beautiful decor in that film came courtesy of Samson's impressive collection of costumes and his distinct interior taste.

My parents had no interest in magick or anything to do with religion or religious practices. On the other hand, they knew Cameron quite well. The artwork that got my dad busted for obscenity was a drawing she did for *Semina*. I'm not sure why she didn't get involved in his defense, but I can't imagine Cameron taking the initiative to go to court or even deal with the obscure hold of the law over art. At that time, too, she was still pretty distressed over her husband's death. Cameron was very much a free-spirited person, and I regret that I didn't hang out with her as an adult because she must have been a lot of fun. She never pushed her beliefs on anyone who was not interested, and she had a wide network of friends throughout the world. I've heard that

Cameron was very close to Juliette Gréco, the celebrated French singer. What I am conscious of is that there wasn't a sinister bone in her body, even though as a kid I knew she was a "witch" of some sort. I have to admit she did kind of look like a witch, but she was a cool-looking witch.

Semina / chapter 8

Due to Wallace's friendship with Cameron, some commentators have tried to establish a "magick" connection between them. But while my Dad respected Cameron's interest in the occult world, he had no interest in it. On the other hand, Wallace admired literature that has strains of the metaphysical. The big book in his life at that time was Hermann Hesse's 1927 novel *Steppenwolf*. Hesse was considered a major writer during the '20s, but he lost favor in the succeeding decades. In the 1960s, he would be rediscovered by, and become very popular with, students and the bohemian reading crowd. But in the '50s, he was nearly unknown.

Wallace discovered *Steppenwolf* as a remainder at Pickwick Books on Hollywood Boulevard. After reading it, he bought most of the copies up and gave the book out to friends. When Wallace was a fan of something, he pretty much became a distributor of that work and made sure all his friends picked up a copy. Not only that, but he became a pen pal of Hesse. They wrote back and forth to each other, but unfortunately, my father's letters from Hesse were all destroyed in a mudslide in 1965. I read *Steppenwolf* many years ago as a teenager, and the book made an impression on me as well. The novel is about a man who has trouble finding himself in a bourgeois society not of his making, and he comes upon a person who tells him about a magic theater that is hidden in a music hall. There, he takes a journey of sorts that rejoins his human nature to that of a

WALLACE BERMAN /
Semina 4, 1959

Steppenwolf, combining beast and intellect to make him whole. I think anyone dealing with the straight world and the tension of that world with the boho scene would easily be attracted to this novel.

Before my family left for San Francisco, Wallace started up *Semina*. This small publication might be called a "zine" these days. It was a collection of loose pages printed on different papers that consisted of poetry, photographs, and drawings. Editions would have a print run of between 150 and 350 copies, all of them done on a hand printing press in his home or studio. I feel that *Semina* was the perfect medium for my father to interact with the world. Most of the copies were mailed or handed out for free. When our family moved to San Francisco, he went to City Lights Bookstore to have *Semina* sold there on consignment. Each one cost a dollar. Nowadays they're priceless, and it's tough to find an original *Semina*, especially one that's entirely intact. Each issue had its individual look and design, though the size of the publication was almost, if not exactly, consistent. Most issues are loose pages but some were fold-outs as well. For sure *Semina* had certain trademark visuals from my father uniting the entire run, but to me each issue is a complete world of its own.

There has historically been a tradition of poets or artists making their publications, not only of their work but also of works that they admired by other artists and writers. A good example is the surrealists, who started up their various publications to publish not only their own work but also that of fellow travelers and artists they admired from the past. The poets in *Semina* include Michael McClure, David Meltzer, and Philip Lamantia, along with older writers like Hermann Hesse, Jean Cocteau, and Antonin Artaud. Through *Semina*, Wallace could communicate with and bring the artistic world closer to his home base, not physically but spiritually. Each person who saw, read, or owned a copy of *Semina* was a fellow member of the club. That's what a publication should do, and *Semina* was very successful in those terms.

The beauty of *Semina* is that it was a periodical made not to be sold on the marketplace. Wallace's intention was to personally hand each issue to a friend or someone he admired. Or, in most cases, he sent it to people through the mail. No one could officially subscribe to the publication, and except for that one issue sold at City Lights, *Semina* never was sold in a retail or specialty shop. So to receive a copy was truly a unique gesture between artist and reader. It was likewise a publication or object that didn't have money value, at least when my dad was alive. In Latin, "semina" means "seed," or the thick whitish fluid we call "semen." It's a perfect name for a magazine given away for free, which would hopefully inspire other publications. Which it has. *Semina* has significantly influenced many printers, artists, and photographers, so its name is satisfactory terminology for spreading new life.

San Francisco / chapter 9

I have to assume that my crippling sense of vertigo started in San Francisco. As a three-year-old, I had a traumatic incident on the staircase leading to our apartment. I was on the steps petting my cat. According to my mom, a homeless woman came up the steps and tried to grab my cat out of my hands. I held on as she dragged me down the steps. My mom found me, after I screamed, at the bottom of the steps still holding onto my cat, but with my tooth penetrating my lip, which left a pool of blood. I have no memory of this, but what I do know is that I have a deep fear of staircases and heights. I couldn't stand to be held upside down or lifted by another human being, aside from my parents when I was a child. For many years George Herms liked to grab me from behind to lift me, and I would scream bloody murder. He kept this up even when I was a teenager! I would get a feeling of vertigo or dizziness, like I was about to faint.

To me, San Francisco was a nightmarish city, not because of its citizens, but because of its architecture and the many hills that make up the dramatic visuals in Alfred Hitchcock's movie *Vertigo* (1958), which was filmed in the city around the time we lived there. To me, the great city of the Bay was a warped landscape played at 45 rpm. I feel that I'm the only person on the planet who had no choice but to come to terms with its landscape that way. The earth spins 1,040 miles per hour, and I could feel its

WALLACE BERMAN /
Tosh Berman, San Francisco, 1960

movement under my feet. What others felt was delightful about San Francisco was a total horror show for me. I remember being frozen in my tracks just looking down Filbert Street, which is reportedly the steepest hill in the city.

As a child, it wasn't much of a problem, because usually an adult was either carrying me around or holding my hand, but as I grew older, my vertigo didn't go away. To this day, in particular locations, I need to hold the hand of a fellow adult, particularly when going up and down staircases. Not all staircases, mind you, just ones that I perceive as grand or big. I am highly sensitive to the size of a staircase and how steep it is. If there is a banister attached to the wall, I can sometimes handle it by myself. The worst thing for me though is when someone is either going down or up the stairs and won't move aside to let me pass. I can't stand to be motionless on a staircase, even for 30 seconds. If I'm forced to walk in the middle of the stairs, it's like a slow painful death to me. The bad part of it all is that people don't realize what I'm going through, nor do they care. As a child, this was my first lesson about how people treat other people. San Francisco was the first urban city that I was made aware of due to a lot of cement pavements and a large multicultural population. As a baby, I knew our house in Beverly Glen, but the first time that I was conscious of being in an urban city was San Francisco.

Despite my crippling fears, San Francisco had a lot of things going for a child like me during the late 1950s. I remember the girl who worked at the bakery would give me a free cookie every time I passed that palace of sweetness, and I also recall rambling around City Lights Bookstore, a place where my father liked to go to browse. A Japanese American gentleman by the name of Shig Murao was the floor manager. Shig first came to attention internationally for being arrested for selling Allen Ginsberg's *Howl* (1956) to an undercover cop in 1957. Shig and my dad used to chit-chat while I wandered within and outside the store. City Lights was probably my first bookstore experience. I never got bored being there with my father because I could people-watch and enjoy the different shapes and colors of book covers. It may have been there that I discovered the physical pleasure of books outside our house, and that a bookstore is a sacred location.

I like how books feel, the texture of the pages, and the beauty of the print on the white page. Being enclosed in a room full of books always gives me a sense of ease and security. At that time, I didn't have a preference for a type of book or even section. I was far too young to distinguish one type of volume from another. A few years later I became profoundly attached to the comic book sections in magazine stands and markets. City Lights didn't have comic books. You had to be crafty to avoid the anger of the newsstand managers because they hated kids looking at the comics.

It sounds silly to describe San Francisco as exotic, but the city had new, sensual, and tasty smells, and the architecture was so different from Los Angeles. Even as a child, I got the feeling that the communities, especially North Beach, were compact in size and filled with people on the same wavelength as their surroundings. Los Angeles is always pop or rock 'n' roll to me, but San Francisco is 1950s jazz and Italian opera music. This particular landscape is what I remember from entering a coffee shop or bar as a child. I was so young that the bartenders didn't mind me being in the location because I was with my dad or both parents. I don't remember North Beach being touristy or beatnik-crazy; it was just a cool, laidback but sophisticated neighborhood. I even picked that up as a child. I was taken with a view of another world, yet with warmth.

Since my father spent lots of time at North Beach, we often walked through Chinatown. Compared to the rest of San Francisco, Chinatown had level streets, so it was a comfort zone for me. There also seemed to be various red objects: red toys, red lanterns, and buildings with red signs. I found the color aesthetically pleasing. I don't know whether my memory is playing tricks on me, or if the connection between the color red and China is clouding my consciousness, but that's what I recall. Another thing I remember is a fake tin can of spinach with Popeye on it. It was in one of the gift shops in Chinatown. Why did that object exist in that neighborhood? My parents bought it for me on one of our walks. This image of Popeye was not my introduction to the character. I must have seen the comic strip in the newspaper or the animation on television. Louise Herms, who the family met at this time, looked just like Olive Oyl, Popeye's sometimes girlfriend. Louise was beautiful, but to me so was Olive Oyl. Besides having innocent crushes on girls I went to kindergarten with, I also had a thing for animated female characters. Betty Boop was another fetish-like fascination for me. I couldn't possibly have defined or understood sexuality, yet both characters struck a deep chord inside me that played for a long time afterward.

My parents also bought me a plastic sword from a Chinatown gift shop, and I enjoyed the fantasy of having an instrument of death in my hands. I would walk with my mom or my dad or both with the sword attached to my arm. I never really played with the sword at home; it was an object I wielded in public. Each face I saw on the street was another character in the story that was in my head. To this day, I have a tendency to look at people, both friend and stranger, and place them in a narrative of my own making.

My obsession with toy guns and knives started in San Francisco. I don't know where I picked it up. My parents weren't into weapons of any kind. I wasn't brought up in an anti-gun culture, but a "no-gun" culture. I must have picked up this obsession from either the medium of comics or the small amount of time I spent in front of a TV screen. I have no memory of watching TV during the late '50s. But somehow I got the idea of fighting bad people and knew that there was a constant struggle between "good and evil." I became obsessed with fighting imaginary criminals. At the

WALLACE BERMAN /
Robert Duncan, 1950s

time I didn't have the slightest idea what "good" or "evil" actually meant. I just knew that evil was bad, and that I was more attracted to the evil characters than the good ones. I took pity on the bad characters. They had to go to jail or, even worse, die.

At a neighborhood café near City Lights, I went up to a pair of police officers who were taking a lunch break. I was drawn to them because of their uniforms and, more significantly, I noticed they were wearing guns at their waists. One of the officers patted me on the head and asked me what I wanted to be when I grew up, so I told him I wanted to be an assassin. My parents, who overheard my comment to the officers, pretended they didn't know me.

Another significant location for me in San Francisco was the home of Robert Duncan and Jess Collins. Robert and Jess had first editions of the entire Oz book series by L. Frank Baum. Over the years, they gave me a lot of their Oz books. I've rarely kept anything from that era, but I still have the books they gave me,

WALLACE BERMAN /
Jess, Topanga Canyon, 1968

which is amazing, considering how many times I've moved. Jess was a man of a few words. I never saw him in painting mode. I imagine for Jess it was just like going to an office to work, but once he was out of the office, he looked very much like—not the wife exactly, but the partner who didn't share the "work" with the family after hours. I think he was the one that made the meals in the household. I remember going to dinner at their home numerous times, which were consistently fun for me because I was drawn to the books. Aside from trips to City Lights, these were probably the first occasions when I paid attention to bookshelves.

WALLACE BERMAN /
Michael McClure, 1958, San Francisco

Jess, of course, was an excellent painter and collage artist. Even as a kid I was called to his work because there was something "comic book" about it, but not in the obvious sense, like Roy Lichtenstein. I feel he got the nature of the comic book or strip. One of his most eminent collages is his *Tricky Cad* (1954–59), a total cut-up of the *Dick Tracy* comic strip. He took all the images, dialogue, and text from the strip and re-imagined it in his peculiar fashion. Regardless of the fact that I was too young to fully grasp the work, I understood it as a child who loved comics. It's fascinating to think how many artists in that era had an obsession with or were influenced by the comics medium. I found myself attracted to that aesthetic. I knew the difference between comic strips printed in the newspaper and artists who took that influence for their artwork. Even as a kid I had a thorough if instinctive understanding of low art and high art, even when the skills and the visuals were very close or in the same family.

My family was attracted to poets, and I think Robert Duncan was the first one I realized was an actual poet. He looked just like a poet to me. He had one angel eye that would wander, and he had the talent to communicate with almost anyone. His humor came off clearly, even to a kid like me. He was gossipy, yes, but with a sharp intelligence to his commentary. Robert and Jess were probably the first gay couple I was ever aware of. Not in a sexual or intimate sense: the fact that they shared a room was not something I was conscious of at the time. But they were clearly a couple, even to me as a child.

If Robert Duncan was my first impression of a poet, and what a poet sounds like, then Michael McClure was my prototype for the romantic poet. He would wear a chunky scarf as if it were naturally appended to his neck. This is not criticism but praise of his unique style, because Michael was (and is) an incredibly handsome man. My earliest memory of Michael is as a Monty Clift combined with just a touch of Brando's *The Wild One* (1953). He never looked like a beat or a beatnik to me. His clothing and attitude and even his voice were a poetic 1950s attitude, and without a doubt, had dandified flourishes. When he read his poetry in public, or privately to my father, he had a way of pronouncing his words like they were sculptures. Each word seemed as if he were making an object positioned in front of his eyes or view. He has the ability to bring a physical, bodily presence to his poetry or words. *Ghost Tantras* (1964) is, I think, his masterpiece, which is him roaring like a lion. Of all the poets we knew at the time, he was the one most interested in sound. Years later, he worked with musicians, but I was always of the view that the music got in the way of his poetry. Just he alone and his voice are enough. I suspected that, somewhere in his past, Michael must have taken a diction class, because of the care with which he pronounced words.

Michael was not natural. There was something artificial in him, and I loved the dramatic aspect of his personality. I have a

MICHAEL McCLURE'S
THE BEARD
Directed by ROBERT GIST
WARNER PLAYHOUSE
755 N. La Cienega Blvd. — 659-0333
OPENING JANUARY 24th

strong memory of dining with him and my parents at a traditional French restaurant, where he ordered the food for the entire table, including yours truly. What I wanted was a hamburger, but I wasn't going to get it at that restaurant. Michael was by no means ordering such food for a table he was dining at. Everything he ordered was very much "grown-up" food, clearly unsuitable for an American kid like me. All I wanted was a piece of meat between two pieces of bread, and I was angry at him for not ordering such a plate for me. Instead, he ordered frog legs and snails. Imagine! Food for a tot.

Michael has a star-like quality. He had a flair no one else had, down to the scarf around his neck. To this day, when I look at a scarf or put one on, I picture Michael. Also, he's one of those poets who know stagecraft. The majority of my dad's poet friends didn't have a commanding style before facing an audience, but I think Michael put a lot of thought into this. Even off-stage, he has a commanding personality. I don't recall frivolous chit-chat with him. He saw the world at the time with an intense awareness. Some poets didn't care how they were packaged, but Michael had a strong point of view regarding book covers, being in journals, and, of course, how his poetry was laid out on the page. I remember one time my Dad and Michael had a very intense discussion about a poster Wallace made for Michael's play *The Beard* (1965). Michael didn't like the poster at first, or maybe not at all, but at the end of the day, my father won the argument. Even though their discussion was heated, there was lots of respect between the two men, which made them good partners on a project together.

WALLACE BERMAN / Untitled (*Beard* poster), 1967

707 Scott Street / chapter 10

Compared with the shack in Beverly Glen, our residence in San Francisco, at 707 Scott Street, appeared to be a mansion. We had the bottom floor and various interesting people rented the upstairs. My parents became the managers of the residence and were responsible for collecting the rent and taking care of the premises. I have no real recollection of being upstairs at all, mostly due to my fear of staircases. At least we had our bathroom on the first floor. I believe there was a bathroom upstairs as well, and the other tenants must have shared it. Louise Herms lived upstairs, before she married George Herms. I found her to be very comforting, perfect even. The poet John Wieners lived on the second floor as well. There he wrote what's perhaps the best known of his published journals, *The Journal of John Wieners Is to Be Called 707 Scott Street for Billie Holiday 1959* (1996), usually referred to as *707 Scott Street*. In the book, my dad figures as "Wally," a character that wanders into the poems and leaves silently. It's a remarkable document of that time in San Francisco, as well as a magnificent book of poetry, which, of course, I read when I was an adult.

I had a friend on the block on Scott Street who lived in a big house with a Christmas tree that was up all year round. On a daily basis, we played at the park across the street from our homes. There was no father figure in his household. Most of the kids I met had a set of parents, so when I was four or five, I was struck by the oddness that not everyone had two parents. I never asked my friend why he didn't have a father. Even then, I was conscious of the fact that I should not ask such questions of a person unless they brought the subject up.

My parents took me everywhere. If there were a gallery opening, I would go. Sometimes, but rarely, they had a babysitter for me. The babysitters that I remember were Leslie Caron, the actress, and John Reed, the artist. The producers of the film *The Subterraneans* (1960), based on Jack Kerouac's 1958 novel, wanted my parents to appear in a club setting, so they demanded a babysitter for me. Why Leslie Caron, the lead actress in the film, had to be my babysitter is beyond me.

John Reed was a rather delightful person. I haven't the slightest idea where he came from, but I knew even then he was an artist. My parents liked him very much. He seemed to be very much of a jazzer in aesthetic and in life. I presume he enjoyed a drink or two, or many. I remember that he smelled like beer, and compared to my parents' other friends, he was the most boho of the set. He always had a beard and wore a cap. I remember a few times when he took off his hat, his hair was all scrunched down and sweaty. He liked to laugh, and had a lazy chuckle. He seems to me to have been a beautiful soul with a hard life. His artwork was much admired by my dad, but I don't think he ever had a show when he was alive. He was also quite close to Walter Hopps; in fact, he used to live in Walter's Pasadena house when Walter was in some other part of the world. Redheaded, with a red beard and freckles, he would have looked like a teen character from a situation comedy if he didn't drink and shaved his beard. My family lost contact with him, especially after my father's death. The last I heard of John, his body was found in the bushes by a freeway entrance.

I started reading around this time, mostly comic books. I was drawn to the illustrations, the inking, and even the smell of the comic book itself. At the time, I didn't have a collection. But

WALLACE BERMAN /
Tosh with Jean Cocteau photograph

I remember my attraction to the medium was immediate. Popeye
was a favorite, and I think I understood the narrative of Popeye
and Bluto fighting over Olive Oyl. That triangle is part of my
DNA, and I later often found myself sucked into the world of a
girl and another guy. I grew out of that type of thinking or feeling
in my very late 20s, but romance or yearning for attention was of
great importance to me. Not in the sense that I needed someone
at all times—God, no—but I think I was meant to be loved from
a distance. This had to do with the fact that I'm an only child.

There is something catlike in that; you want someone to come up and pet you, but not hang out too much afterward. I much prefer objects: the vinyl LP, for instance.

The first time I became aware of a vinyl LP was in San Francisco in our house on Scott Street. The album was *Lotte Lenya Sings Berlin Theatre Songs by Kurt Weill* (1958). It was an LP I couldn't have escaped from even if I wanted to. Not only was it played on a constant basis in our household, but my German grandmother, Martha, also owned a copy, so when I visited her, I heard it there too. It's a fantastic album on many levels. The songs by Lenya's husband Weill and Bertolt Brecht are brilliant. The melodies steeped into my childhood like Peter Lorre's voice calling out to a child in the Fritz Lang film *M* (1931). Also, one of the first TV shows that I can remember was *The Ernie Kovacs Show* (1961–62). The program used Lotte Lenya music for its theme song, which was weird enough because that show was such an odd one for a small child to watch. Even as a teenager, I couldn't escape: The Doors recorded "Alabama Song" (1966) and later David Bowie did a version (1980) as well. I can't ignore the three recordings of that song. It is not about love or hate. The melody and the song are stamped on my personality.

With that in mind, it's probably not so strange that I was raised with an image of Jean Cocteau always somewhere around the house. Cocteau was a poet, and he made poetic novels, poetic drawings, poetic art, and of course, poetic cinema. Cocteau's definition of cinema was "poetry written on light," which is, in theory, an excellent explanation of movies. As I mentioned before, Wallace never talked about why he liked an individual artist or art movement, but he often showed his affection by putting the artist's image up on the studio wall, or wherever he did his artwork. The house on Scott Street had homages to the great on its walls. Someone like Cocteau made such an impression on Wallace, I think, not only due to his skills as an artist and filmmaker but also

WALLACE BERMAN /
John Wieners, at 707 Scott Street, San Francisco, 1959

for the way he transformed his world into an artistic landscape.
Cocteau's taste reshaped his world as his personal platform. Wallace was attracted to this artist who conveyed his signature with not only poetry, but also with films, prose, drawings, and his own outsize personality.

At the time, Cocteau's poetry was published here and there in English. My dad published one of the poems and a drawing in *Semina*, but Cocteau's films made the deepest impression on Wallace and his circle during the early '50s. A family friend and filmmaker from the Bay Area, Lawrence Jordan, owned a 16mm print of Cocteau's *Orpheus* (1949). He had an incredible collection of 16mm film prints, and he would treat us to a movie after dinner. I remember I was very fond of Lawrence's little handmade books of stills from his favorite films. Each book was focused on one film. He made one of Eisenstein's *Ivan the Terrible* (1944), as well as Buster Keaton's *The General* (1926), among others. I presume he took photographs of the movie screen. These private showings were a real treat for me as a kid, not only for the exposure to such remarkable films as a child, but also for the seriousness of the proceedings, the sense that what we saw on the blank white wall was something incredible. Lawrence would never show anything less than fantastic. Even with the films I didn't pick up on, owning to my tender age, I had a delightful time sleeping in front of the images flickering on the wall. The comfort of being in a dark room with my parents and their good friend made me sleepy, and that feeling has stayed with me forever. I remember watching a variety of films over at his house, but without a doubt, dinner was always spaghetti. So to this day, when I think of *Orpheus* or *The General*, I immediately think of spaghetti with tomato sauce.

San Francisco life, though fabulous for me, became difficult for Wallace, due to the beatnik culture that sprang up during the late '50s. Always a sensitive soul who felt the vibe of his times, he was not comfortable living in the city, especially a city well known to tourists for beatnik activity. He loathed to the very core of his being to see a bus full of tourists stop by the Coexistence Bagel Shop and call attention to him as a beatnik. With the success of his great novel *On the Road* (1957), Kerouac inadvertently created a culture of people who were fascinated and alarmed by the beats. They became a joke for mainstream culture, with a TV show, *The Many Loves of Dobie Gillis* (1959–63), having a beatnik as one of the main characters. This funny figure—Maynard G. Krebs, played by Bob Denver of later *Gilligan's Island* (1964–67) fame—became the iconic representation of what a beatnik was supposed to be at the time. Thus, anyone who wore a plain sweatshirt, sandals, and canvas pants was part of the beatnik conspiracy. Which may have been true in a cultural sense, but the beats were too unorganized of a group to overtake the youth of the Free World.

When it began covering the beatnik phenomenon, the mainstream press invaded the beats' personal space, and such space was crucial to a countercultural figure like my dad. All of a sudden his favorite hangout was overrun by tourists who wanted a look at a real "beatnik." San Francisco became a magnet, meanwhile, for kids who wanted to join the beatnik revolution, as well as for reporters, who commented on, made demands of, and then took the piss out of a group of people who were uncomfortable in the media glare in the first place. Kerouac, for example, had a tough time going from beat writer to very famous person. It didn't gel with his sense of culture, nor did he want to be spotlighted in such a way. Allen Ginsberg, on the other hand, was a natural for the media. He was extremely articulate, and he was comfortable with the press and how it worked. But to my dad or someone like Kerouac, fame was a depressing process. By no means did Wallace have "Jack Kerouac" fame, but even a touch of it drove him batty. Wallace in a sense aspired to be invisible. He didn't want to destroy mainstream culture, but he preferred to live in its margins. My dad refused to conform his particular taste or art to another's standard, and he needed distance to work, to view, and to comment, in his way, on a world that he was both part of and alien to.

The *New York Post* sent a journalist by the name of Al Aronowitz to San Francisco to write a series of articles on the Beat Generation. More likely, his assignment was to expose the inner workings of a beatnik and his or her world. Aronowitz did his research well, for he had already interviewed Jack Kerouac, Neal Cassady, and, of course, Allen Ginsberg. Wallace, for some odd and now forgotten reason, agreed to be interviewed for the *Post*, but immediately regretted it. The interview took place that afternoon, and by the evening Wallace had arranged to get his friend Artie Richard to help him get the tape back so they could destroy it. They found Aronowitz in his motel room with the audio tape. There and then, my dad destroyed the tape in front of Aronowitz. The thing is, Wallace also destroyed the interview with Kerouac and Cassady, which was also on the tape. This, one would think, would exterminate the relationship between these two men. But Wallace and Al became friends, and later, in the '60s, Aronowitz became famous for introducing Bob Dylan to the Beatles, as well as turning on the Fab Four to marijuana.

At the same time there was a growing drug problem on Scott Street. Speed was the narcotic of choice for the upstairs residents, which would have been perfectly OK if it hadn't attracted undercover narcotic officers to the household. My father, being naturally paranoid, was alarmed when a stranger came to the house—especially if he were a friend of John Wieners. My dad was convinced John only picked up men who were undercover cops. Due to this fear and the depressing drug scene on the premises, Wallace decided to move the family to the idyllic community of Larkspur, north of San Francisco.

Larkspur / chapter 11

In Larkspur, we rented a houseboat, and the only entrance was either from a boat or from a single boardwalk from the main street that went over the marshes. The houseboat always seemed freezing to me. I remember being numb with cold because there was a broken window in my bedroom. It was a window looking towards the river. The river attracted a bitter wind, but we also had ducks going "quack-quack." I thought of these ducks as my pets and remembered the simple joy of feeding them bits and pieces of bread from the bedroom window. I could hear the ducks in the morning and sometimes in the middle of the night if something or someone disturbed them. I always wondered if they felt the cold as well. The water must have been freezing, so I felt sympathy for their wet feathers and beaks.

The structure of the houseboat itself I always considered part of nature, in that I got the sense the water could pull it out of its foundation and send it merrily down the river. I could imagine waking up one morning and being in the house, but floating somewhere in the Pacific Ocean, like the house in *The Wizard of Oz* (1939) that goes up with the tornado. I can't forget the sense of movement of the water; I couldn't avoid the feeling of a life force pushing against our home.

On the boardwalk, I felt nervous because I was walking on a higher level than the ground. If I wasn't on the ground floor of

Tosh Berman with photograph of Shirley Berman, Larkspur, 1960

some secure structure or even outside, I felt like I was floating, which was unnatural, and not a pleasant experience. The vastness of the sky or the inside of a large structure provokes in me the alarming realization that I am indeed minuscule in the world, and therefore vulnerable to architecture, the steepness of a hill, or the height from the ground. The boardwalks were built because of the river; at certain times of the year the water would rise, and that area would be flooded. I have no memory of the river flooding; I just recall being in the presence of dust and weeds. For most people, I

WALLACE BERMAN /
Tosh Berman, Larkspur, 1960

think, the boardwalk was a thing of great beauty, but to me, it was just a bridge to get from one place to the other. I thought that if I fell off the boardwalk, I'd never get back on again, that I might just disappear and drown in the dust and weeds, or get eaten up by whatever lived in that god-forsaken vegetation.

For the first time, my father had a separate studio away from the main house on the property. The structure was perhaps at one time a storage unit, but my dad converted it into a studio and dark-room. The studio space was dark, small, and full of objects, with photographs on the walls. The space between the studio and the house felt very much like being on a boat. The ground right under me seemed to go with the current of the river, which was gentle and felt alive. This is the spot where my father took photographs of me, some in the nude and some not. Along with my mother, I was my dad's favorite subject matter for photographs. Some shots were of me playing around the property, but a lot of them were Wallace posing me in specific positions or with certain objects, usually a toy machine gun or a broken doll I was attached to. Many images were inspired by my obsession with toy guns and knives.

By this time, I was a confirmed comic book reader. I loved DC comics, especially *Batman*. Men who wore masks to hide their identities always intrigued me. In my head, the Batcave had the perfect interior for a child: a crime and chemical lab to engage in research to fight crime, and lots of dark corners. The fact that the Batcave was beneath a mansion was another plus for me. I imagined the Larkspur house being attached to an underwater lair, a place that would be safe from criminals and nasty spirits—my spiritual home, at least in theory. All of that was flowing through my head while my dad took photographs of me. To be honest, I don't know if I ever wasn't performing for an audience inside my mind. Even to this day, as I write, I feel like a performer.

My mom had to work in San Francisco. She took the Greyhound bus, probably an hour and a half each way. She worked for a wine merchant whose customers often came in and helped themselves to a bottle or two without paying. My mom brought this up with the owner, who said that those particular "customers" chose not to pay in the everyday way of a retail business. While my mom worked regular day hours, my dad was responsible for my well-being. He made me lunch, took me to kindergarten (which was walking distance from the house), and kept an eye out for me. I couldn't play in the studio, but I could sit there or stand by and watch my dad work. He would lose himself in whatever

WALLACE BERMAN /
Tosh Berman, Larkspur, 1960

he was doing. As a kid in Wallace's world, I could Zen myself into a state of quietness and patience. I never needed to get attention from him or my mom. I instinctively knew my dad had to do his work, and there were times to jump up on him and for sure times to remain quiet and just be there.

The worst aspect of my father taking care of me was his cooking. He used to make me fried egg sandwiches, which I am sure he made with an enormous amount of love but which in reality were torture. I loathed his cooking, especially his egg sandwiches.

WALLACE BERMAN /
Semina Gallery (Exterior), Larkspur, 1960

I hated the soaked bread more than anything. Even as I write
this, I feel like I'm going to gag at the thought of a runny egg on
a moist piece of barely toasted bread. Then again, I have to wonder where he even learned to cook such a horror show. He never
actually lived alone, so either his mom would cook for him, or
my mom would. And I don't see the possibility of either of them
teaching my father the finer points of preparing food in a kitchen.
No, I think he experimented in the kitchen, and I had to pay the
price for being in the wrong place with the wrong person at the
wrong time.

In Larkspur, my father started a gallery, called "Semina" after
his periodical. The gallery was situated on the boardwalk between
our house and George Herms's residence. It was an unusual place
to show art, since there was no ceiling and most of the walls had
burned in a fire sometime before my dad ever saw the place. The
flooring in the structure also had huge gaps; the floorboards were
rotting due to the open air, which exposed it to bird shit as well

WALLACE BERMAN /
Semina Gallery (Interior) Larkspur, 1960

as water damage from the nearby river. There were barely walls
left. For Wallace, this was the perfect place for a gallery. The little
wall space still intact was used for the artworks. In this gallery, he
showed George Herms (probably his first show) and the photographers Charles Brittin and Edmund Teske. The structure was so
open to the elements it had a treehouse sort of vibe to a little kid
like me. It was the proper location for me to rouse my imagination while acting out stories that were stored in my DNA. Since
I had no close friends really and was just an only child, I had

elaborate storylines that went through my head, usually based on a favorite comic book character like Batman or a TV personality like Zorro. I can still feel the cold that ran through the gallery. It became apparent that part of the world—Marin County—was always cold.

One of the main reasons Wallace had removed himself from San Francisco was the intrusion of the media on beat culture. The reporting had no depth and didn't even try to understand the art that was being produced by these young artists. With his desire to be invisible, Wallace was allergic to the prospect of being interviewed. Yet for some reason he occasionally allowed it to happen. I remember the day a reporter and a photographer for a San Francisco paper came to Larkspur to interview my dad and some of his friends. It was a very awkward afternoon. There's a photograph of me, my dad, and some friends looking like a gang caught during a heist. Funnily enough, my father took a photo of the reporter and photographer, and they too look like they're thinking: "Oh my god, we gotta get out of here!"

There was only one movie theater in Larkspur, and it was (and is) called the Lark, an old art deco theater built in the '30s. This was the spot where I saw my first movie in a proper movie theater. My father took me to see something that he was looking forward to, Roger Vadim's *And God Created Woman* (1956), starring Vadim's then-wife Brigitte Bardot. The owner wouldn't allow me in the theater, even with my father. I must have been four years old at the time. Wallace made a huge scene till they let us in. It's no exaggeration to say that the first woman, besides my mom, to make an impression on me was Bardot. Bardot's beauty struck me hard, and I believe it set a pattern to my sexuality. Perhaps the theater owner's concern was reasonable: he just wanted to protect me from the passion of Brigitte Bardot.

I have little memory of the film, except for the part where Bardot did her dance, in front of men who seemed to share the same amount of desire as the movie theater audience. Without a doubt, Bardot represented an ideal woman for the male bohemian set. It had more to do with her attitude than her undeniable beauty. The greatest sirens of the cinema all have incredible character, which sets them apart from other people. It's not their figure, but the attitude of the body that makes them so naturally desirable. In the beat world, some women expressed a look that was both natural and sensual at the same time, and Bardot represented that type of woman. My father always had a photograph of her in his studio; he must have collected them from magazines. As I write, I have two Bardot photos in my eyesight. I've even published her one-time boyfriend Serge Gainsbourg through my imprint Tam-Tam Books. It seems childhood never leaves. It just continues with facial hair and erections.

School / chapter 12

Wallace didn't have any concern about schooling or the nature of schools. He was thrown out of Fairfax High School for gambling, so to him, school was not that big of a deal. Some parents have a vision of their child: that he or she will go off to college, get rich, and become a doctor or perhaps the head of a multinational corporation. But I don't believe Wallace ever had any vision of my future. At least he never told me his thoughts on my non-existent future plans. My memory of school is that I wasn't a serious student. I would become a very dependable C– student: average, not caring either way. I don't think I had a problem making friends. But I often feel that I was thrown in the backseat of a car and the driver took me where he wanted to go, so little was the say I had (especially as a tot) in my formal education. One remarkable thing I did have in my favor was parents who surrounded me with books; my curiosity engendered a lifelong reading habit in me. So, in a way, I didn't need school. What school taught me was the feeling of being an outsider. My fundamental sense of alienation without a doubt came from there. I remember craving to be liked by the teachers but never getting their approval or attention. Whenever they called on me, I felt they were saying, "Oh dear . . ." and, of course, "Why is Tosh wearing pants with a hole in his crotch?" A question I couldn't possibly answer.

School was a necessary experience for me, but not a good

one. My kindergarten teacher in Larkspur was gorgeous. I felt like she didn't pay enough attention to me. I wanted to be closer to her, but I also felt I wasn't important enough for her to be concerned about me. I don't know whether I remember her because my memory is tainted by her rejection, or whether I just think I remember because I have two class pictures with her. I flunked kindergarten once and had to take it over again. One picture, taken the year after I failed, has me holding up the school place card with its name and the date, as if to taunt me for my failure. I almost never return to these photographs. The memory of those years is already disagreeable and writing about them just makes the picture fuzzier. To this day, I never can live it down. How can you fail kindergarten? You play, you nap, and that's about it.

Nonetheless, when I do look at one of the photographs, I remember a girl there I considered attractive. Her mysterious ways tempted me. I don't remember her name or anything else except that I was drawn to her beauty. It was a crush, of course, and having one at such a young age is sort of a mystery emotion to someone who can't even understand why humans are attracted to each other. But sexuality came early to me, not in the sense of the physical act, but definitely in the way feelings occur when you see a girl and like her. It was pure emotion. And when I think of her now, I still have the same feelings for her. She wore a lot of knitted sweaters with plaid printed dresses. There was always some dirt on her blouse or dress. I had a fixation on the stains because I believed they were a clue to her personality. Her beauty was so perfect and her dress sense immaculate, except for the dirt smudges on her blouse or sweater. One might think it was an indication of poverty, but I found even that imperfection alluring. I had a sensitivity to class and wealth differences, and without a doubt, I was at the time attracted to those who didn't have perfectly clean clothes, which is not saying much for a little boy who had holes in the crotch of his pants.

Tosh Berman (Front row, second from left) Kindergarten photograph, 1959/1960

Clothing had an impact on me, because while I was conscious of a beautiful face, what the girl wore expressed another side of her, perhaps a world that she lived in, and clothes were a window to peek through. If she'd worn something I didn't like, I couldn't have loved her that much. But the fact that she wore a sweater over her dress made a huge impression on me. I also have a faint and charming memory of her wearing Mary Jane shoes with white girlie socks. The entire package was so superb; everything she wore was like a map from A to B. But I don't remember talking to or being friends with her. I suspect our relationship was distant, even though I sat right by her in class.

It was the first time I got physically close to someone I found incredibly attractive. I remember I didn't want to talk to her because there was nothing for me to say. I lacked the vocabulary to express what I felt inside, because I didn't know what I was feeling. Regardless of the fact that I sat by her, she never acknowledged me in any manner, except for a slight smile that came from nowhere. I don't know if it was a passing thought, or if she just noticed me being me, acting like a dork. The only time we made eye contact was when she leaned in my direction to reach for her folder or schoolbook. There was sometimes a smile on her lips when she knew I was watching her, but I pretended I was looking over her shoulder. I think she knew otherwise, which was an erotic/romantic feeling for me. When I see her in the class photo, I can remember her walk and the intuitive way she sat straight up in the school chair, but I have no memory of her voice.

After two tries at kindergarten, I was finally allowed to go to the first grade, but the problems just did not stop. Concerning my schooling issues, my highly educated guess is that I'm slightly retarded. My parents never addressed the issue, probably because I never required them to do so. I think I was dreading the moment when my dad and mom would sit me down and say, "Son, you are mentally challenged." In actuality, I don't think my parents would have done that; my guess is they would've changed the subject if I asked. The problem I had—and still have—is that if I'm given a set of instructions on how to do something, I find them impossible to follow. The best thing for me is to let me figure something out in my own way. I must experience the solution, and I can only do that in my fashion. I can make deadlines because I have my system for finishing up something. But I cannot do things in someone else's way.

I made friends with a pair of brothers my age who lived on the boardwalk about two or three houses down. It was the first time classmates invited me to their home. It was weird. Their mother made us grilled cheese sandwiches, which for me was totally exotic. Before they ate their sandwiches, the mom and the brothers bowed their heads down to pray. I just followed them, because I believed they reckoned all people in the universe followed this practice. But to me, it was a remote procedure. I didn't understand then, and I still don't. I can learn to say thanks to the person who made the cheese sandwiches, but I didn't understand the importance to thank or chant "good things" to a higher being due to all the work their mom did.

The brothers also had a vast collection of Hardy Boys and Tom Swift Jr. books. These novels were tailor-made for the adolescent boy with adventure in his heart and passion for reading. I loved these books, not only for the stories but also for their design. The first book outside of City Lights or our house that made me realize how much I physically love books was a Hardy Boys book. At the time, I didn't know that *the book* was an object that would have such an impact on my life. What intrigued me about the Hardy Boys and Tom Swift Jr. series was that they invited the reader to participate in the adventure. I marveled at the bookcase in my newfound friends' bedroom, with all the Hardy Boys books in numerical order; there's a fetish quality to shelving a set of books in order. The brothers' world seemed complete to me. It would be a couple years down the line before I finally had my own collection of Hardy Boys books together via used bookstores in Santa Monica.

Beverly Glen II / *chapter 13*

In 1961, we returned to our home in Beverly Glen. My mom missed her family—though her parents often visited us in San Francisco—and I think my dad just missed Los Angeles. And even Larkspur was too close to San Francisco to avoid media interest in beatniks as a pop culture phenomenon, which drove my dad nuts. The house in Beverly Glen was on a very steep hill called Crater Lane. Around this time my phobias made a huge return to my world. I had to go through dirt, mud, branches, insects, and various reptiles (mostly snakes and lizards) to get through the front door of our house. I never felt safe in this environment. My Uncle Don had been living there while we were up north, so it didn't seem like a fresh beginning, more like coming home after a holiday outside of Los Angeles. When we moved away from Beverly Glen, I was still a baby so I hadn't been conscious of the hill. Being a tad older, I now had to face it.

Crater Lane is so steep that it represents a sense of gravity gone amok. Everyone who walked up the hill resembled Jacques Tati doing his iconic walk, in which his torso is going forward, but his legs are dangling back. This might be the main reason I like Tati's work so much. But in my un-cinematic life at the time, I had a great fear of going up or down the dreaded hill. I didn't

Wallace Berman and John Wieners at Beverly Glen, 1962

feel attached to the pavement, as if I was going to fly off that road. The distance looked longer to me than it was in actuality, I would lose my bearing, and my heartbeat would change. My body temperature went up. I also had the fear I'd be pushed down the hill or made to fall, so didn't trust anyone to help me while I was walking up the hill. The fear would grip me mentally and physically as I put my feet on the pavement.

I never saw my father lose his cool, but the one thing he couldn't understand was my phobia. I was conscious of the fact that it disappointed or disturbed him, but I couldn't help it. Just seeing how he reacted, I felt I could never go to him and seek assistance. Not out of fear of being punished, but more out of shame. Being a kid, I found it challenging to articulate my feelings or my fears. I just felt totally unable to find help within or outside of the family. All I knew was that people had no trouble going up and down the hill, or up and down a staircase, but for some reason, it was my secret dread. Having a fear that you can't share with anyone is a weird position to be in, in life. I had no choice but to hide my fear or somehow take a different route to get up or down that hill. What I did instead was go through a neighbor's yard, where there were short concrete steps that led to Beverly Glen Boulevard. I told my father and mother I could go down the hill, but actually, I would use this passageway to the street below. It was a devious practice, but I did what I had to do. And there was no way in heaven or hell I would go down or up that hill by myself.

Once my father found out I was still having difficulty going down the hill, he took me up to the house to spank me. It was a horrible scene because he was crying. He didn't know what to do, and was in a panic mode. This was probably the worst moment I had with Wallace. I felt bad because I felt responsible for him feeling bad, but I don't think he understood how real this problem was for me. I don't believe it ever dawned on my parents that they should take me to a doctor about it. A child psychologist I'm sure was way too expensive for my family. On top of that, I think Wallace had a profound suspicion of psychologists or anyone needing to chat with one. Wallace was a very self-reliant type of guy, and I can't see him ever going to a doctor unless it was an emergency. So major things like getting my teeth fixed were put aside due to finances, and I don't think Wallace ever thought it would be a problem then or in the future. He was wrong. He had crooked teeth, but mine were terrible. Normally parents would get their child's teeth fixed, but my parents never brought the subject up.

Not only the Crater Lane hill, but also any decent-size museum would give me the jitters. I couldn't stand to be in a large room with a huge painting or work of art on the wall. Additionally, I would have a panic attack if the floors had patterns or the walls had any textural wallpaper. In situations like that, I tried to focus on something that would not make me ill, but everywhere I looked there was some pattern or object that felt like it was going to fall on me. One thing that was a total no-no was to look at the soaring ceiling. My knees would buckle once I looked upward. I remember going to the Victoria & Albert Museum in London with my parents, and in this one enormous room, there was a replica of Michelangelo's David. By the time I looked up to his knees, I was feeling a loss of gravity, as if some force was pulling me away from safety. My parents had to lead me out of the gallery. I couldn't do so myself. I would lose direction or walk into the walls. It's embarrassing; I was utterly useless in those situations. I feel sorry for my parents, who had to go through the ordeal of removing me from the premises.

I am not sure if my problem was medical or mental. Even now, when I'm under stress, the phobias come back. They're always around the corner, and I'm never sure when I'll hit that place. My problem made me feel outside the human race, a one of a kind, but not in a good way. I felt like a freak more than anything else, so I tried to keep it a secret. I would ignore the feelings that were stored up in me until I eventually knew I had to leave, because if I didn't leave the perceived area of danger, I felt the room or the landscape would swallow me up. There are still traces of that fear deep within me.

There was also a problem when I went to school. In the second grade I was on the ground floor, but sometimes a teacher would ask me to go upstairs to borrow something from another classroom. I was terrified at the thought of using the staircase. I got up to the third or fourth step and started feeling shaky. I went back to the class and told the teacher I had to go to the nurse's office right away because I felt sick. Which on the one hand was a lie, but on the other hand I did feel nauseated. The teacher never caught onto my odd illness; I'm sure the thought of someone being afraid of using the staircase was totally out of the ballpark. Somehow I was successful in avoiding the dreaded concrete stairs for a whole school semester. But I already felt panicky about the future in second grade, knowing that the third grade would be upstairs. Eventually, I was able to climb up and down the stairs, but only if there were people in front of me, and only if they weren't chit-chatting on the staircase, because it was important that they go up and down without delay; it cushioned the space's impact on me.

If my anxiety were color, it would be gray. The temperature would be chilly. I was always in fear of embarrassment that someone would find out about my phobias. I was also hesitant to go to unfamiliar places, in fear that the ceilings would be too high, the staircase would be too steep, or the structure would be located on a hill. Of course, this was a big problem when we lived in San Francisco. I often wonder why my parents were comfortable in such surroundings. It was almost as if they went out of their way to find areas of the world that I found totally unsuitable for my delicate sensibilities.

Special Education / chapter 14

My father had a unique way of keeping me in line at social events. If we were sitting at a dinner table with adults and I said something inappropriate, he would kick my leg underneath the table. It could be confusing, however, because Wallace had a nervous tic in his leg when he sat down. One of his legs would shake up and down, but if you watched him above the table, you wouldn't ever notice it. If he were deep in the newspaper, the leg would go 100 miles a minute. This would only happen if he were totally lost in thought or reading. He was a calm man, at least outwardly, but the constant movement of his leg while sitting down told me otherwise. I never recall him telling me not to do something. It was mostly a kick under the table, or some other physical but non-violent form of action to let me know I was going out of bounds socially. A lot of it I had to think through. I picked up that, when an adult wanted to discuss something adult-like, I should shut up. Still, it was always questionable in my mind what to do or not to do. So if I was sitting with him, it was tough to tell if he was upset with me and wanted to quietly let me know by kicking my leg or if he just had his tic and kicked me by accident.

I never shouted in pain or surprise. But I sometimes didn't know why he was kicking me. What I do know is that sometimes a child wants to be the focus of attention when adults are around, and while my parents brought me up among grown-ups, it didn't mean I was a small adult or I deserved extra attention. My concerns or interests did not significantly interest a grown-up, and if I opened my mouth for too long, a swift kick under the table did the job. But I was never dismissed from a table or a party full of adults. This is, in the long run, a very effective way to raise a child. I learned manners by being with adults. I also realized even as an egotistical young child that there was a difference between a kid and a grown-up.

Most of my childhood was spent with adults. I had no lasting play pals of my age that I can remember. If I did, it seems like I got along OK with them. I only lost friends when they moved or, in some cases, died. I did have a problem with the school system, or more likely it had a problem with me. When I was in second grade in Beverly Glen, I got kicked out of Warner Avenue Elementary School and sent to special education at another school called Nora Sterry. It was just an elementary school that had a special education department attached to it. The reason for my removal from regular school is, to this day, a mystery to me.

What I do know is that my parents were called in and told I had a problem and needed to go to a special education class. My mother said that the teacher pointed to a six-inch-high stack of papers and when Shirley asked to see those documents, the teacher refused to let her look at them. She told my parents I had trouble putting a wheel on a wooden toy car, and therefore, I had an issue. I had also failed kindergarten, which I'm convinced was the root of my educational problems. The other problem is my father. Wallace never accepted the concept of school, and he passed that stance to me as well. I think he could have related to a trade school, but for the rest, he didn't think much about it. So his attitude and the teacher's reaction towards me were equally death blows in terms of getting anywhere with school.

The special education or "needs" section of Nora Sterry shared the same space with the "normal" kids and classes. We had lunch and recess together, but once those ended, it was back to special education. I shared my space with a handful of colorful children. One was a Japanese American named David who was full of anxious energy. For instance, he ate colored chalk. If memory serves me correctly, he preferred orange chalk. He was a sensitive child with an orange tongue, but he was riveting. He was quite vocally expressive. On a volume dial of one to ten, he was always turned up to at least a solid eight. There was nothing subtle about him, but he had such a sweet personality. He was a kid who very much acted like one. I think that was his only problem; he was just too much kid for a grown-up's taste.

There was also Tom, who looked like the boy version of Steve McQueen's character in *The Great Escape* (1963). He was nice but very guarded at the same time. He talked really fast, and his eyes would dart from one part of the room to the other. He possessed a full range of facial tics and had a hard time concentrating on anything and everything. My memory of him is that he had two types of shirts. One was the classic button-down 100% cotton checkered shirt, and the other was a gray sweatshirt, again like McQueen. At the time, I considered gray sweatshirts the coolest thing to wear. This was the first time that I noticed another male's personal style of fashion, the first time I remember being impressed with a guy because of his clothing. He had his blond hair cut very short and big blue eyes. His lips were thick, which I remember because he always licked them to moisten them. He could sit in a chair quietly, but his various tics and nervous tongue would be going a mile per minute, like the world moved too slow for his body.

There were just two girls in this classroom. One was a cute little Japanese American girl who never spoke. Not a word. When the teacher asked her a question, she would just nod "yes" or shake her head "no." Sometimes she smiled after a question. That was charming. I remember she made me a present; I believe it was a flower made out of color tissue paper. I don't recall the gift so much as that a girl paid attention to me. It was such a great feeling, to receive a gift from a very attractive girl. Rarely did I receive such attention, and when it did happen, it was like a small explosion went off in my body. Her silence never bothered me, and I think she was comfortable with my presence and my lack of demands on her—hence the gift. I think she could speak but just refused to, and my guess is that something traumatic had probably happened to her. I could only assume she never spoke at home either.

The other girl in the classroom was Sandra. It is hard to define what a sexual experience is with a child at such a young age, but I have to say, Sandra was my first sexual experience with another body. Not touching, mind you, but in the sense of my awareness of her body in front of me, and her mindfulness of having her body in front of me. I used to take the school bus to Nora Sterry with her. It seems she was as crazy as I (whatever that meant to the education system at the time). But for sure she provided my first sense of erotic adventure. We sat at the back of the bus, and Sandra invited or allowed me to use my fingers to explore the forbidden areas of her body. I have no memory of actually touching her, but she exposed herself by lifting her skirt or dress above her knees. It's hard to believe that the school bus driver wasn't aware of our activity; we were the only kids on the bus. The whole situation was like *The Story of O* (1954), but on a child level, of course.

Sandra wore cotton panties with little flower prints. She pretended she was warm so she just naturally lifted the dress up to her stomach, saying, "It's so hot on the bus." The implication of what she said made such an impression on me. Also, I liked the intimacy of the moment. Sharing a desire was almost as important as fulfilling that desire. One time we both got off the bus at her request, and she tried to pull me into a gas station bathroom. I didn't go in with her because I considered it too dangerous; I couldn't have been more than 10 years old. But for sure that was the first time the sexual aspect of my character emerged from my introverted personality. The intimacy of being driven in an empty school bus with a driver who paid no attention to us is something I will treasure forever. It was fantastic. I don't know where she is now, but I am hoping Sandra still has that spirit.

There was a difference between the normal kids and the weirdos—and I do mean *weirdos*—since we had our classroom apart from the regular school. It was evident that we didn't belong to the other side of the hall or schoolyard. The regulars had a different outlook on life, for sure. For one, they didn't eat school property like paper, colored chalk, and so forth. Second, the normal girls were exquisite-looking in that romantic image of young beauties who don't have a care in the world. On the other hand, Sandra and the Japanese American girl had that crazy sexy thing going. I had the impression they couldn't articulate their passion, but they sure could show it, and their insanity added something unusual, intense, and fun. Sadly, being mentally challenged, I really couldn't approach a girl from the other side of the tracks, meaning just across the schoolyard.

There was perhaps one girl among the regular students who liked me, a very pretty "normal" girl. She would call me on the phone and spell out "I love you": I.L.O.V.E.Y.O.U. She did this very slowly, and I was just shaking with excitement by the time she reached the letter "Y." I told her I couldn't spell, but if she could read it out to me, I would be most grateful. I think I was trained to flirt at that point. My training came from experience, and how the girl would react to what I told them. I'm convinced that sexuality and the need for love and attention come to us at an early age. It's not a penis/vagina issue, but more of the need to have someone like you, whether it's love or just a super intense reaction you desire from someone else. I spent hours on the telephone with the girl who could spell, and considering how long it took her to spell out a word, I had a significant amount of free time then. But it was a specific period of intense feeling. I was too bashful to convey my need for her love. The situation came to a head when I threw a cookie at her on the schoolyard. It was an indication on my part that I liked her, but she started crying when the cookie hit her forehead.

One of the normal boys came up and hit me in the face. He then kicked me when I fell to the ground. I don't know what was worse, the beating or the fact that I was struck down in front of the girl of my desires. The thing is, I realized what I'd done was totally wrong, but I couldn't express my desire in any other way. What made everything worse was the fact that the most popular boy in the school beat me up. Did I deserve to be hit by this young knight in shining armor? As I hit the ground, slightly bruised and bloodied, I realized I was in the correct position. It was all my doing, and I had to pay my debt for my appalling judgment. I've rarely regretted anything in my life, but to this day, I honestly feel sorry for having thrown a cookie in that girl's face. I was misunderstood, and getting beat up by the boy all the girls liked was one of the most painful moments in my life. But on the other hand, it's good to push your limits—even when you're wrong, because you learn from your mistake—or to be able to step outside of yourself to see how your actions alter the emotional landscape. It's an incident I still draw on for creative ideas concerning my writing.

The one nice thing about that school was its festival, which I think happened twice a year at that time. They had games and food, and it was obviously an event that parents could attend as well as the kids. One of the things I loved about the festival was that they had booths covering the entire schoolyard so no one could play basketball or any other sport. For some reason, that gave me lots of pleasure. I liked seeing a place that was once a horror show to me change into another type of landscape, where imagination and desire take over the image of school athletics and schoolyard life. For me, the school festival was all right. I was very attracted to the booths with food, especially the plastic bags of homemade cookies for sale. There was a carnival aesthetic that was geared toward the children, not the grown-ups whatsoever. Surely this would lead me to hang out at the Santa Monica Pier later in life. Wallace never went to any of the school functions, especially the festivals. Instead, my mother and grandmother Martha would go with me. Since my dad was the only one in the family that drove, he would be in the car outside the school gates, reading a newspaper. My dad was a patient sort; as long as he had a paper to read, he was happy sitting behind the steering wheel. I often ask myself why he didn't take the extra three steps to go inside the school festival. His silence and demeanor expressed a certain amount of contempt for the academic world that was deeply rooted in his psyche.

At the festival, I won a goldfish in a plastic bag full of water. The thought of having this living thing in my hands made me uneasy. It was the first time I felt a sense of responsibility. Of course, the goldfish died within a night or two. But I do remember getting a bowl for the fish, and I had it right by my bed. One day I woke up, and the fish was floating on its side. I'd always suspected that demons came out while I slept, so I instantly knew that one or two had killed my first goldfish. Or maybe it was the ghost of that old lady in the rocking chair that everyone could see except my family. She may have killed the goldfish.

Secret Headquarters / chapter 15

As a child in San Francisco, I became a fan of Walt Disney without in actuality seeing any of his films or cartoons. I mostly knew his work through the *Mickey Mouse Club* (1955–59) and *Zorro* (1957–59) TV shows. Also, my grandparents Dodo and Martha bought me board books, and they were usually Disney-related. Being a child of the early 1950s, I couldn't avoid the world of Disney; it was virtually impossible. I never had a love for the Disney cartoon characters, but Zorro had a huge appeal for me because he wore a mask and seemed to be a very soft man when he was Don Diego. I loved the duality of the feminine man and the male masked hero.

From a young age, I was always attracted to comic strips and comic books with a masked man or woman. Looking back, it was almost a sexual mania, but I liked the idea of someone hiding his or her real identity from the world. In my imagination, I often thought myself as "Tosh," but a Tosh whose real identity was a masked figure fighting for good (or evil). I also needed to have my place and I needed time to be alone. I get physically and mentally drained when dealing with the public, or even another person. Some people have to be with more than one person or a group on a regular basis; I am not one of those people. For me, the mask serves as an excuse to run into the world but remain hidden from the populace. In an odd way the masked Tosh is the real me. I imagine the writer Tosh is the same as the masked Tosh.

The everyday Tosh is a character I made up to deal with everyday issues or social obligations.

I learned how to read early via comic books. I was attracted to the illustrations or artwork more than the stories themselves, as well as to the paper stock and the scent of the comics. There was something so fragile about the newsprint they used at the time. Nowadays the comic book page is of higher quality, but in my childhood, it could easily tear or yellow if placed in direct sunlight. I would go to secondhand bookshops and raid their comic book section. The copies I was attracted to were the ones that weren't taken care of—bent pages, loose bindings—the ones that had that "thoroughly read" look. Comic books at the time weren't meant to last forever; they had a decaying aspect that I found quite beautiful. There was a textural pleasure of holding an old comic book, and even smelling it. The scent of an old comic was a combination of mold (due to dampness, I imagine) and ink.

I was also attracted to the advertisements in the back of comic books for adventuresome items, such as a log cabin. My dad bought me one through one of the ads. In the illustration, it looked relatively large, with a beautiful realistic drawing of a boy around my age standing by his new log cabin home. I remember the child in the ad was wearing a Davy Crockett outfit and coonskin cap. The way it looked in the ad, I imagined I could live in this log cabin all by myself. Perhaps I would have to hunt down animals for my food. The only animals I had at the time were my cats, and surely I didn't want to eat them. But in my imagination, there were wild boars, and maybe a cow or two in walking distance from our house and my soon-to-be new log cabin residence. When the package arrived at our Beverly Glen home, it was one of the happiest moments in my life—till I opened the box. The cabin was a large sheet of plastic with a design on the outside that resembled a log cabin. What you had to do was attach it to a large table and then go under that table. I was disappointed.

The artist and close friend of my dad Ben Talbert had a stash of comic books that I read whenever we visited his home. The production values were up there, but the costumed heroes were entirely unknown to me then and are still unfamiliar to me now. The superhero titles I remember him having were *Blue Beetle, Nature Boy*, and *Captain Atom*. They were obscure to me because they didn't belong to the world of either Marvel or DC comics. They were more like the B-movies of the comic book industry. Where I bought my comics, there were only DC and Marvel and, at times, Archie or Gold Key Comics, which did tie-ins with TV shows. I never saw *Captain Atom* on the newsstand. I got the impression that perhaps they were distributed or sold only in specific backwoods communities. Being a child, I wasn't familiar with the world of eccentric literature, or even aware of the concept. Nevertheless, I knew there was something quite weird about these odd comics. But Ben was a connoisseur of the strange publication, and this was no doubt a serious collection to him, though probably to no one else in the world.

I also had a serious collection of comic books based on TV shows: *Lost in Space*, Walt Disney's *Zorro, Mister Ed, Maverick*, and *Wyatt Earp*, among others. I preferred the comic book versions to the shows themselves. TV shows were very abstract to me, because I had to sit in front of the TV set at a particular time, and then that was it. The experience might have stayed with me, but physically I had nothing to show for it. The comic book is a real product, and therefore seemed more tangible to me. Also, my parents restricted the amount of TV I could watch per day. At my grandparents', no problem! I could watch TV day and night. But no one ever told me to put down those comic books. I could spend endless amounts of time focusing on the illustrations.

It was probably at this time that I was introduced to the concept of a brand name, by reading DC Comics. I totally knew what I was getting on the page. The same goes for Dell Comics.

When I became a young teenager, I totally changed my allegiance to Marvel Comics. Once introduced to the world of *Spider-Man*, *The Hulk*, *Nick Fury*, and *The Fantastic Four*, I couldn't read DC anymore. Marvel successfully added a sense of realism to its super-heroes, even though they had special powers and wore silly costumes. The genius of Stan Lee & Co was their ability to add angst to the main characters, making them virtually three-dimensional figures. DC heroes were quite flat and one-dimensional; now, of course, one can read some depth into something like Batman or Superman, but for a kid, it was flat. Marvel opened up new feelings and situations that an angst-driven kid could easily identify with.

In Beverly Glen, I had my "Secret Headquarters," which was a space that was entirely mine. I must have gotten the idea from the comic books. To be more precise, I saw the hideout as something between Batman's Batcave and Superman's Fortress of Solitude—a fantastic name for a secret headquarters! My fortress was in the backyard underneath some growth from a tree. In this space, I hid some stuff, most likely a toy gun and other toy weapons. No one knew about this location, and the fact that it was 10 feet away from the backdoor somehow made it more of a secret place to me. And believe me, this location was a total secret. Well, I'm sure my parents knew it was there, but they respected that it was a secret, and never mentioned among themselves in conversation, in case the room was bugged.

I spent a lot of time there, and to this day I haven't forgotten the essence and scent of the greenery and the big tree that covered the area. It was a tree with large limbs full of green leaves that touched the ground yet left a beautiful space to walk into: perfectly refreshing, especially on a hot day, and dream-like as well. It was the first location I thought of as truly and entirely mine. I moved some of my books in there as well, noting which ones could last in the outdoor weather. But mostly I would enter and just sit there and let my imagination go. It wandered everywhere, but always came back to that place, and a lot of the time I imagined myself designing the interiors of the space, though I enjoyed it as it was: wild and, it always seemed to me, ripe. It wasn't as grand as the Batcave or as odd and cold as the Fortress of Solitude, but nevertheless, it was a place where I could go and be by myself and not be bothered with the evil forces out there, on what was known as Earth. To this day, I think of my house that I live in now as a version of that secret headquarters.

I used to imagine my father was a crime fighter, and I would help him in a manner that was very much like Robin working with Batman. Perhaps Batman was that type of fantasy for a lot of kids. I know there is talk about a homosexual element in Batman, but what if it isn't homosexuality? What if the fantasy is an expression of kids wishing their dads were Batman and they were Robin? I think that's a stronger fantasy than the sexuality of Batman and Robin. I imagine millions of kids believe in this fantasy, and that's why Robin has endured for so long. The fact that a child can read Batman and think of him as a father is both charming and disturbing at the same time; a son joins his father in fighting crime, yet he knows Batman will protect Robin, and maybe vice versa. Looking back now, it's evident that as a Robin, I didn't protect my dad in the end.

James Bond / chapter 16

One thing my father and I would do on a regular basis was to see James Bond movies, which always screened at the Chinese Theater on Hollywood Boulevard. I must have been seven or eight when I saw my first Bond film. Oddly enough, Wallace never took me to see a Disney movie or something that was more kid friendly. As in Larkspur with Roger Vadim's *And God Created Women*, starring the great Bardot, Wallace only went to films he wanted to see, and my opinion on the matter meant nothing to him.

The Chinese Movie Theater made a huge impression on me. Walking through the main door with the huge banner announcing the current Bond film gave me a sense that I was part of a spectacle. The theater itself was fake Oriental, which was the perfect setting for *Dr. No* (1962). Also, my mother had told me that bats were living in the theater, and though I never saw a bat in there, I imagined that they were up there somewhere watching the audience. I recall watching the Bond films and expecting a bat to fly across the projection light—thereby rendering a Bat-signal on the screen—but alas, that never happened.

The whole packaging of the Sean Connery-era Bond films was delightful to me. The films were like an amusement park ride: the Ferris wheel takes you up, and you're on the top, and you're waiting for the moment when the wheel starts moving again. I rarely remembered the narrative or plots of the Bond films. I recognized the girls, and I always remembered the opening credits scenes. The most exciting part of the Bond movie experience is at the very beginning of the film, when the iris eye of the camera opens up to Bond walking across a soundstage, and then aiming his gun towards the audience. I could watch that forever. I always had a slight anxiety attack thinking we wouldn't make it to the opening credits of a Bond film. The car ride to the theater was always a sensitive point of time for me. We were always on time, but the fear of missing the first five minutes of the opening credits would make me nervous and give me a slight stomachache. The thought of missing the opening sequence of a Bond film almost got a phobic reaction from me. Also, the film starts before the credits, and it's always the best fight or daredevil scene in the Bond film.

Marcel Duchamp / chapter 17

The first big art opening that I was conscious of was the Marcel Duchamp retrospective at the Pasadena Museum in 1963. I was nine years old, and I'd been to other art openings with my dad and mom, but for obvious reasons, this is the one I have the strongest memory of, because, for once, everyone dressed up for this opening, which led me to believe this was something of large cultural importance to my dad's community. I also very briefly met Marcel Duchamp at the opening. Before the exhibition, I'd never heard of Duchamp. There were images of his artwork in our family home, mostly pictures from magazines that Wallace cut out and put up on the wall, or from various art books we had around the house. For instance, Duchamp's *Bicycle Wheel* (1913). At a young age, I was always impressed with the machinery of a device that affected me. I didn't ride a bike, but I clearly saw them being operated by various people in my life. It was art for nine-year-olds! The bicycle wheel on a stool spoke directly to me. It was an object that I identified with, and it didn't seem odd this bicycle wheel would be in a place of honor, such as a work of art. My parents had always admired a well-built piece of machinery. Wallace loved tools, like a hammer or a hand drill, and he owned an Italian racing bike given to him by a friend. He would use it, of course, but mostly the bicycle stood in the Beverly Glen house as an iconic design of beauty. I remember I used to spin the bicycle wheel and make a sound with it.

Seeing Duchamp's *Bicycle Wheel* in person was very impressive to me. Having seen an image of this piece before in a publication made it like seeing a celebrity in person. I think my first thought was to touch it, but I was sophisticated enough to know, even that age, that one shouldn't touch art objects in a museum or gallery. The whole exhibition room—and to this day I can't recall how large the show was, even though it was a retrospective—was full of objects and printed matter of all sorts. The textural aspect pleased me, more than a room of someone's paintings. Grown-ups had to address the theory, humor, and concept of what was and what wasn't art, but to me, at the time, the bicycle wheel was something to be admired, and it was nice that this Frenchman took the time to express gratitude for it. Walter Hopps, who curated the show, introduced my dad, mom, and me to Duchamp. The artist bent down to reach out for my little hand, and I remember when he shook it, he gave a wisp of a smile across his closed lips.

This stayed in my mind because at that moment I realized that this person was very important, and I also got the feeling of just how the room interacted with him being there. The exhibition was memorable not only for the art itself but also for the presence of Duchamp. When my dad walked into a room, people were conscious of his presence. I witnessed this again with Duchamp. People were nervous, and I could tell they looked up to him. I knew he was of importance, though I wasn't sure why. I got the impression he was excellent at what he did, and we were all there to acknowledge that fact. I'd never felt that way at the previous art exhibitions I'd gone to with my parents. On one level, he wasn't that important to me, but on another level, I instantly liked him. And even more important to me was how my teacher reacted when I told her I met a French man at a museum in Pasadena, the night before, who had this bicycle wheel in his show. She must have read about the opening or exhibition in the newspaper at the time, because she was very impressed that I had been there and met him. In the past, I had trouble in getting this teacher's attention, and this was the first time that she acknowledged me in such a fashion. It was my first lesson in how fame can affect other people, and how they may react to you, if you're close to a celebrity of some sort.

WALLACE BERMAN /
Untitled (Jack Ruby), 1964

JFK / chapter 18

The first time I experienced a death was the assassination of President Kennedy in 1963. As a kid, I was glued to the coverage; it was the first time I knew of an incident that caused the entire country to be wired to the same images. Everyone was upset. When Kennedy was shot and killed and my teacher announced it, she broke down and cried. It was a massive thing for a kid to see in a teacher's classroom. Teachers got mad, or they were nice, but they never cried in front of the students. Before Kennedy, dying to me was something that happened to a bad guy in a movie or TV show.

The Oswald shooting was another strange experience, especially watching it live on television. I remember watching a *Tarzan* movie and then the film was interrupted with live footage of Jack Ruby shooting Lee Oswald. I was equally shocked regarding the shooting and at the same time disappointed that my favorite *Tarzan* film was disrupted. Until then, everything in real life and on TV was fully organized, planned out—then a shooting took place that turned the world into a chaotic environment. At nine years old, I was starting to make critical judgments about life. The shooting seemed impossible, and yet there it was in front of me in black & white, on a TV set. All of a sudden, no one had all the information together to be put in a single perspective. I soon realized that there was life before and after Kennedy's murder. Before things to me seemed sane to a certain point, then madness took over after. And Oswald getting shot on TV seemed so unreal, yet very real at the same time. I felt distant from the violence, but I knew it wasn't like the violence I saw on my favorite Western. It was different, and it had emotional aftereffects.

The next passing that would hit home was the death of Ben Talbert, the artist friend of my dad's as well as the owner of that vast comic book collection of oddball superheroes. That was in 1974. The thing I remember with Ben's death was how it was announced to me. I remember I was in the car with my dad, and he casually brought up that Ben died. It wasn't a big statement, just a by-the-way comment. I know that he felt very close to Ben, so this death must have had an effect on him, but I couldn't tell in the car that afternoon. His telling me like that made me feel distant from the fact of Ben's body no longer being on this plane. I wondered right away what happened to his comic book collection! Wallace wasn't comfortable speaking of death, especially that of a friend, and as far as I know, he never brought it up again. I never knew my father or parents ever going to a funeral or memorial. I don't think they did.

Wallace's thoughts on people were very private; that code of privacy was a huge thing for him. I wouldn't say Wallace was secretive, but he was concerned about the right to privacy. As an artist, he was obsessed with the work speaking for itself. He didn't like art-talk or commentary on works of art—particularly by the artist. Personally, I can't understand the need for artists to chat about their work. Visual artists use talent and skill to make a piece that is not language, so why do they need to verbalize or articulate a job through language?

Andy Warhol / chapter 19

I got into *Tarzan* because of Johnny Weissmuller playing the jungle man in the film series from the '30s. They were on TV on a regular basis throughout the late '50s and '60s. It was at our home in Beverly Glen that Andy Warhol shot some of the scenes of his first full-length film, *Tarzan and Jane Regained . . . Sort Of* (1964). It seemed perfectly natural for me to play "Boy." I have a full memory of Taylor Mead and my father's fight scene in the film. I also remember Naomi Levine, the woman who played Jane. And I totally recall my role as Boy, the son of Taylor Mead's Tarzan. What I don't remember is Andy Warhol. I know he was there, but he left no memory for me whatsoever.

I recently saw the film, and it struck me as a masterpiece. Sadly, my wife refused to sit through it, and she left before I came on the screen. I then gave the VHS tape to my mother, thinking that she might be overwhelmed with emotion seeing me on the screen at such a young age, but alas, her only comment was, "God, what a horrible film." I had and still have a tough audience. Watching the film at the Egyptian Theater many years later, I was terrified seeing myself on the big screen. The scary thing was seeing myself as a little boy, who is clearly terrified of the surroundings at that time. My memory of that day is one of pleasure yet, when I see myself, I look so scared, probably due to the camera being on me, and the presence of these strange people in our living room. The

expression on my face as a young boy was very much the same as mine as I watched this film. I have a good memory, so it troubles me that I can't remember Warhol. I've been told that is not an unusual occurrence when one thinks of Andy Warhol. He was there, yet not there. That whole generation of people of my youth consists of phantom figures at the very least, and at the most, they put a stamp or tattoo on my brain. But Warhol is a ghost to me.

What I think is interesting is how Andy Warhol was affected by Los Angeles. Warhol was a fan of Hollywood cinema and a great admirer of the Hollywood studio system. He had to come to Los Angeles to make his first feature-length film. I was chosen to play Boy because I was the only "boy" around at the time. The whole process was totally laidback; it would have to be, if my dad were taking part in the film. I think he admired Warhol's take on culture and probably saw his early, more minimalist work. Wallace had a great appreciation for the New York City lifestyle. It wasn't for him, but he followed New York events with high intensity. He probably knew more about NYC events than a native New Yorker, mostly through art magazines (which were pretty much New York-oriented) and especially the *Village Voice*, which at that time was a great weekly newspaper. Norman Mailer was one of the original editors, and until the 1970s it had incredible coverage of New York culture as well as some focus on the underground scene. The newsprint media of the 1960s were a lot of fun, and very energetic in their coverage of the social as well as the art scene. The importance and success of the underground press of the time were very impressive.

Compared to the immediacy of the print media, TV was so old-fashioned in that era. TV at the time represented a world more imagined than real. There were shows from time to time that

WALLACE BERMAN / Taylor Mead filming *Tarzan and Jane, Regained . . . Sort Of*, 1964 expressed something to an audience—for instance, *The Smothers Brothers* (1967–69) and later, *All in the Family* (1971–79)—but the majority had their heads stuck in the sand, refusing to acknowledge the world outside the boob tube. The underground newspaper was one of the few outlets (along with underground radio) where you could connect to the culture as it was happening at that moment. It was educational and exciting to pick up the *Voice* in those days. After my dad had read it from front cover to back cover, I would pick it up to read the music and film sections. I was a young teenager at that point in time and was totally enthralled with the music and film worlds of the mid-1960s.

Dean Stockwell / chapter 20

My parents had strong friendships with a group of people who, by chance, were ex-child actors. These people knew each other when they worked in the movie studios and stayed connected to each other till they were adults. A lot of them had severe lives due to the demands made of them when they were children. I can see them being attracted to my dad and his world. There is a strong connection between the artist making his art, and the film world making movies. Actors being involved in the filmmaking process can move into the world of visual art-making. The two worlds are not that far off from each other.

Being a child actor in the Hollywood studio system is probably not that creative an endeavor, yet it's part of the process of making art; the whole factory approach must have offered some way to foster these actors' talents for something creative in the future. Child actors come from a very insecure space, due to not having normal childhoods. The ones who were friends of my father—Russ Tamblyn, Dean Stockwell, Bobby Driscoll, Billy Gray, and even Noel Harrison—were drawn to his talent. I think he brought them into a world where they didn't have to worry about the past. All of them were, all of a sudden, in a world that became "now." Wallace encouraged his friends to do art, and he gave them the room to experiment and be themselves. He was never a teacher, but people brought their work to him to get some judgment or guidance. Wallace never said "no" when asked to look at someone's work. Russell, Dean, Billy, and Bobby wound up being pretty good visual artists. Wallace was at least ten years older than them, so in the framework of a family, he would be the big brother, but I never felt there was anything there except friendship. It was a sincere friendship with equal give and take. I loved them all. I have very little memory of Bobby Driscoll because he was around when I was a very young child, but Dean, Russ, and Billy were very much part of my childhood.

I don't remember a time when Dean was not part of my life. As I write, I wear tinted prescription glasses, which is exactly what he wore most of the time. Besides Walter Hopps, Dean is my clearest childhood memory of a man wearing glasses. Unlike Walter, Dean didn't need to wear them on a regular basis. Not long ago, I saw David Lynch's *Mulholland Drive* (2001) with Justin Theroux, and throughout the film, Theroux wears the same type of glasses that Dean wore. I'm convinced that Lynch had Dean in his mind for this particular role, because, of course, I'm aware of Dean being in *Blue Velvet* (1986).

Dean was an active reader, and I know he had a thing for H.P. Lovecraft and science fiction novels. He also loved baroque music and the Beach Boys. He was the only one in my father's circle who liked the music of the Wilson brothers. Dean spent a lot of time in Beverly Glen with Wallace, as well as later in Topanga Canyon. If there were a second male presence throughout my childhood, it would for sure be Dean, although by no means was he a father figure to me.

Dean liked to take our family on early morning road trips, usually somewhere beautiful, like the middle of the desert or the darkest part of the forest. I remember these trips as pure enjoyment. We went to places like Death Valley or Big Bear, where I just remember going by the river—or was it a lake? I never paid attention to where we were going; I just went for the ride, as part

WALLACE BERMAN /
Dean Stockwell, 1963, Beverly Glen

of the family package. I remember the weather more than the scenery: chilly, brisk, with bright sunshine. Tasting the water from the river was a new sensation for me. I'd never had something so cold, yet extremely clean-tasting, in my mouth. For someone like me raised in the urban world, this taste of nature was an entirely new experience. There were camping grounds that had campfire areas where we cooked meat and hotdogs over an open fire. I think Dean and my mom equally did the cooking. We also made hobo coffee, which I didn't drink at that time, but I remember that smell, and it was the only time I liked the smell of the coffee. The real treat was going out for breakfast at some log cabin place, maybe attached to a hotel. The food was excellent, just the breakfast basics, but almost TV-like in brilliance, plates that didn't disappoint the eyes or the taste buds. Scenes of cowboys eating food in the open air always looked incredible to me. That's what I think of when eating by a campfire or in a tourist restaurant in the area; it strikes me as unreal, and the idea of such food is probably better than the actual food served in the countryside.

Dean loved nature, and nature to me always seemed like a movie. Maybe it was because he took the family to beautiful spots, but they never seemed real to me. Death Valley was somehow more real when I watched it on TV as a kid. The sand dunes were an alien landscape I couldn't wrap my head around. Due to my sense of vertigo, I couldn't walk on the dunes, because I immediately lost direction, or succumbed to the feeling I was somewhere specific but nowhere at the same time. I had a vague fear of entering the desert and never coming back if I kept walking on the dunes.

Dean and Wallace had rough patches throughout their friendship, but these never seemed to last long. An incident that comes to mind was once when Dean began to talk about acting. I remember Dean's girlfriend at the time, Toni Basil, was there as well. Somewhere in the conversation, during a car journey, Wallace mentioned he thought that acting was a craft, and not an art. Dean for sure thought of it as an art. Wallace's point of view was that acting was a skill, and skill falls under the category of craft. It was clearly the wrong thing to say to both Dean and Toni. They were furious at him, and a big hunk of that trip was spent in uncomfortable silence. The coldness between Wallace, Dean, and Toni lasted till the next afternoon. It made for an awkward ride, a trip that seemed to last hours. Dinner was awkward, as well, only the raw sounds of forks and knives hitting plates and nothing else.

For a kid, that type of vibe is hard to take. Like when your parents are having an argument: you're not angry; you just feel trapped. I thought for sure that Dean and Toni would just dump us in the middle of the woods. I also would have thought my dad, realizing this was a serious subject for them, would apologize, but I don't believe he did. Come to think of it, I never heard Wallace apologize for anything. It wasn't in his DNA. Even if he were right, shouldn't he have been sensitive to Dean's thoughts on the subject? I think acting is a combination of craft and art. A jazz musician who takes a piece of someone else's melody and does his take is, of course, using a learned craft, but the art is about choosing what to leave out or to bring in for a performance. I should have sided with Dean and Toni on this, but I didn't want to show disrespect to my father. It would have been like ganging up on him. But I have to admit I had a slight fear of being abandoned on the side of the road, with just my father and mother. In other words, never piss off the driver.

Dean never talked about his existence as an actor to me or to us as a family. On one level, I got the impression that he didn't care for the lifestyle or the job at all. Acting was something to do to pay the bills. There were films or projects that he worked on as an actor that were of great importance to him. *Compulsion* (1959), *Sons and Lovers* (1960), *Long Day's Journey into Night* (1962), and even *Blue Velvet* were crucial works to him. When Dean was serious about his work, no one was a better actor. When he did TV guest spots in the 1960s, I could tell he cared less, but still, even when he wasn't trying, he was good, and when he was deeply interested in the character or film, Dean was exceptional.

The other disagreement I recall coming between Dean and my dad was later at the Mermaid Tavern in Topanga. Dean was putting on a production of Picasso's only play, *Desire Caught by the Tail* (1944), in the main room. Wallace was going to have an exhibition at the same place in the same room. He asked Dean to remove the props that were set near the stage. They were more than likely heavy and not easy to move, but Wallace wanted them removed for his show. When it came to his artwork, Wallace never compromised with anyone. To argue with him was a foolish procedure; if a mountain had to be moved, so be it.

The households of my father's friends were all different from each other. Dean's house in Topanga was very woodsy and dark and smelled like the forest he took us to. His home in Laurel

Canyon was the same. I can't imagine Dean living anywhere except in a wooden house with firewood near the front door. Dean worked on his art in the living room, which was also the main social area of the household. I recall a bathroom and walk-in closet downstairs for Toni. Dean and Toni would pretty much share the living room as a workspace. Their house struck me as equal in the division of the workspace, but my recollection of it is filled with Dean's furniture and art. Toni herself has an impressive collection of art, but I don't remember it being part of that household. Their home used to be owned by Joel McCrea, the great actor and Hollywood star of the 1930s. I've been told that he had haunted the house for many years. I think it was Toni who told me when she was in the bathroom, she looked in the mirror and saw a face behind her, which sounds like typical Topanga.

Overall, I liked visiting Dean's house with my parents or dad. He had a vast collection of records. He was a giant Glenn Gould fan, but he also had excellent taste in pop music. In 1965, he mentioned he liked the Beach Boys more than the Beatles, which at that time was a ridiculous statement, but now? Dean also had a large organ with pedals in the living room, and he could play it. Later on, he would give the organ to Neil Young. He was one of those guys who could pretty much do anything once his mind was set on doing it. In the '70s, Dean took up Kendo, a Japanese martial arts practice. He became friendly with his teacher and brought him everywhere in the canyon, including our home. I remember the teacher being quiet. It wasn't a teacher-student relationship, but more like artist to artist.

As a kid, I found it odd that Dean never discussed his work as an actor, because his work was something magical. He's had such a long and fantastic career. Dean was a child actor, but unlike Bobby Driscoll, he didn't stop there. He did theater, TV, and film side by side throughout the '40s, '50s, and '60s. I have a feeling he wasn't comfortable with the Hollywood promotional world, but there were a lot of actors not into the biz at that time. Dean also loved the cinema and was a regular filmgoer like my parents. I remember he had a thing for Antonioni films. I can easily imagine Dean being in an Antonioni film. His character and mood fit the pictures. While Wallace had many friends and an active social group around him, Dean seemed to be his best friend; they had a long history together. Without a doubt, Dean loved him, and while they did have their disagreements, I think my dad loved him back to a certain degree.

In the presence of Dean, I felt very much loved. It wasn't until years later that our relationship soured; we split over something that Dean and my father would have argued about—the use of Wallace's artwork in a film project. In fact, this argument has set us apart for life (at least so far). I've seen Dean from time to time, like every 15 years or so. We usually hug, and then there's no further communication between us, which is hard to believe, considering how close we were as family unit and friend. But the truth is, when someone in a circle dies, the whole structure of the family or a social group changes. It's like shifting sand. Life flows, even in death.

WALLACE BERMAN /

Toni Basil, Crater Lane, 1964

Toni Basil / *chapter 21*

From the age of nine to around 21, I felt very close to Dean's ex-girlfriend, Toni Basil. I identify her that way simply because he was my gateway to knowing Toni. She was the one person who represented glamour to me, due to her work as a dancer and choreographer and her range of work-related friends like Elvis Presley, Mick Jagger, Brian Jones, John Lennon, David Bowie, and so on. And, of course, my mom and dad and their circle of friends. Toni was the one who made introductions and secured us invitations to the other world that co-existed alongside Wallace's social set.

I don't know how or where Dean and Toni met, but their life together exerted an attractive pull on me. I liked the world they orbited in, especially Toni. I was drawn to Toni not just because of her placement in this landscape but also because of her personality, which was pretty wonderful, due to the fact that she was a young girl but still an adult to me. I believe there's ten years' difference in our ages, which, when you're an adult, is nothing. Realizing she was so young when I was a child, I felt she was totally approachable. She knew I loved music and all the tidbits that go with that world, and both her talent as a dancer and her appreciation for art in general made her such a special person at that particular time. She went to high school in Las Vegas, where her father was an orchestra leader at one of the many casino nightclubs. From the very beginning, one gathered, Toni came from a very particular background. There's usually an individual in every social group who ties all the personalities together and pushes them forward, and I think Toni did this for us by having one foot in the rock 'n' roll and movie business world and the other planted firmly in the bohemian/beat scene. She's also extremely beautiful; when she walked into a room she lit it up like Technicolor. I imagine if one has dated Toni, it'd be tough to be with any other girl, even though I never had a childhood crush on her. She was more of a big sister than anything else, but I could never tell her that to her face—only in this book!

Toni was an important bridge between my father and the pop music world. I often felt she had more in common with Wallace than she did with Dean. They both had a strong sense of what was going on in the street, culturally speaking. My dad knew literature, and he had a more in-depth knowledge about jazz culture due to his age. But Toni, being from Las Vegas, understood the pop aspect of jazz, as well as the medium of dance. She was one of the original go-go girls on the TV show *Shindig!* (1964–66), as well as a background dancer and choreographer for various Elvis and beach blanket rock 'n' roll films. At the same time, Toni was working with the artist and filmmaker Bruce Conner on his fantastic short film *Breakaway* (1966), which strikes me as the perfect collaboration between them. Let's not forget the importance of the Lockers, the dance troupe she organized and choreographed. Years later she would become famous for her song "Mickey" (1982). Why Toni wasn't as huge as Madonna is a complete mystery to me. Maybe she didn't have Madonna's drive or hunger, but of the two, Toni is clearly the genius.

I always felt that Toni was at the center of a culture that is interesting to me, and I believe my dad and the others did as well. Without Toni, there wouldn't have been a connection between Wallace and Brian Jones, or Dean and Neil Young, or Bruce Conner and Devo. She was also part of the Monkees' world. She choreographed the famous dance sequence between herself and Davy Jones to the great Harry Nilsson composition "Daddy's Song" in the Monkees' only film, *Head* (1968), which was written by Jack Nicholson and in many ways was a kiss-off to the Monkees' mythos. Toni invited us to the set and we met Micky Dolenz, who was very stoned. For a 12-year-old Monkees fan like myself, it was a great moment—thanks, again, to Toni.

Aside from her work as a performer in films like *Easy Rider* (1969) and *Five Easy Pieces* (1970), Toni should be considered a significant director. While my dad was working on his film *Aleph* (1966) and Russ Tamblyn and Dean were working on their art films, Toni was working with Bruce Conner on *Breakaway*, and she would go on to be a crucial figure during the music video era. She was among the first artists to realize that the music video would become essential, and that it could be used in quite creative ways well beyond being a commercial business card of sorts. Toni made perhaps the earliest video album, *Word of Mouth* (1983), which contained her recording of "Mickey." Of course, she was surrounded by a lot of creative and talented people, but it was her vision that made her stand out, at least in my eyes. She would go on to direct David Byrne in the Talking Heads video of "Once in a Lifetime" (1981), as well as directing two David Bowie tours and a Vegas show for Bette Midler. No wonder I'm such a fan of Toni, and a great admirer of her essence as an artist.

WALLACE BERMAN /

Russell Tamblyn, 1963

Russ Tamblyn / *chapter 22*

One night, Russell Tamblyn was throwing a party and Dean called and asked if he could bring two friends. Russ said "sure" and asked him their names. Dean said, "Wallace and Shirley Berman." Russ heard "Shelley Berman" instead of "Shirley Berman." At the time Shelley Berman was at the height of his stand-up career and, being a fan, Russ was excited to meet him. When he answered the door, Russ was shocked to see Dean with a beat-looking couple, neither of whom was Shelley Berman. But the initial disappointment turned into a deep friendship between my parents and Russell and his then-wife, Elizabeth. She was an English showgirl, and I loved her right away. She always paid attention to me when the family was together, and she could cook, which, at the time, was an unusual skill for someone from the UK. In their household there was Elizabeth, Russ, and Elizabeth's "Mum." I haven't the foggiest idea what Mum's given name was, but she liked to drink and seemed way older to me at the time. Then again, anyone taller than me appeared to be ancient.

Visiting Russell was my first time being in a movie star's home. Number one, it was large, and two, it was really large. I have only a flicker of a memory of the upstairs, because everyone who entered that structure immediately went downstairs to the party room. It had table tennis and a pool table, and there was another room devoted to a full-size bowling alley, and, of course, a large swimming pool outside. Unlike Dean, Russ had photographs on the wall from his acting career. He received an Oscar nomination for *Peyton Place* (1957), and the nomination was up there in a frame. There were images of Russ as a child actor, and many from *West Side Story* (1961). Once he started to hang out with Wallace and other artists, he began to replace the photographs from his acting career with art he was making. Sometimes he painted or collaged over the photos and even the award citation from the Academy. In a sense, I think Russ was acknowledging his life as a visual artist over his career in Hollywood. Wallace opened a door for Russ to make art, and make art films, and, once he entered that mental space, the door closed shut behind him. Of all of Wallace's friends who had worked or were still working as actors, Russ changed the most. He arranged to show films by Dean and Wallace, as well as Bruce Conner, in his home. Russ used his bowling alley as a theater, with the screen placed where the pins would be. After that, I don't think Russell used his bowling alley for bowling; it became a makeshift theater for artists' films.

Russ was the first famous person I became close to while realizing he was famous. I had seen *West Side Story* before meeting him, so he was the leader of the Jets to me. I'd known Dean since I was a baby, so I never made the distinction between him on the movie or TV screen and him in real life. Russ was also unique because I discovered him outside of my parents. My grandmother Anna took me to see *West Side Story* as a child, and I remember she fell asleep during the movie. She'd prepared a meal that she smuggled into the theater, so I had lunch there as well. I liked the film a lot. For one, the music spoke to me. And too, I had never seen a musical before. I must have been seven, and that type of world was foreign to me. A decade later, *A Clockwork Orange* (1971) would have a significant impact on me as a cinema-goer, reminding me of *West Side Story* because both films dealt with gangs. I had a thing for groups on the big screen. I also loved

The Great Escape, because, in my mind, it was also a gang story. A World War Two prisoner-of-war gang, but nevertheless a gang.

Like Dean and Toni, Russ and Elizabeth felt like extended members of the Berman family. At that time, both Russ and Dean seemed to turn their backs on their acting careers and concentrate on making art. Russ got into it big time when he met Wallace and rekindled his friendship with Dean. Russ and Dean were both making collages, and were excellent at it. Dean's work was more textural, and I remember he did a whole series of collages with paper currency. A lot of his work looked like animation to me. There was something very methodical about his work, very well thought out, almost a science. My father liked things to look messy, even punk like, but Dean's work was neat, precise, and organized. He's very much an underrated artist. Russ on the other hand makes me think of George Herms. His work is about sensuality and not so much precision. As far as I know, Russ didn't write poetry, but he became very close to Jack Hirschman, another poet who was close to the Berman clan. Nevertheless, Russ was a big reader of poetry, and he has a deep appreciation for it. It's no surprise his daughter Amber Rose is a published poet as well as an actor.

WALLACE BERMAN /

Billy Gray, 1962

Billy Gray / *chapter 23*

Billy Gray may be the first person I recognized as an actor in my dad's circle of friends. Unlike Russ, who was a star to me first, then a family friend, Billy was a friend who happened to be on my TV set at the same time. The show he was in, *Father Knows Best* (1955–60), was the iconic family show of the '50s; even though we didn't have a TV set, I was well aware of this series. Billy played Bud, a typical male teenager in a family with two sisters and a mom and a dad. It was a television manual showing what an average American family is and should be. Alas, life is a bit different from that. As a boho kid, the show had an effect on me. It was the first show I watched that exposed me to the straight world that was outside our door, maybe even next door.

The funny thing is, watching the TV show was very much like knowing Billy. He looked like he just walked into my TV set and lived in it for half an hour, with a window I could watch him through. Billy in the TV show was not all that different from the Billy I know. Apparently, he was playing a role, but in everything else, he was very much "Bud." His character was so sweet and decent, and Billy in real life was the same way. The only difference was, Billy liked to smoke pot. In many ways, Billy was (or is) very much like a grown-up kid. His girlfriend at the time, Helena, was a very dear friend to Toni Basil, and close to my family as well. Even though they were a couple, their lives were not bound together. Billy was very much a man of his world. I never thought of him as being part of someone else's life. He was truly an All-American youth. He had that spirit of being an adventurer, and he was a huge fan of motorcycles. I remember Billy going right up a mountainside with his motorcycle, and it impressed me he could do something like that without falling off. It was the closest thing I'd seen in real life to Steve McQueen in *The Great Escape*.

After his TV show ended, Billy stayed in contact with his fellow cast members. He was very close to Lauren Chapin, the actress who played his little sister; she had a lot of problems with her family and life after *Father Knows Best*. The same goes for his TV dad, Robert Young, who had problems with alcohol and depression. The happiness depicted in that show was a mere fantasy. Over time, I think Billy felt remorseful about the show as a representation of something he felt was untrue. But then again, that's the nature of show business: to sell illusions.

Compared to Wallace's other close friends, Billy was very practical. The mechanical aspect of his personality was so unlike my dad and the other child actors. He was always working on inventions. I'm sure he had money in mind, but I also have a feeling he liked to work with his mind and body together. He has a natural ability for engineering. When I look at a piece of machinery, it is very much a foreign object to me, but to Billy, it is a functional object that can be easily figured out.

Billy was the perfect friend for a young tot like me. He was magnificent at telling stories, especially my type of stories. Whenever I was at an adult party and Billy was there, he would spend some time with me. I remember being at parties and getting sleepy. I would be placed in the party host's bed; even when I went with my parents to parties, I was still encouraged to go to sleep at a particular time. In situations like that, Billy would tell me a bedtime story, and it was always the scariest episode of *The Twilight Zone* (1959–64). Billy would tell me the story in great detail, even with sound effects, before I fell to sleep. Billy is a natural with children. He doesn't talk down to them.

Dennis Hopper / *chapter 24*

Another friend among the actors my dad was close to was Dennis Hopper. Dennis first met my father at Stone Brothers Printing, the studio that Wallace shared with Bob Alexander. Legend has it he brought James Dean with him to the studio, though my mom can't remember if this is true. She clearly remembers Dennis at the studio. My first impression of Dennis was not as an actor, but as a friend of the artists. He bought art from his buddies, and his taste in friends, like his taste in art, was superb. What made him unique is that he was totally open to the world of small galleries. Dennis had a taste for the visual arts, and its social world as well. In a way, he reminds me of Brian Jones of the Rolling Stones, in that he came from a very small and contained world—the entertainment world—but, like an ant separating himself from the queen, Dennis struck out to see what was around that world. Therefore he brought others to the landscape of galleries and friendships with artists. He was a citizen of the Beverly Glen household, among all the others who came to the house on a regular basis. It was only years later I realized Dennis was an actor—a working actor—when I saw him on an episode of the TV show *The Defenders* (1961–65). He played an American neo-Nazi and was quite intense in the role. Although Dennis was far off from the world of the Nazis, he was clearly a very intense man. That would have been my initial impression of him, and even now, when I think of him, I think of the flame-like intensity he showed for his life and his work.

When I knew Dennis, even up to my father's death, he was a man of the art world, as well as being an artist himself. I was amazed to see him on TV for the first time, when I was around eight years old. Like seeing Dean or Billy on the tiny screen, I didn't find it that odd, because I knew they were actors, though I was surprised that Dennis made his living this way. Of course, Dennis had an incredible career in films, especially *Rebel Without a Cause* (1955) and *Giant* (1956). But I didn't see *Rebel* till I was a teenager, and, to this day, I've still never seen *Giant*. During his relationship with my parents, he did appear in a film called *Night Tide* (1961) that's known not only for being his first starring role, but also for including Cameron in a strong role. Since it takes place in Venice, California, and I knew Dennis and Cameron so well, *Night Tide* is more like a home movie to me than a Hollywood film.

Whenever I picture Dennis throughout the 1960s, he's always with a camera. Which isn't odd, because my dad always had his 8mm camera with him as well. I never saw Dennis take a photograph, but I knew he was quite serious about photography. At the time, he took photos of bands like The Byrds, Ike & Tina Turner, and the Jefferson Airplane. This, I reckon, was a commercial job, where he was hired by either the bands or their record companies. It was years later, way after my dad's death, that I came upon his book of Dennis's photographs, mostly images from the civil rights struggle as well as portraits of the artists that he knew. He was one of the leading photographers and collectors of L.A. artists, and he made no distinction between the art worlds of New York City and Los Angeles. Dennis even took images of the British art dealer Robert Fraser in Los Angeles, as well as in his gallery in London. Though he's never identified in the picture with Fraser, Dean Stockwell is there in the background.

Robert Alexander at Stone Brothers Printing, Los Angeles, 1957

The young actors around Wallace all most likely met through their profession, but being visual artists was what really connected them. I wouldn't say Wallace was the sole cause of these actors getting together, but he was a major magnet for these talented people who were looking for an outlet for their creativity. Dennis's best friend was no doubt Dean. They knew each other before meeting Wallace, but they became tight through the art world more than through Hollywood. At times, I felt a tad nervous around Dean and Dennis when they were together in a room. I often felt that they would try to outdo each other or do things neither would have done if the other one hadn't been there as well. Once we were at Dean's house, and Dennis was on the telephone talking to a woman who I knew at the time. She was a typical face in Topanga, and I remember her being stunning. Dennis was trying to get her to come over, whining and pleading with her. I felt weird to be in the same room overhearing this conversation. There was nothing sinister about the call, but Dennis was, for sure, stoned and he was totally focused on seeing this girl. Dean was entirely focused on Dennis, and my dad and I were just sitting on the couch trying not to pay attention to anyone, except for Russ, who was there as well. But I did sense this grouping of Dennis/Dean and then there were the rest of us.

While Dean and Dennis were sharing the telephone, 100% focused on getting this girl to come over, my dad started to play with Toni Basil's microphone. He turned it on and began to do a low-grade Vegas comedy routine, telling atrocious Henny Youngman jokes with no punchlines at the end. Russ and I were laughing hysterically at Wallace's routine and just the surrealism of being in that space and time. All of sudden, Toni approached the front door from the outside. Wallace threw the live mic to Russ, who caught it, and when Toni walked into the living room and saw Russell holding her mic, she totally lost it. Wallace meanwhile had changed his whole body language and pretended to be reading a book on the couch. So Russ was trying to explain that he wasn't playing with her equipment, and my dad just totally ignored them, like he was lost in the book. Meanwhile, Dean and Dennis didn't stop pleading with this woman on the other end of the phone to come over.

There were many nights with Dennis and Dean. I heard from someone who was there when Dennis was living in Taos, New Mexico, that he and Dean were dancing waist-to-waist at a local bar, where such behavior was clearly a no-no. It was a more-than-likely dangerous situation, and Dennis was probably armed at the time. Many years later, I saw David Lynch's *Blue Velvet* on the big screen. Seeing Dean sing Roy Orbison's "In Dreams" to Dennis reminded me so much of their relationship. Lynch captured the dynamic of those two together. It's a scary scene, because of the undertone of violence and sexual menace. But I thought it was actually a very real portrait of Dean and Dennis together.

George Herms / *chapter 25*

My father's closest friend who was a fellow artist with no other occupation was George Herms. As far as I know, George is California-born and -bred. He's a classic assemblage artist from the beat era and has always been closely associated with Wallace. Wallace always supported George as a friend and fellow artist, and now he's the last beat-era artist standing. Louise, who was married to George from the late '50s to the late '70s, was the woman I was closest to during my youth. She was also my mom's best friend during those years. There was something frontier-like about Louise. She was strong, and I think she had to be, to be with George for so long. They had two children: Nalota and Lillybelle. Both were friends of mine, though I was at least two years older than the girls.

For many years, first in Larkspur and later in Topanga, George and his family were our neighbors, and it's almost spooky now, thinking back, that we were never that far from their home. The Berman family lived with Louise when we were all on Scott Street in San Francisco. She was one of the tenants upstairs. I have a faint memory of her at that time. Interestingly, I have a more active memory of the record albums in the house than the humans who lived there, though John Wieners is very much a deep-seated memory to me. My earliest memory of George and Louise as a couple is in Larkspur, and if my memory is correct, Nalota was delivered at their home. I know Louise was a Christian Scientist,

WALLACE BERMAN /

George Herms, Topanga Canyon, 1965

which I think meant she didn't believe in being under a medical doctor's care. Their home was very much a shack and very similar to our home just down a ways on the same boardwalk.

Wallace gave George his first platform, a show at the Semina gallery, which was the structure directly between our home and their pad in Larkspur. As far as I know, George and Louise were the first ones in our social circle to live in Topanga Canyon, which was where they lived after we moved back to Beverly Glen. George had a chaotic lifestyle. His studio was a total mess, and he was the type who would sneak into your space and take that as well. His "stuff" seemed to have a life of its own and it just got bigger and bigger. As a kid, the thing that struck me the most was that there was nothing new in his studio. Everything was from the junkyard, and there was a lot of it. Many years later, after my father's death, George was living in Downtown Los Angeles with Margaret Nielsen—a superb artist, by the way. What was hysterical to me was that George had the whole studio floor, while Margaret had a little space in the middle of the studio to do her drawings and paintings. Her area was entirely cut off from the world of George, surrounded by his junk pile of materials to be used for his assemblages. Her tiny space reminded me of West Berlin before the wall came down, smack dab in the middle of East Germany. Her studio was immaculate and precise, while George's was as dark and gray as East Berlin during the 1970s. He had East Berlin, but he allowed Margaret's West Berlin right in the middle of his space, although, if memory serves me, it had been Margaret's studio in the first place.

George was also the first performance artist in my life. I remember countless events or performances where he was half naked and blowing into a discarded water hose. At first, it was kind of interesting. Then it became annoying. But he's been doing that routine for the past forty-something years, and it's always a hit with the crowd. Lucky for him, he gets a new audience every ten years or so. George's message is "love" with the last letter turned either backward or forwards. You can't argue against love. He loved many. Wallace and George shared a love for be-bop jazz and the boho lifestyle. The difference between the two was that George liked to attract attention, whereas my father went out of his way to defuse the attention he got. The more he ignored people, the more attention he got—that was Wallace. George, on the other hand, didn't mind being in front of the public. He's extremely intelligent and an exceptional assemblage artist, like Wallace. He is also a man of great social grace and charm. Rarely have I met someone who doesn't fall entirely in love with George on first meeting him. George is a naturally great designer, and his work is very "George," which is the wonderful thing about his artwork; there isn't anyone out there like him.

It is rare when the name "George Herms" doesn't bring up the name "Wallace Berman," and I guess the reverse could be said. Their friendship was strong, and they hung out for years, but their works are very different from each other. I always felt that Wallace's work was very textural, with layers of meaning and mystery. George, I think, is much more vaudevillian, with broad humor. Rarely did his work comment on the world of politics directly, whereas Wallace used the language of that world and transformed it with his sensibility. Also, though it doesn't show in his work, George was very much part of his community, even becoming the president of the Topanga P.T.A.! His interest in politics was also personal, in that he believed one could change things from within, or that's the impression I got. Although at first glance he appears anti-structure, in fact, he had or has a great belief in society and all the tools that come with it. Wallace, on the other hand, never voted or showed any interest in any matter with the P.T.A. George wanted to be very much part of the system, and my father wanted to ignore that world. In that way, they were total opposites of each other.

Music / chapter 26

I never heard my parents talk about money matters. In Beverly Glen, my mother went out to work while my father stayed home and took care of me. The financial end came from my mother's work, but it was at this time I realized that my father was working as well, making art. Being raised in this household affected my notion of work. My mother had to get up early, get dressed in work clothes, and go to work. On the other hand, my father never had to get dressed for work. He got up, had his coffee (always with milk and sugar), looked at the mail, read the newspaper, listened to music, and then went to his workplace, which at that time was in the corner of our living room. I think I preferred my father's concept of work to my mother's. Then again, she was bringing in the money for us to live, to eat, and to pay the bills. I don't believe my father was making money at the time. He would win card games here and there, but a regular salary was not part of his world whatsoever. Similarly, I work every day, though my work doesn't always equate to earning money. It wasn't till I got married and had to deal with household expenses and bills that I became properly introduced to the world of finance and the hard fact of how not having money can affect one's lifestyle. Having a grown-up relationship with a partner is a shock to the system, not just in terms of living with someone, but also in figuring out who pays for what and how to get money.

Wallace never had assistants helping him make his artwork. He was very much a solitary figure in his studio, and only his close friends and I were allowed in while he was working. He was highly focused, and he didn't have a telephone in his workspace, which in effect was cut off from the outside world. I had a "job" with him; I had to look after the music in the studio/workspace. Either I would pick the records, or he would tell me what he wished to hear. He would ask me to play particular 45 rpm singles for him. I think Wallace liked the single because, in theory, the single is just one perfect song; it's sort of like him picking out the perfect image for his grid pieces. He would hear a song on the AM radio and immediately, or as soon as possible, go to the local record store in Westwood Village to purchase the record. He used to play the Supremes' "Baby Love" (1964) over and over again, about 25 or 30 times in a row. Other records that stay in my mind are the Rolling Stones' "(I Can't Get No) Satisfaction" (1965) and lots of Motown. The songs after a while became trance pieces to me. I lost the melody and went into a trance, and I wonder if my dad did the same, if it helped him focus on his work.

Most of my father's work is untitled, but some were named after songs: one is "Papa's Got a Brand New Bag" (1965) and another is the Phil Spector/Righteous Brothers hit, "You Lost That Lovin' Feelin'" (1964). Both are great records with strong, poetic titles. "Papa's Got a Brand New Bag" (1964–65) is a large piece Wallace made while under the influence of that song. It was eventually sold to Robert Fraser in London. It's a beautiful mixed-media piece consisting of drawing, collage, and Verifax. I remember him slowly putting that piece together. Time wasn't that important to him; he would get in a no-time zone when he was working, which was another reason to play a song over and over again. It destroyed any sense of the hours going by.

James Brown was a critical figure in Wallace's world. Toni Basil arranged for my father to meet him while he was shooting *Ski*

WALLACE BERMAN /
Phil Spector, 1965

Party (1965), a beach-blanket-type movie made in the snow. My dad showed up on the set and was escorted to Brown's dressing room trailer. Once they met, Brown showed my dad his closet. Being a clotheshorse, my father was impressed with Brown's wardrobe as well as the man himself. Both were on separate planets, but Wallace enjoyed that aspect of stardom. He had an incredible respect for those who were in show business. Like his literary heroes, he saw performers as beyond the every day, and he had great admiration for people who had the ability to entertain on a stage.

"You Lost That Lovin' Feelin'" was a song that hit my father intensely. Phil Spector went to the same high school as my dad, but even though they shared the same social world, their temperament was entirely different. But Wallace had lots of respect for Phil, in that he was someone with a vision, and in many ways, built his own world. I'm not sure why my dad loved "You've Lost That Lovin' Feelin'" so much, but it grabbed him like no other

Music / 147

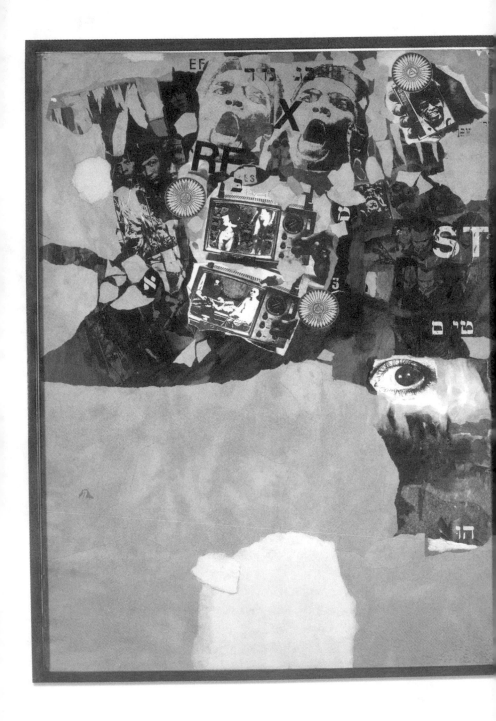

song. The artwork that he named after the song captures the essence of Spector at work. In many ways, it's a beautiful portrait of another artist doing what he does best.

Wallace had a one-day show of his artwork in his studio in Beverly Glen. After the show, Wallace was contacted by Spector's people, who said that he was interested in seeing "You've Lost That Lovin' Feelin'," as well as other works. Spector showed up with his wife at the time, Ronnie Spector, and their driver. Spector was small, and very gangster-like in appearance, and I remember he had a walking stick with him. When Spector saw "his" piece, he took the cane and pointed it at the work and said he was going to buy it. I think, even though he's in prison, he still has Wallace's artwork in his collection. Eventually, I hope it becomes part of a public collection, because it is too great a piece to be hidden away. Wallace did remain in contact with Phil over the years, which may have been how he was introduced to Spector's great friend, Lenny Bruce. Recently my mother told me that they once saw Lenny at a comedy club, and part of the show was to spotlight someone in the audience, and Bruce would make fun of that person. The light hit Wallace, and Bruce went to him, looked at Wallace, and said to the audience, "This man is an angel," and then went on to find another victim in the crowd.

I later ran into Phil at Wallace's opening at the Timothea Stewart Gallery that took place a couple of years after his death. Phil came to the opening with his bodyguard and they were acting very strange. I found out later he was going up to complete strangers and saying stuff like, "See that guy behind me? All I have to do is say the word, and he will beat you up," or something to that effect. My friend Gary, who (we've been told) looks exactly like me, approached Spector at the opening. Phil thought that he

WALLACE BERMAN / *Papa's Got a Brand New Bag,* 1964

was talking to me. Then Gary said to him, "You think I'm Tosh, but I'm not." Spector insisted that Gary bring me over. I went over there not knowing what had taken place, and I said, "Hi, Phil. " He looked at me for at least 30 seconds, and then said, "How do I know it's you?" It was an excellent existential type of question, and I wasn't sure how to answer it.

The Fortunes' "You've Got Your Troubles" (1965) and the Kinks' "Who'll Be the Next in Line" (1965) were two other songs that Wallace was fanatical about. It's funny, I share the same love for these songs, but I'm not sure if it's because they're simply fantastic or because they're songs Wallace was attached to. If there was some music that he loved, more than likely I loved it as well. In a lot of father/son relationships, some objects or activities bind the two males together. For me, this bond is the music Wallace loved. There is no way that I can separate the memory of those songs from the presence of my dad. They represent not only the time period but the essence of my father as well. When I hear them, I immediately think of my dad.

Frames / *chapter 27*

On Crater Lane, right across the street from our little shack, a friend of my father's moved in. His name was Billy Jahrmarkt—aka "Billy Batman," founder of the Batman Gallery—and with him were his wife Joan and their two small kids. One was a bit under my age, and the other little boy was maybe three or four years old. The Jahrmarkt family lived with no possessions that I can remember. For some reason, I think the kids slept on the living room floor, so maybe the place was just a one-bedroom structure. It had a den downstairs with a separate entranceway. I'm assuming that this was Billy's playroom or studio. The main part of the house was very minimal. It almost had a feeling like it was a hideout for a gang on the run. As a small boy I wandered over there to play with the two boys, and the mom, Joan, would make us chocolate milk with chocolate syrup. I was intrigued watching her make the drinks, because my favorite part of the drink was using the spoon and stirring the syrup till it disappeared and dissolved into the milk. She served the chocolate milk in large glasses, and I remember sitting around the kitchen gulping it down with the brothers. She also made us sandwiches, which tasted so different from what my mom or dad made for me.

Billy was very kind, and he had two passions that I picked up on as a child: heroin and guns. Billy and Joan's home was modern compared to our house; he had some family inheritance. I don't remember him ever having to go to work. He was pretty much always around the house while I was there playing with his two sons. Heroin I didn't see, but I knew of its presence, I think, due to my parents. What I did see was Billy's gun collection, which was something out of James Bond. Billy presenting his guns to me was like Q in the Bond films showing 007 the latest devices. I remember one that had a long barrel, and I think it came with a shoulder brace. It was a beautiful object that looked like it came right off the big screen. He would lecture me about how guns were perfectly safe when handled properly.

The Jahrmarkt family resembled an All-American family, and they were perfect neighbors. But they had an edge to them. Even at a young age, I understood that. I remember that their record collection was a lot of contemporary folk music. Pete Seeger albums come to mind. Guns and Pete Seeger were a very strange combination. The kids were great but wild like their parents. One of the boys shot me, point blank, with his BB gun. I had the worst black and blue mark on my arm, and it stayed for a while. He just stared at me to see what I would do. I screamed in pain. He was disconnected from what he did. He had a pair of beautiful blue eyes, like his mom's, and they read empty when he shot me. Not long afterward, Billy and family moved to Afghanistan so he could indulge in his other favorite activity, heroin. Ironically, for someone who went out of his way to show me his gun collection and swore to me that anyone could handle it, he accidentally shot himself in the stomach, and died a few days later.

But while living on Crater Lane, Billy was kind enough to provide the downstairs of his home for Wallace's use as a studio. It was essentially a den with a small sink area and a toilet. The room itself was tiny, and in its entrance were large pieces of plank wood, supported by a series of sawhorse stands that made them into one large worktable. There was barely room to walk around the table, and I remember the only other object around was a

WALLACE BERMAN /
Billy Jahrmarkt aka Billy Batman

small, portable turntable in the corner. I have a memory of the smell of wood, which Wallace liked as well. He always had pieces of wood around his workspace. He also had a thing for metal. There is magic in wood and metal, and both were suitable for my dad's aesthetic pleasure. Wallace loved hanging around a hardware store the same way I like to spend time at a record store. Later he made his wooden frames for the Verifax pieces, and lovingly he would stain the wood a darker color. Often he went to Sid Zaro to do his framing, but he also did the job himself sometimes, and I was called on to assist him in work.

Besides controlling the record player, my studio job was to hold the artwork steady so he could screw the frame onto it. There is one true sign of a Wallace Berman-made frame: the screws on the artwork. If you see those screws, it means he made the frame, and more than likely, I helped him. At this point, I'm probably expected to mention how much I loved helping my dad frame his works, but the fact is, I hated it. It would take him forever to hammer a nail or work a screw into the frame. I had to hold the art up, until my shoulders were about to give out, and then "bam!" and more little "bams" to hammer that perfect nail in that perfect place. It made me sad that a particular art collector, the owner of some of my dad's artwork, had the frames removed and replaced with shiny metallic ones. The collector reportedly said, "At last, I found the perfect frame for Berman's artwork." Maybe so, but I went through a lot of boredom and stiff shoulders for those frames, and I like my dad's frames better. That collector is lucky that he changed the frames after my father died. If Wallace were alive, he would never have approved the modification.

There was a movement around that time to use the United States postage system as a conceptual way of presenting art. Wallace used postcards to make art pieces, as well as to communicate with his friends. These works were not made to be shown in galleries or museums or anywhere else in public, but they do hold up as art, as well as a diary of sorts. It's worth noting that his work in the '50s, and in the '70s right before his death, reflected more on the personal than the public. In both decades, he was making sculptures that dealt with his inner world of artmaking. The '60s work dealt with the outside world, especially the Verifax transistor radio collage; the radio in a sense broadcasts images via music. This work was intended as a commentary on the culture and politics of America and beyond.

My father had a particular style when working. The music just had to be right, the mood perfect, to make the moment at hand an inspiration. Wallace was fanatical about perfection in his artwork. He never took himself seriously; in fact, he was goofy. But when it came to his art, Wallace was extremely serious. He spent a lot of time on one piece, sometimes just studying it, looking at it from different angles. My mother told me that he would sometimes place the artwork on the ground and look at it from between his legs—an odd angle, of course, but who am I to argue with genius?

Wallace was particular about who bought his work. For instance, a bank wished to purchase a piece by my dad for their corporate art collection, and he said sure. He made a piece called "Bank Statement," with an image of a woman giving a man a blow-job superimposed over the document in question. For some reason, the bank declined to purchase the artwork, which is too bad, because I'm sure it would have made a great conversation starter at the bank's next board meeting. If someone purchased his artwork, Wallace would show up at that person's house and hang it up himself. For him, the work always had to be presented in an individual matter. It didn't matter who owned the work; Wallace felt he, not the new owner, should have control over how the work would be displayed. The owner acquired not only the artwork but also the company of my father and his handy skills in hanging his work.

Whether it was due to the failure of his Ferus Gallery exhibition or just to his relationship with the art world, Wallace refused to stage shows at commercial galleries. I think he was nervous about being part of someone else's business. He didn't want to be in a position where he had to do a show once a year or anyone put him on a schedule to produce art. He had no problems doing book covers for friends, but he disliked the idea of a solo show at a commercial gallery. He rarely, if ever, commented on the relationship between his work and the gallery system. He loved going to see exhibitions, and he was friends with numerous art dealers, but for whatever reason, he wasn't comfortable being tied to one. What he did, instead, was bring his artwork to a dealer and tell him how much money he wanted for it; after that, the dealer could sell it for as much as he wanted. If he only wanted $500 out of the deal, Wallace didn't care if the dealer made $20,000. He wasn't egotistical or concerned with money matters in that way.

Wallace was also quite charismatic. Women and men, boys

and girls were all attracted to him. To me, he was a dad, but to others, he was a god, especially to those who had an interest in the arts, and on top of that, he was pretty good-looking. He was quiet, but that silence made him special to the people around him, and attracted attention from those who didn't know him as well. He loathed the spotlight, and couldn't care less what people thought of him. He never did interviews, and as far as I know never spoke about his artwork, but he devoured issues of *Artforum* and books on art. He was aware of every "ism" that was out there in the art world, and he usually was for it. The mixture of being private yet so open to the world made my dad a unique personality. There was no generation gap between us, and he was very friendly with all of my childhood friends. Yet I always felt an age difference with some of his friends, at least in an aesthetic sense, since he was more on top of what was happening at the moment, while very much aware of the past. In his Verifax collages, some images transcend time. To see the present he needed the past, and through the past, he could see the present. Who knows? He maybe could also see the future.

Smellwise, it's Royal Lime aftershave lotion that reminds me of Wallace. The last time I saw Royal Lime was in Japan about ten years ago. It was a traditional aftershave, but it disappeared over the years until I could only find it in a discount shop in a port town in Japan. Memories and scents fade, yet once in a while, you can capture the essence of both if you set your mind to it. Even thousands of miles away from my home, long after my father's death, the sight and scent of the Royal Lime aftershave lotion brought the memory back to me. By just opening the lid of the sample at the gift shop, I was immediately back in Beverly Glen. It reminds me of when my face was very close to my father's. In fact, I loved it when he shaved, I think because of the smoothness of his face, but also because of the smell. Shaving represents something fresh to me. I picked that up as a kid, noticing my dad's face. I never liked him with a beard.

Brian Jones / chapter 28

When I was around 10 years old, I purchased my first 45 rpm single. I didn't have a job, so I have to assume that either my parents or, more likely, one of my grandmas gave me the money. I purchased the Yardbirds' double A-sided single, "I'm a Man" b/w "Still I'm Sad" (1964). I must have seen the Yardbirds on *Shindig!* Jeff Beck was in the band, and I remember his style more than anything else. I liked his face, his haircut, and the way his suit fit him. There's nothing wrong with the album format, but to me, like my dad, the 45 rpm single is seven inches of magic. The Yardbirds record was avant-garde to me as a 10-year-old. What impressed me about the Yardbirds' version of Bo Diddley's "I'm a Man" was the final 50 seconds of the record when the dueling electric guitars and percussion become totally manic and intense.

The intensity of the rave-up made me swoon. I'd never heard anything like it in my life, and to this day, it makes my lower spine shake. It was pure noise, but rhythmic and tribal, and it left me with a sense of the whole world collapsing in exhaustion at the very end. Then you flipped the record over to this fantastic, spooky ballad, "Still I'm Sad." As if the manic quality of "I'm a Man" wasn't enough, the morose sadness of "Still I'm Sad" touched me in a very vibrant manner. What a brilliant title for a song! And the combination of both titles is fantastic as well. It couldn't have been random. It must have been fate. It's pure poetry, pure noise. I learned how to operate my parents' turntable by playing both sides of this single over and over again. Each side pulled me in a different direction. The angst, anger, and sadness moved from the vinyl into my heart.

Shindig! (1964–66) was, for my mental state, the perfect TV program. It didn't last long, but compared to other shows, its few moments on the TV screen lasted forever for me. Each show was 30 minutes long, and within that half hour, you got the best artists of the U.S. and the U.K. That show and the radio were my connection to the world that I found equally glamorous and essential to my well-being. As I mentioned, TV programming was very conservative, even at the height of the 1960s. Very few shows dealt with my culture, and *Shindig!* was the one I was plugged into like an electric cord in a socket. It wasn't only the Beatles and the Stones; there were a lot of wonderful one-hit wonders who disappeared after making that fantastic single. It was a series of blissful moments for me.

Toni Basil invited my dad and me to go to the dress rehearsal for *The T.A.M.I. (Teen Age Music International) Show* (1964), starring the Beach Boys, the Supremes, James Brown and the Famous Flames, the Rolling Stones, and other incredible artists of that time. This, to me, was ground zero for everything that was good in life. It was a cinematic version of *Shindig!* with the same dancers that were on that show, like Toni. *T.A.M.I.* was a cultural sampler of pop music that was groovy in the year 1964. There were at least a dozen acts, and each did one or two songs, and some did four or five. It was an amazing spectacle to watch the film in a movie theater, but to be at the actual dress rehearsal was almost unthinkable. Sitting down in the empty Santa Monica Civic Auditorium to watch the Supremes do a soundcheck with curlers in their hair was an out-of-this-world experience. I was also impressed that the Beach Boys did their soundcheck in their full stage uniforms, which were white pants and striped shirts. I found the juxtaposition of the Supremes looking raw and undressed with the slickness

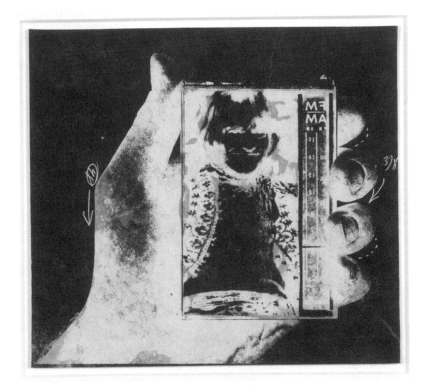

of the Beach Boys surprising. The Rolling Stones were the ones that impressed me the most. My first estimation of British culture was Hayley Mills, but the Beatles and the Stones made a huge impression on me, as well. Being in an empty theater and seeing the Stones mingle among the vacant seats was a dream that had a 3D effect for me. They looked exactly like their photographs, like they'd walked right off their first album cover into my world.

Toni introduced Mick Jagger to Wallace and me. Mick rubbed the top of my head and said, "Cute tyke." My father also met Brian Jones, which was the start of a lasting friendship between them.

Wallace, at the time, had his 8mm Bolex camera pretty much attached to his hand. He didn't obsessively film everyone or everything, but if something caught his eye, he shot it. The weird thing is that he had the camera with him at the *T.A.M.I.* soundcheck and he could clearly have shot film there, but he didn't shoot one piece of footage. Instead, he waited for the movie to be released, and then went to Westwood Village to film it off a movie screen. I think he was more interested in getting the grainy effect of the film stock, and he could do that by capturing images from the big 35mm screen. He was almost like a journalist. Whenever he shot or took a photograph of someone, it was a very subjective view of that particular subject. On the other hand, when he used the secondhand material, including images from another movie, it was almost as if he was reporting an incident or a feeling. "Indirect" is a mode of operation for a lot of Wallace's work. It's interesting to me that he didn't stay for the actual concert; he could have shot images from the live audience point of view. I remember being disappointed that we didn't stay for the show, but I never questioned my dad's need to leave. I think he got what he wanted out of it.

Sometime after the dress rehearsal, Toni Basil brought Brian Jones over to the Beverly Glen house, just to hang out. As a child owning Rolling Stones albums of the time, I found it odd to see one of the guys on the covers suddenly show up in our living room. He was the first famous person I met that I respected due to already being a fan of him. At the time, he was a teen idol, but he was also seriously considered by many (including me) an extraordinary musician. He had his mystique within the Rolling Stones framework. If you look at the label, you can see that the Stones' original songs were written by Mick Jagger and Keith Richards, but I got the impression they weren't the real force behind the band. It was this beautiful blond-haired guy that had the focus. The fact that he was blond, while everyone else in the band had dark hair, made him stand out in all the photographs.

(I have to presume that the Stones later had a lifetime ban on anyone blond joining the band.) And Brian Jones was in truth the outlier and pioneer in the band. It was he who developed the whole 1960s dandy look, he who took a real interest in the counterculture. The Stones were very much a bunch of guys who were faithful to their environment, but Brian went out to locate more compelling people. Whether it was social boredom, or unhappiness being in the Stones' framework, he was active in discovering a new world. Part of that new world was my father and mother. And, I guess, me as well.

My impression of Brian was that he looked exactly like the figure on the sleeve of *Aftermath* (1966). In my first memory of Brian at the Beverly Glen house, he's wearing a black turtleneck sweater, white jeans, and desert boots, precisely what he wore on the album's back cover. Often when you see a famous person in person, you notice the difference between the image and the real person. With Brian, there was no difference. As a child, I found that shocking. I was very shy around him due to his stature in the pop music world. At my age, I was totally surrounded by that world through the medium of vinyl, radio, and countless magazine articles, as well as being utterly seduced by the imagery of British pop music. What was truly wonderful was how Brian, at least in the presence of my family, was very down-to-earth and incredibly sweet.

Whenever the Stones were in Los Angeles, Brian would come to the house to listen to records and drink wine all night. I went to bed the regular time for a child, and I remember waking up to see a lot of record cover albums on the floor, as well as a wine bottle or two. Even if I fell asleep before Brian showed up late at night, I knew he'd been there just by the records being on the rug the next morning. Mostly jazz recordings, but also Glenn Gould was part of the soundtrack for these late night meetings between Brian and my parents. He never played a Stones work-in-progress. I do remember Wallace asking him about the guitar sound in "Satisfaction." Brian explained to him the fuzz box gizmo the guitar was plugged into made the sound, which was unusual for its time. Other than that, I don't think there was any mention of the Stones or their music between the two friends.

When we moved to Topanga years later, Brian would call Wallace from London, just to chit-chat. If Wallace wasn't home at the time of the call, Brian chatted with me. The other strong memory I have of him was when he came to Topanga Canyon, I think around early 1967, to see my dad, and brought Keith Richards with him as well. They came up in a chauffeured limo and called my dad up on the car phone, which was a novelty at the time. I never got over my nervousness to see Brian, again due to his star status, but when I didn't go downstairs to see him, he eventually came up to my room to say hi. To me, he was very kid-friendly. I didn't find him self-centered, but a decent and sweet guy. When I came down the stairs with him, he sat himself down with Keith and they immediately went through their clothing to remove various narcotics. Even their shoe heels had a secret storage space for drugs, and both went through their hats and jacket lapels to remove each item and place it on the table in front of them. Within a minute or so, the living room table became a pharmacy of various drugs. My dad, being my dad, was concerned about the welfare of the driver who was waiting in the car, parked outside the house. Brian said not to bother, it was his job to wait. Brian wore a purple velvet suit, a white silk ruffled shirt, and a floppy hat. Keith was dressed in a similar fashion, but I can't remember his outfit, except that it was colorful. They were dressed as a couple in a sense, in that they wore similar suits and hats that late afternoon. They stayed for hours, till Wallace suggested they go to the Corral, a bar that was close to our home. I didn't go with them, and that was the last time I saw Brian.

A year or so later, my mother came up to my bedroom in Topanga to let me know that Brian died. I have no memory of Wallace mentioning his death that day or making a comment about it. But I remember riding in the car with him, and stations KHJ and KRLA were playing Stones songs non-stop. Brian's death was a big deal because I was a fan of him and the Stones, and he was a friend of the family. This was another crucial moment of going through a death of a public figure, like the JFK assassination, coupled with the fact that I knew him. I think of him often, because the time during which I floated in his private world was for me magical. He and Kennedy introduced me to the thought of someone on this planet not being here anymore. It was a shocking realization for me.

To this day, I think of the Rolling Stones as Brian Jones and friends. I do like the Stones after Brian left or was kicked out, but they became an entirely different band. The Brian-era Stones was like a group of musicians in pitch darkness, and once he was gone, a light went on, as if it was a well-lighted room. The magic was gone, and what was left a remembrance of something once truly great, but now just perfectly OK.

WALLACE BERMAN /
Anna and Shirley Berman

Grandparents / chapter 29

I was raised with no religion whatsoever, nor did I learn any language except English. I bring this up because people always ask me about the Hebrew language on some of my father's artwork. I tell them it's visual poetry or something in the line of Lettrist literature. Wallace liked how the letters worked against stone or any of his assemblage pieces. He did study the Kabbalah, but I don't think his interest in it was a spiritual quest of any sort. Kabbalah deals with numbers, and that fascinated Wallace, especially with his interest in gambling. Many of my father's heroes were interested in the Kabbalah, like Baudelaire, Duchamp, and Artaud; every fascinating lunatic in the arts, it seemed, had an interest in Jewish mysticism. Like with my father, I don't think it was spiritual, more a game of sorts. Kabbalah has a strong pull for visual artists and poets, I think, because it's very open-ended, yet systematic at the same time. My dad was a game player, but he was not tied down to a game's rules or practices. He treated games as a map so he could follow a specific road, but there were alternate routes as well.

As far as I know, Wallace had never been inside a Jewish temple or a church. Once in a while, I see his name attached to Cameron's interest in "Magick," but that's like saying anyone who reads Aleister Crowley must be a follower of his beliefs. Wallace never participated in magick ceremonies. He had friends who took an interest in that world, but he was utterly indifferent to magick and all its offshoots. His feelings about religion and all the cult activity can be reduced to Frank Sinatra's very profound quote: "Whatever gets you through the night is OK with me."

On the weekends I would stay with either one grandmother or the other. I liked both places and women equally. Grandma Anna, Wallace's mother, allowed me TV privileges, as well as sweets. So did Shirley's mother, Martha. The big difference between them, concerning yours truly, was that Anna encouraged me to go outside, which meant long walks with her in the Fairfax district. She would go about marketing, and I would hold the groceries. I did hear my Grandma Anna speak Yiddish, never with my father, but with people in her neighborhood: the butcher, the baker, Jewish shopkeepers and their employees. The household she shared with her brother Harry wasn't a religious home. I liked to spend time at her apartments; she had two in my lifetime, both located in that same neighborhood. The main reason why I liked the Fairfax area of Los Angeles was its location in the city, not in Beverly Glen or Topanga. I could fall down the stairs and end up in the capital of that particular Jewish world, which was the Farmer's Market at Third and Fairfax.

There are locations in life that never leave you. I have often dreamt of an indoor/outdoor newsstand that has every magazine imaginable. I would wake up in the middle of the night trying to figure out what this newsstand was. It took me decades to realize the newsstand I'd been dreaming about was the one in the Farmer's Market, where Anna bought me comic books. It was a great magazine stand that had all the comic books I liked. To get there was like walking through a maze of food stands and small shops. This particular location was my own personal Oz. Yet even though I still live in Los Angeles, I've never been back to that newsstand since I was a child. Why disrupt a perfect dream landscape? I would stand in front of the magazines till Anna bought me one or two comics. I had my technique down: I would look at two comic books for a long time. She told me that she would buy me only one, but I wouldn't move, trying to make a decision about which one I wanted. Eventually, she had to give up and buy me both, because for sure I was not going to move till I got both. I also used this technique on my other grandma, Martha, but it never worked with my parents! I still use it with myself. After a long period in front of the merchandise, I usually decide to get everything I want.

After the comic book buying session, we would have lunch at the food court, which usually meant a hamburger and a milkshake. My dining out choice was always the hamburger. It didn't matter if we were at an Italian or Mexican restaurant, I would still order a burger, fries, and a milkshake. After lunch, I would convince Anna to take me over to the toy store near the food stalls. At the time, I was totally enamored with the doll figures of characters from TV shows. I never actually had one, because they were quite expensive, but I did get board games tied to my favorite shows of the time. I was obsessed with all the James Bond-era spy shows, such as *I Spy* (1965–68), *The Man from U.N.C.L.E.* (1964–68), and so forth, so I had games based on those shows. I haven't the foggiest memory of actually playing the games, but I was in love with the concept of having such a game based on my favorite shows. It was more of a visual object than something to play with.

I also liked the fact that the Farmer's Market was—and still is, I imagine—a tourist attraction. I have always enjoyed locations that tourists flock to. There is something lovely about a tourist shop selling useless items. It's not about the merchandise, of course, but the remembrance of a location; the cheap items represent something more profound to the buyer. Even as a small kid I took a certain amount of pride in living (at least on the weekend with my grandmother) in an area of the town where people came from all over the world to have profound experiences near my favorite newsstand. For some reason, I never think of it as my father's old neighborhood. More than likely he slept here but usually went off to Central Avenue or Hollywood to the jazz and dance clubs. So my idea of Fairfax was very personal and, compared to a canyon area, it represented life at its best for me. Also, the spacious CBS Studio on Third and Fairfax meant a lot to me, because famous TV shows were shot there. Television City, it was called. Many of the CBS variety shows I watched were taped there, so every time I walked by as a child, I felt the presence of showbiz, which thrilled me to the bone.

Anna's first apartment was on the second floor. Luckily, my grandmother didn't have a problem holding my hand while walking up and down the staircase. Once I was in the apartment, I was in there, for good till my grandmother had to leave, or my parents picked me up. Only a few times did I descend the staircase by myself, and I remember hitting a solid wall of fear—it was that strong. By good luck, Harry and Anna moved into another apartment that was on the ground floor, so I didn't have to deal with the staircase anymore on future visits. Living with my grandmother and her brother was a woman named Esther. She had red hair like Lucille Ball, which must have been dyed, now that I think about it. She used to have a large bedroom in their apartment. I remember she had to move into a senior hotel located in the same Fairfax neighborhood. Anna and I visited her every weekend. It was my first time in a senior home, and it didn't seem much different from the apartment, except the food tasted very bland (Esther would allow me to eat her lunch). Anna brought her food every time we visited Esther because the hotel food wasn't so hot, and also due to the cultural habit of bringing food to another. I don't recall any time that Anna didn't bring food with her as a gift, especially when visiting a neighbor or friend.

One time Anna took me to a barbershop to get a proper haircut. It was your basic young boy's haircut of the 1950s. I know it

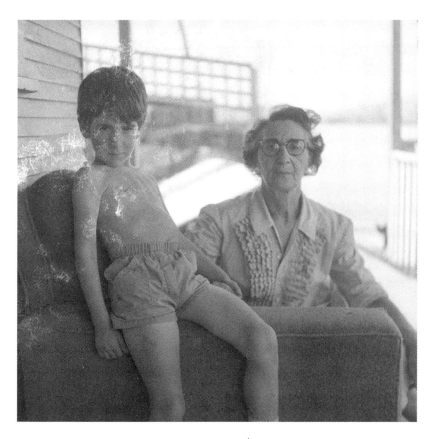

WALLACE BERMAN /
Tosh and Anna Berman

made my grandmother happy. Sadly, my dad wasn't as delighted, and I think it caused a big rift between mother and son. My parents were quite focused on my hairstyle as a child. My dad may have forced me to wear a hat until my hair grew out. The initial impression I had of the barbershop was the smell of the hair oil. I liked it. I had no strong opinion about that haircut, except it felt good to have my hair cut by a barber. I would see a reflection of myself, and it was hard for me to keep my eyes off my image. I had never seen myself with such a square haircut before. I was just amazed to have that type of "do" on top of my head. It was like looking at someone else, but alas, it was truly me!

Family visits to Harry and Anna's consisted of coming there early for dinner and my father reading the newspaper, which at the time didn't strike me as strange, but looking back, it's ridiculous behavior on my dad's part. My mom had to carry the conversation, though naturally, Wallace should have been doing so. He undoubtedly loved his mom and Harry, yet there was a certain amount of tension on his part when he took a trip to Grandma's. He was close to my cousins, Shelley and Paula, as well as to his sister Bea and her husband, Dave. The most enjoyable visits to Anna's household were when Dave and Bea and family were there because Dave enjoyed arguing for the sake of it. I remember he would make comments like, "Humans can live without love." This was not set forth as a subjective point of view, but a scientific one, in other words, a fact. He would also add some arcane information on that subject. Of course, he would draw Wallace into the conversation, and it was fun to see my dad in a sense get sucked in. This wouldn't happen with his friends like Dean, Russ, or George. Only Uncle Dave could draw Wallace into these debates that had no end or results. I remember as a child being entertained by Dave's statement of purpose. Getting my dad involved was a bonus. If it weren't for Dave, Wallace would just read the paper before and even after the family meal.

My mom and I felt uncomfortable with Wallace reading the paper at Anna's house. Wallace had a slight passive aggressive streak, and when it came up, it was annoying as hell and awkward to deal with. "Why did he do that?" I would wonder. I assume that he had a deep unconscious anger with his mom, which was silly because she was a lovely woman, cream on the top of this yucky world. She probably didn't understand my father's lifestyle whatsoever, and it probably caused her a certain amount of worry as well. She got along well with my mom, so there were no mother-in-law problems in the relationship. My father once owned the entire run of *View* magazine, which was a New York surrealist publication edited by the poet Charles Henri Ford. It had some new talent, like Philip Lamantia, but it mostly featured a lot of exiled surrealists, who were in America owing to World War Two. Anna threw out the entire collection, not realizing its importance to Wallace. I don't think this action amused him, and I got the feeling that even years later my father was deeply disturbed by the loss of his *View* collection.

By profession, Uncle Dave was a TV repairman. Wallace would bring our TV set to Dave when it broke, because usually it just needed a replacement tube or new picture tube. When Dave opened the back of the set, there was an electric scent. The tube batteries had their smell, and I recall them being rather dusty as well. It was during these visits when I realized that the TV set was a family member. I cringed if we got the bad news that the TV set would not make it past the operation. On the other hand, we had the best TV doctor possible. Even so, I always think of Dave more of a thinker or intellectual than a guy who worked with tools, most likely due to his usual discussions of subjects that were almost philosophy-oriented, rather than political. Education was an important part of that family. My cousins Shelley and Paula became a lawyer and librarian, respectively, and I always thought of them as being very intelligent. As their younger cousin, I looked up to them, because they too offered opinions and were very much part of the discussion around the table. My immediate family wasn't like that. It was one of silence. When we had people over, we had lively discussions, but when it was just the three of us, I have no memory of actual conversations going back and forth.

My cousin Shelley had a collection of 45 rpm singles in a case with a handle. She gave it to me when she wanted to clean out her room as a teenager, and I was thrilled to receive such a wonderful gift. I distinctly remember Elvis Presley's "Jailhouse Rock" (1957) as one of the records in the case, and at home I played that song over and over again. The thing that impressed me about Shelley's collection of singles was that none of them were obvious hits at that period in her life. We never spoke about music, but she had a specific and keen aesthetic in choosing her songs—unless she obtained the singles from someone else. But I doubt that. In my teenage years, I also received music from my cousins on the other side of the family, Greg and Jeff. Both were very much into music, and, in fact, were musicians. One of the great things about music is that it makes a community, and one can easily join, just by loving it. The beauty of music is in the actual sharing. Even in the Internet stage of our world, music is still something to share, whether legally or illegally. The impulse to take music from one's home to someone else's is strong for the music lover.

Wallace was close to his nieces. Their lifestyles were entirely different from his, yet the Berman side of the family totally accepted Wallace. I'm not sure if they totally understood his stance in the world, but they did accept it. They took great pride when he was acknowledged either in the press or an exhibition. Wallace also shared his artworks with them. I remember once that he showed his 8mm film *Aleph* at Dave and Bea's home. I don't know what they thought of it, but my memory of that evening is a good one. Wallace would never go out of his way to convey his deepest secrets to his mom or the family, but he did share his life with them, especially his life as an artist. But while he was very receptive and open to a degree, he was still very enclosed in his world and very much in his own landscape. I could tell when he was in deep thought. I had no problem with him in that mindset and adopted it from him. It would have been one thing if I saw him only twice a day, but I was with him on a constant basis, so instead of finding his remoteness difficult or weird, I not only accepted it, but also learned how to adapt it to my mixture of character.

On the weekend, if I wasn't at Anna's, I went to my mother's parents Martha and Dodo's house. Usually, I was dropped off on a Saturday morning and stayed till Sunday morning. I watched a lot of TV at Anna's house, mostly cowboy films on Saturday afternoons: Kit Carson, Hopalong Cassidy, and early Roy Rogers. I loved them because the cowboys were cleaned up and the bad guys always had a slight five o'clock shadow and, as a rule, sneaky eyes. You could tell they were guilty just by their looks. Of course, they wore the black cowboy hat, and they mostly hung out playing cards at the local saloon. They were shifty, sometimes drunk, and very much show-offs regarding their gun skills. They remind me of my later years in Topanga because there were men there who adopted that sort of look during the hippie era.

I was a serious reader of the weekly *TV Guide*. I was fascinated with the technology that TV brought to my life and surprised I could watch such amazing stuff in my home, as well as at my grandparents'. I would map out my schedule for the day by what was on television. Sometimes there was a conflict when I wanted to watch two shows that were on at the same time on different channels. This would cause a certain amount of anxiety for me. The schedule, as I remember it, began with cartoons in the morning. I loved *Looney Tunes* and *Tom & Jerry*. Whenever there was a conflict or a chase scene between two animated animals, I was glued to the set. The Coyote's battle of wits against the Roadrunner was pure bliss for me. I laughed hysterically when the Coyote ran off the mountain cliff and realized what he had done. After the cartoons came the Westerns or *Tarzan*. It was amazing to spend an afternoon watching an old serial or film and being swept away by the adventure.

At the end of those movies, it was time for a break, which meant either eating lunch or going out to explore the outside world with a grandmother. With Anna, that meant the streets of Fairfax, but with Martha, it meant Topanga, mostly playing by the pool in the backyard. Then came night, dinner, and various

Western TV series, including *Gunsmoke* (1955–75), *Wagon Train* (1957–65), and *Bonanza* (1959–73). I much prefer the movie cowboy films of the '30s to the TV Westerns. Still, I did have a thing for *Have Gun – Will Travel* (1957–63), *The Life and Legend of Wyatt Earp* (1955–61), *Bat Masterson* (1958–61), and, of course, James Garner in *Maverick* (1957–62). I was attached to the cowboys who were dandies. The only "serious" Western that I admired was *The Rifleman* (1958–63). I think I was drawn to that series because of the relationship between the father and son, which sometimes reminded me of my relationship with my dad.

Mudslide / chapter 30

I'm often drawn to the feminine side of life, but the one masculine thing in my life was Wallace. There is softness in both masculine and feminine. It is a matter of shades of gray. Wallace didn't represent a hard world, but his stance was aggressive as well as smart. He admired the art of boxing, which I think was more important to him as an art than as a sport. The way a boxer behaved in the ring enticed my father's interest. I often watched boxing matches with him, totally bored, especially when the two fighters danced around each other. I, of course, wanted to see the punches connect so I could see the opponent on the ground and perhaps bleeding. For Wallace, that wasn't the compelling part of the match; it was the dancing that he liked. Now that I'm older (but not wiser), I can see the aesthetic of such a sport and also the psychology that each boxer brings to the ring. To win or lose isn't the issue, so much as how one performs in such a setting. Losing isn't bad if you lose with your principles intact. Wallace was, if nothing else, a masculine man who had principles as well as a moral code, of his own making, of course. What I learned from him is to take the failures and just get up and raise your head up high, to draw from them a degree of knowledge and, on a very basic level, a life lesson.

We lost our home in 1965, a couple of days after Christmas. I was 11 years old. Wallace was in a federal building obtaining one of his first official documents: a passport. He had the urge to visit New York City, Paris, and London. Wallace wanted to take the trip by himself, which is something he never did as a young man. He wasn't a great traveler. In fact, Wallace almost never actually traveled. In a way, his reading of books and publications was a form of travel for him, which he could do without leaving the downtown library or his home. So the decision to travel must have been life-changing for him. The odd part, which fits in perfectly with Wallace's personality, was that he planned to visit New York City, London, and Paris all in one weekend. Whether that's even possible, I don't know, but he didn't want to spend more than a weekend away from Beverly Glen. Wallace must have heard of Raymond Roussel, who famously didn't leave his hotel when he traveled around the world. That was a myth of sorts, but Wallace took this to another level. He probably didn't consider the time zone changes or the possibility of losing a day while flying to Europe. My guess is that Wallace didn't plan to sleep on this trip (except maybe on the plane), and he would be on the move constantly.

While Wallace was out at the passport office, my mom and I were in the house in a heavy rainstorm. We heard a giant rock hit the back of the house. The house was on stilts, built on a steep hill. Up till now, we had survived numerous earthquakes of different sizes, as well as rain and the occasional fire. There had been close calls, and I even remember having to evacuate the house once due to a fire in nearby Bel Air. My mom wanted to see if there was any damage from the rock, so she took me by the hand to go outside. I don't even remember wearing rain gear because we were just going to step out for a second or two. Once we got to the pathway, the house was crushed by a massive mudslide. It was the first time in my life that something I had always seen was gone seconds later. Like the structure had never existed. If we had stayed in the house, we would have been crushed to death. I'll never forget the roar of the wood being smashed or the out-of-body experience of watching this disaster take place, dragging everything I'd ever owned into a wet slush of nothingness. To this day, I remember the presents I lost that Christmas. One was a *Man from U.N.C.L.E.* gun and badge set with a membership card to the U.N.C.L.E. organization. Even worse was the loss of the albums Dean Stockwell had given me for Christmas: the Rolling Stones' *December's Children* (1965), *Herman's Hermits on Tour* (1965), and *The Animals on Tour* (1965). The shock of losing the new albums, as well as every other album and single I owned at the time, was one of the worst things that ever happened to me.

The only things I had were the clothes I was wearing at the time of the mudslide. I didn't have an extra pair of socks, underwear, or any other clothing. All were lost. I remember that night we stayed at Carol and Charlie Patton's house, which was a block up from Crater Lane on Beverly Glen Blvd. I think our heads couldn't accept what took place, and it probably took a couple of days to realize that we indeed lost a great deal of stuff, including a lot of art made by friends, various family items, clothing, of course, and personal photographs and documents (like my father's letters from Herman Hesse). But being inches from death didn't weigh on my 11-year-old consciousness as much as losing the Herman's Hermits album. Worse things have happened to others, of course, and at least we weren't physically hurt. We just had to start over again. Even though it's been over 50 years, the incident is still a prominent one in my life. It was a hard lesson, but I realized that life could change quickly, and you can lose possessions as easy as obtaining them. We were poor, and anything given that Christmas was a financial sacrifice of some sort.

Luck, as usual, was on our side. Billy, Joan, and their kids, who lived across the street in the house where my dad's studio was, were out of town. We stayed in their home while they were away, so we weren't completely homeless. Still, I remember I came down with a horrible virus, which I'm confident was from stress due to the mudslide. I don't remember my school situation at the time; most likely I was on vacation for the winter holiday. But I do remember horrible images. Neighbors and others came to the hillside to dig up stuff we owned and reclaim it as treasure for themselves. Often we returned to the property and found strangers digging up the hill to look for objects. Perhaps they suspected that there was money buried in the mud. The weird thing was that these individuals did not appear to be hurting for any goods or comfort. I think they just wanted to get something for free and didn't have a thought in their heads that it might be an insensitive act on their part. It was the first time I came upon cruelty in a societal manner. It was appalling and emotionally draining, not only from the loss of our possessions, but also from seeing those fellow humans go on private property to dig up goods, without a thought of the moral issues involved. It was an eye-opening experience that never left me.

Topanga / chapter 31

When our house in Beverly Glen was destroyed, Dean Stockwell bought us the Topanga house. I don't remember if there was ever a discussion of what house to buy; I think Dean saw the house on Artique Road and purchased it outright. He gave it to us, and when the Berman family moved in, the golden era of Topanga started. I think my mom was uncomfortable to get such a generous gift from a friend, but Wallace wasn't the type of guy to feel either guilt or shame at accepting such a great present as a house—in my mom's name, mind you. Wallace refused to have anything under his name. For a moment or two in his history, he probably didn't exist on paper, except for his driver's license. He didn't have a bank account under his name. Our family didn't have checks or credit cards. My dad's choice of currency was cash and art. He often traded his art for food. Joe, who ran the Topanga Market, accepted artworks from Wallace in exchange for credit at the store. This barter method of payment for goods suited Wallace's sense of capitalism. Everything was under my mom's name, including the car (she didn't drive), the house (gifted by Dean), and anything else that needed a legal signature. As far as I can tell, there was no concrete reason why Wallace didn't want to sign anything. His "why" wasn't something he conveyed to me. Somewhere down the line, Wallace chose not to participate when he was told he had to. He didn't like to depend on someone else's system.

WALLACE BERMAN /

Tosh Berman, Topanga Canyon, 1966

We moved into a community that was already full of Wallace's friends. Dean, Russ, George (whose home we could see from our front porch), and Billy Gray all lived in the canyon. For Wallace, Topanga must have been like a large clubhouse, with his major social life only minutes away. I, on the other hand, immediately felt I was miles away from anything that interested me. Even going to the local drive-in market on Topanga Canyon Boulevard was at least a 30-minute walk. I would go there just to read the labels because I was bored in the canyon. For a glam-obsessed teenager, it was a nightmare of a place to live. I remember my first full day in Topanga, in our new house. Beverly Glen had seemed very lush, shady, and green to me. Topanga was hot and dusty, and there were lots of pick-up trucks everywhere, which of course meant that my dad sold his car and purchased a pick-up truck. Not a macho American pick-up, but a Japanese pick-up truck called a Datsun: much cuter, but still a pick-up truck. If the whole family were going out, I would have to sit in the middle between my mom on the passenger side and my dad and the gear-shift. Wallace would constantly hit my leg while changing gears. I missed the privacy of having the backseat of a car all to myself. Life was evolving in a lot of ways for me.

Before he built his workplace on property my parents purchased next door, Wallace's studio was in the garage, below the house; it was not a large space, but it was perfect for Wallace to do what he had to do. He had an old couch by the entrance and a large worktable that was a giant, thick board attached by a couple of clamps to two or three sawhorses. There was another worktable about as long as the room built into the concrete wall. Beyond the two large tables, there was little room to walk around. The rest of the space was filled with books and discarded and cut-up magazines my dad used for his artwork. He had work lamps, but no direct lighting in the studio, so it was mostly dark, cold, and damp. It was a perfect spot for him because there was no way to reach Wallace unless you approached the front door of the garage. As usual, there were no telephones in his studio.

The entrance to the actual house was the living room, and it was tiny. Around the living room was an open kitchen area, and that was even smaller. The house, when you get down to it, was very much like the shack in Beverly Glen. The big difference was the addition of an extra bedroom for my parents. What sticks in my mind about my parents' bedroom are the two large posters of Jerry West and Wilt Chamberlin of the Los Angeles Lakers hanging over their bed. Both of my parents were Lakers fans, but I thought those two posters were a bit much. Some years later, after my father's death, I noticed a knife carving on the bedpost of a heart with the initials "WB+SB." Even though we had our own rooms, the space was very contained, and the only thing I liked about the house was the front yard, with the steps leading to the house. The previous owner of the house built a restraining wall at street level, also another wall in the front yard as well. There were seashells in the wall, which strikes me as some poor person's idea of high class. The garden was charming and private from the street view. At the time, there were hardly any other residences on that part of Artique Road. After living in this house for a few years my mom and dad built a porch facing Artique Road, which had a spectacular view of the outside world, as well as George Herms and his family's house across the canyon. But the porch held no interest for me.

Despite his refusal to put the house in his own name, Wallace was, in his way, very community-oriented. For instance, he didn't mind making and posting images of undercover cops in the canyon or doing design work to support keeping the canyon property free from land developers, and he also donated artworks to various anti-war organizations. He never ripped off anyone, and he was quite honest about his inability to obtain credit to pay someone back (I was never aware of him borrowing money from friends).

I'm sure he had a beer tab at the Topanga Corral, but he was a citizen of good standing in Topanga, so his name was worth the credit. He never asked for a discount. I think he believed everything was worth whatever the seller was selling the merchandise or service for. As much as possible his art was his currency. He was not anti-society or anti-art world; he liked society, and he loved the art world. But he liked to be in control of his world within that world. It was only years later that Wallace started to sign his artwork. I think someone convinced him that it was imperative that an artist sign his art.

The one constant in my father's life was his role as an outsider, in that he didn't want to join any organization or institution where his name would be known. This was an obsession with him. He donated artwork to various agencies that were against the Vietnam War, but never, as far as I know, offered to sign a petition against the war. While everyone was going out on the streets, he was retreating to his workplace to make art. At times, I believe, his only language was art. He never commented on his work, because he felt very strongly that the art could do this itself. The way he got himself involved with art and making art was entirely non-verbal, and the whole idea of the artist writing about his or her work was a foreign concept to him. Also, he seemed not to care whether others liked or disliked or even paid attention to his work. Most artists like to communicate with the public, either by making the art or talking about it. Wallace never felt the need to do such things. He liked putting on his special one-man shows because, I think, the exhibition itself went beyond the art making. Wallace loved making the announcements for the shows, which were just as important to him as the work on the wall. He was very conceptual in thinking out how the work should be laid out in the exhibition. Even in group shows, my dad insisted on absolute control on how his work would be hung in the space. This alone is not such a weird thing for an artist, but what made him unusual was that he saw the exhibition as another form of art. He may have been like Duchamp in that sense.

At the height of our Topanga years, I noticed a slight change in Wallace's behavior. Topanga in the late '60s and early '70s was on the surface a paradise but, in fact, it was tainted with paranoia. The fear of undercover cops was pretty intense. It was a combination of fear and competition with the outside world. To live in the canyon, you become aware you're in an environment that exists outside of the "norm," which is a world hostile to the hippie and every freethinking libertarian. This, of course, was a grand version of the paranoia that ran through Topanga like a flu virus, whether due to the amount of pot smoked between the beach and the valley, or the nature of how canyon space traps negative feelings within its borders. Topanga was very much a small community, and the thing that bonded everyone was a sense of paranoia. Wallace would often get off the chair when he heard a car approaching the street outside our house. He would stand by the window, sort of hiding, to see if anyone would get out of the car, or where the final destination of that particular automobile was. The road stopped in a dead end, which I think made Wallace even more curious why anyone would drive up the street if they didn't live there in the first place. He would never talk about it, but at times I felt he was fearful of someone. Perhaps a figure from his past gambling days, I was never sure. He never talked about it, but his actions showed caution and concern whenever someone drove up Artique Road.

Throughout my life, I've only had pot as secondhand smoke. It never affected me, nor did I ever have an urge to smoke a joint, which is strange considering that my father smoked it every day, and when I was in junior high and high school I was surrounded by potheads. Not only adults, but also my fellow school chums. I pretty much ignored that culture. It was not a moral choice or a bad feeling about weed, just a total indifference. I just didn't care. To be honest, I can't tell the difference between someone who

WALLACE BERMAN /
Shirley Berman

smokes pot and someone who doesn't. I never witnessed anyone
acting evil under the influence of pot. Also, I don't like the sensation of the smoke going down my throat or my mouth. As far as
I know, Wallace never actually smoked cigarettes. My mom did,
yes. My dad may have taken a toke of a Sherman cigarette here or
there, but pot was his main vice. Even with that, he would smoke
every day, but he could make one joint last a few days. He just
took two hits and put it away for the next day. Or he would smoke
it socially with others.

He told me as a teenager that he tried everything at least once, but the only other drug I ever saw around Wallace was LSD, and that was less than a handful of times. I think he took acid in Beverly Glen, but I have no real strong memory of that. When we lived in Topanga, he took acid once with Dean, and watching them that afternoon was boring but scary at the same time. The scary part was that, during his trip, my father was out of the loop. His behavior wasn't off-the-wall, but basically, it was just him lying on the couch or outside on the patio furniture, looking at the sky. Asking him for a sandwich that day was, for sure, totally out of the question.

The drug culture, especially in Topanga Canyon, was un-yielding. I wasn't into it because I just wasn't into it. On the other hand, my friends in junior high and high school were into it, as were their parents. In Topanga, there was no cultural divide between teenager and grown-up. It was very much a small com-munity that abandoned the outside world. It was a utopia for some, but to me, it was a very restricted culture. You either got stoned, or you didn't, and if you didn't—then why not? Many adults offered me a toke of pot or whatever, but my father would step in and say something like, "He's naturally high." The concept of getting high was very much a desired state to be in. For me, ever since I was 10 years old, the ultimate high was turning on the turntable and amp, and letting the music take me somewhere.

On the beach side of Topanga Canyon, I loved the Santa Monica Pier. I have a cozy memory of the family visiting the pier on a cold, rainy night. My parents had a friend, Jim Elliott, who lived on the top floor of the merry-go-round building known as the Santa Monica Looff Hippodrome, which houses the carousel. My parents' friend had parties at his apartment there, and it was always a magical place to visit as a kid; how many apartments had carousel music drift from the bottom floor? Meanwhile, down below, the sideshow attractions and games just glistened in the rain, and the ocean had that dark intensity when you looked out—nothing but blackness. You can feel it's out there. In the electric light at the end of the dock, you could see ripples of the rain hitting the ocean. That was a happy place and time; the weather, the nighttime, and the scent of the pier was like a cocktail, and everything worked perfectly. Nature is not natural to me unless there is a pending storm that will kill or wipe out a crowd of people. I usually fell asleep at these parties and was placed on a bed full of coats and purses. Once the party was over, or my parents wanted to leave, I would wake up feeling lethargic, but the late night weather on the pier was like having water splashed on my face.

On the other hand, Malibu is a crappy community that I find to this day dull and depressing. The difference among Venice, Santa Monica, and Malibu is quite great. The problem with Malibu is the power of wealth made the beach into a private backyard, when in fact the very nature of its design should be open to the public. The strange relationship between privileged residence and the sand and ocean always seemed odd to me. Also, me being me, I was always paranoid that someone could get on "my" beach with little effort or time. I suspect nature itself hates Malibu. Historically, there have been numerous mudslides, floods, and fires in the area, and I think that's nature's way of not accepting these people. But they still come, they still purchase a home, and they have a sense of entitlement in an area that apparently hates them.

On the opposite side of the canyon is Woodland Hills, which is full of tract homes and the ugly Topanga Plaza. For a short period, there was a record store in Woodland Hills on Topanga Canyon Boulevard that stocked glam rock American releases. Warehouse Records was located at the intersection of Topanga and Ventura, and it had a small import section where I would buy my first Sparks release. It was a beautifully designed album graphic with a flimsy cover that tore easily, but it seemed extra special because it came from somewhere in London. London, at that time, was a land that held a sense of fantasy for me, which was that it was a city full of people who have good taste—unlike Woodland Hills and Topanga of course.

Topanga Elementary / chapter 32

In general, school was extremely tough for me. In subjects I wasn't interested in—which, in all honesty, were most of my classes—I was a very slow learner. Or maybe I should say "non-learner." My primary weakness was (and still is) math. I don't understand the logic of it. I can understand 1 + 1 = 2, because I can put one finger up in my left hand and one other on the right hand, and see there are two fingers up. But past the number 10, I'm utterly hopeless. Making the change at a cash register is a total mystery to me. When a particular price comes up, and the customer gives me a bill, that's bad enough, but when he or she gives me change with that bill to get a certain amount back, that's impossible for me. My brain is not wired to figure things like that out. Throughout elementary school in Topanga, I found myself in a state of embarrassment. I tried my hardest to comprehend, but I just didn't understand the logic or the formula to get the correct answer. I often pretended to understand; though it was evident to me that I was stupid, I didn't want my classmates to know!

Topanga Elementary School was in many ways a better school than Nora Sterry Elementary in Sawtelle. For one thing, I wasn't in a room full of disturbed children, and second (and most significant), no one there seemed to want to hit me. When I first showed up at class, a lovely redhead by the name of Lisa See was the first person to address me, and she did so in a very charming manner. She was friendly and totally open to the idea that I could sit by her in class. For me, it was love at first sight, because I wasn't used to getting attention in the first five minutes of a meeting. Of all the people I met in Topanga, Lisa was and will always be my favorite. In that time, the boys played with the boys, and the girls played with the girls, but I would have rather played with Lisa. I didn't care what the game was or what type of toys we would have played with. It would have been better for me to be with her. Taking that seat next to her was the best thing I did during my education. Lisa was and still is a beautiful redhead. I remained close to her up to high school. I lost touch with Lisa after my school years but I have kept track of her because she became a very successful novelist. Her great-grandfather was Chinese, yet in my youth, I didn't pick up on her Asian roots. Without a doubt, she was the first Chinese redhead with freckles I had ever met or seen. I loved her voice. It was a pure melody because she laughed a lot, and when she did, the world would turn into a Technicolor movie. She would have these mood swings, but I rode them like I was on a luxury yacht in troubled waters. I took the school bus with her, and I remember a dark cloud going across her mind, and she would put on a face that to me was totally charming. I never questioned her on anything, I just fully accepted her.

The Topanga Elementary School was right in the middle of the canyon. It had a long driveway that led to the school. I can't remember one teacher, which is quite strange. I vaguely recall one of the male teachers—he reminded me of Deputy Dog—but I don't remember his personality or even if I liked him. I do remember the fear of leaving Topanga Elementary to go to Parkman Junior High School in Woodland Hills. The boys in Topanga all had long hair, and all we heard from the other side of the world was that Woodland Hills was a hostile place if you were from the canyon and had long hair. We went on a school trip to the junior high campus, and the first thing that happened to me was that a student there came by and pulled my hair hard. I remember the word "fag" coming out of the mouths of those students on a consistent basis, as they walked by us, as an insult towards us newbies. It is no exaggeration to say that I hated it with every cell in my body. All the stories I heard about Parkman were true. After that day, all I could think about was the moment when I would have to be a student at that death camp. On the other hand, the older girls there were beautiful, but there is a significant difference between boys of 11 and 12 and girls that are around 14—forbidden love, of course, on the male side of the world.

Collector's Items / chapter 33

My father, on rare occurrences, loved to shoplift in front of me. He would take me to the local market in Topanga Canyon, and as he spoke to the owner, he would steal the food and other items right under the man's nose. I would like to say it was a financial or food need, but I think he liked to keep his hand in small-scale crime. There was nothing verbal; the action alone was significant—something to awaken us from boredom. I think my father felt comfortable sharing this outlook on petty crime with me. I also remember once he went to the lumberyard to purchase a piece of wood at a particular size. They cut it to size, sold it to him, then helped him load it in the Datsun, leaving the rest of the wood on the ground to be put away later. But before he left the yard, he quickly put the rest of the wood in the back of the truck. I would watch at these times in horror. I was so afraid he would be caught and then sent to jail. Or, worse in my mind, he would be arrested and handcuffed, and I would be abandoned by both the cops and my father. In all honesty, I think he did it to give me a thrill. He was funny that way. Of course, I never asked him, and it's odd, given my past, that I never ended up as a thief.

As far as I can remember, the only thing I've ever stolen in my life was a Baby Ruth candy bar. I shoplifted the candy from the Beverly Glen market that was down the hill from our house on Crater Lane. I remember I grabbed the candy and put it in my pocket, but I didn't run off quickly. I thought that I should stay and look around so I wouldn't look suspicious. After I left the market in a leisurely manner, I went up the hill and buried the candy, because I didn't want to get caught with the goods. The candy meant nothing to me, except that it was my favorite food at the time. The combination of chocolate and peanuts in a chewy texture was one of the great pleasures of my childhood. But stealing this candy bar had little to do with my enjoyment of Baby Ruth, and more with pushing myself to a moral limit. I wanted to do something that was obviously wrong, to see what it felt like to do such a crime. The stolen candy bar represented a line that I crossed. The fact that it belonged to someone else and I took it had a lot of meaning to me. Owning something usually gives me a sense of security, but in this case, it was completely the opposite, and the fear of getting caught with the stolen candy was an extreme high of sorts. I knew what I did was wrong, and that was part of the kick. Stealing to me is morally evil, but I never understood people who claim they don't understand the need or passion for thieving. How can you not know the thrill of committing a theft? Knowing that fun, I knew I wouldn't want to do it again; once was enough. If I had done it again, I could see it turning into an addiction.

The primary commercial activity at the Topanga Canyon Shopping Center was the market, which to me had one thing going for it: it sold *Melody Maker* on a weekly basis. God knows, I was the only one in the entire canyon who was even aware of *Melody Maker*. It was magnificent. It was like giving a thirsty man in the desert a very expensive brand of bottled water. What threw me was the fact that the market only carried three copies of each issue. I bought one every week and, as far as I could remember, no one bought the other two copies. Everyone complained the prices at the market were too high, but even I, at that age, could figure out it cost more to maintain a market in the middle of nowhere. It was a great food market, but I much preferred the market down the street, Fernwood Market, where my grandmother worked as a butcher.

Fernwood had comic books, which, after *Melody Maker*, were my primary reading matter. They carried all the titles I liked, including Key Comics, Marvel, and DC. My grandmother bought me one or two every weekend when I stayed with her. She worked there on Sundays, and I would hang out with her behind the meat counter. Once a guy approached me in the market with some literature, and he asked me to read it. It was a comic book that was beautifully illustrated, and stated that black people are monkeys. So there was that element in the canyon, as well. That this gentleman would want to give a 12-year-old that comic book was and is very creepy. But that was Topanga in a nutshell. I often feel that remote areas of the world are a breeding ground for racists, and Topanga is nothing short of remote. I remember at some shitty Topanga party overhearing a stoned hippy saying when the revolution came down, the blacks would spare the canyon. He was told this by H. Rap Brown, so he claimed. I can't imagine Brown talking to such an idiot, but, then again, maybe he was stuck there on the way to Malibu or something.

In Topanga Canyon I developed a fascination with collecting comic books. I was mainly interested in DC and Marvel. I was obsessed with getting every Marvel comic possible, particularly *Nick Fury and the Agents of S.H.I.E.L.D.* and *Spider-Man.* I would stack all my comics as neatly as possible in numerical order. If I had issue number one of *The Avengers*, then issue number two would have to be immediately under it. My bedroom became a comic library. I would spend hours in my room just focusing on what I had or wanted. I often traded with friends, who shared the obsession as well. This took up a significant amount of time, because one had to use psychological powers to get the other collector to give up a particular issue. In short, I had a great time with my collection of comics.

One late afternoon, after school, I went to my room to enjoy my collection. As I looked at one of my stacks of comics, I noticed something quite odd. One of the titles on the top of the stack had "Collector's Item" stamped across the front cover. Was it printed on the actual page? No, I could see another device had stamped it. When I looked down at the next title, it too was stamped "Collector's Item." The one under that, the same. Finally, I went to the middle of the pile—the same thing: "Collector's Item." I went to the last comic in the stack, and it was stamped "Collector's Item." At this point, I also had some comics stashed in my sock drawer. This was the section for comics I hadn't read or fully processed yet. I went through comics in the drawer and they too were stamped "Collector's Item." I found myself in panic mode. At the same time, I was struck that my collection of comics was under attack. Who in their right mind would stamp every issue, every comic in my personal collection?

I was nearly in tears when I approached my dad. I was behind him as he sat in the rocking chair reading the newspaper. I tapped his shoulder, and he turned to face me. On his forehead, stamped on his skin, were the words "Collector's Item." I remember that I screamed.

This cured me of collecting comic books. On the one hand, it was a hysterical practical joke, but on the other, there was something serious behind this prank. Wallace never sat down with me and said why he did this. In fact, we had no conversation about it at all. What I did do was get rid of the comics, because I felt they weren't mine anymore. I think I traded them off either in a used bookstore or among friends. Now that I'm writing this, I think of his entire collection of *View* magazines being thrown out by his mom. More likely Wallace did this on impulse, yet how could he forget the hurt when his magazine collection was tossed into the trash? In a way, Wallace may have felt foolish to have had such deep feelings for his collection of *View* that he had to lash out, not at me, but at the thought that such a collection could be so precious. Like everything in his life, his humor had some serious ingredients mixed in.

Around the same time, whenever my parents went out, my mom would complain she had nothing to wear, a common complaint. Except one day, as my mom went to get dressed to go out with Wallace, she discovered her entire closet was missing. Wallace had removed every article of clothing and hid it all in another location, somewhere out of the house. Again, this is hysterical on one level, but on another level, it's quite cruel. And I don't think my dad did it to be cruel, but somehow he wanted to teach her a lesson not to complain about one's property. I can't speak for my mom, but for me, to this day, anything I own is super special to me. As I look at my library and music collection, I shudder to think what would happen if I lost them all. The truth is, nothing would happen. But to be taught that in such a manner was funny and disturbing at the same time.

WALLACE BERMAN /
Topanga Seed

The Grinsteins / chapter 34

Although my parents had the reputation of being recluses, I don't remember them ever missing a museum opening or an opening at the Ferus or, later, at the Nick Wilder Gallery. I was raised in an environment of wine being served in clear plastic cups. Since I was very young, I have been wandering around in large rooms with many people. And when I was a tot, I mostly saw their knees. Usually, children don't go to art openings, but my parents took me to every opening possible, including the great Duchamp exhibit in Pasadena. I met him face-to-knees. He was kind enough to bend down to shake my tiny hand, of course. Los Angeles was full of social activity around art, and there were numerous openings as well as private parties focusing on artists. For whatever reason, it is often thought that New York City was the place for the arts, but I didn't get that impression at all. I'm sure New York has more museums (especially in the past) and even more galleries, but quantity doesn't beat out quality. I think there were key galleries in Los Angeles that were important to the artist, the collector, and even more so, those who liked to look at art.

Nick Wilder, by the way, was just an ultra-charming guy, especially when he was drunk. To me, he was the archetypal art dealer: Handsome, well dressed, and fun. He was unbelievably chic, was gay, and had probably the best gallery in Los Angeles during the '70s. What I found impressive was his dress style. He had a suit with a polka-dot bowtie. As a teenager, I adopted that look from Nick. I can't say I knew him, and the last time I saw him was after my father died. At that point, he became a painter. His comment that struck me was that painting shouldn't be text-related because he had a problem with reading. I thought that was kind of smart.

The art dealer is primarily a retail store manager. But like managers of little stores, art dealers can shape a culture by using their spaces to show particular artists and match them (ideally) with the perfect clientele. It doesn't always happen that way, but dealers like Irving Blum, Robert Fraser, and Nick Wilder were people who had great style. Putting together a collection, whether a record collection or a collection of knick-knacks, takes lots of talent. You really can't just collect names to make your collection interesting. For instance, you may want to buy art from a particular artist, but maybe you only want to collect a specific period of that artist's career. A good art dealer can reach out to a client to encourage them to build up a collection. If I had money to spend, I would for sure go to a specific gallery, once I knew that dealer's taste and expertise.

Wallace, contrary to his image, was very fond of art dealers and their galleries. He just didn't want to be owned by or associated with one or two galleries. This was not a judgment call against a specific dealer or gallery, but more of a need to be a free agent with his artwork. The dealers knew that, and I think most, if not all, admired him for his work, and they also liked him personally. His relationship with the dealers was never negative, as far as I can tell. He was profoundly fond of the people who bought his work. If Wallace didn't like you, he would not sell you his work. Generally speaking, of course—lack of food on the table can change one's mind from time to time. But overall, he was fond of the people he dealt with in his professional world.

Wallace was very close to various individuals who bought his artworks. As I mentioned, rarely did he sell work to people

Wallace Berman working on *Topanga Seed*, Topanga Canyon, 1974

he didn't know. He liked the personal touch of knowing the customer. The perfect collectors in Los Angeles at the time were a couple, Stanley and Elyse Grinstein. Stanley passed away in 2014, and Elyse just died very recently. Not to be so cliché, but hearing about the passing of Elyse Grinstein was like Proust's character biting into his cookie and unleashing his memory. I don't exactly remember my first meeting with Stanley and Elyse since I was nothing but a child, but I guess it was at their gallery/workshop Gemini G.E.L., either in their office or perhaps at an opening.

What I do remember is the big picture, the Technicolor memory of the numerous parties that took place at their home in Brentwood. Thinking back, a lot of my most pleasant memories are located in that house. I don't believe my parents ever turned down an invitation to their home. To be invited, and to be there, was a splendid thing.

Elyse and Stanley collected art. They collected art because they obviously loved art. They also loved artists. Their relationship with artists was magical. The Grinsteins were the focal point of the artists' landscape, which included, of course, the artists, but also anyone associated within that world. It was not a private club. Their parties were way more than that. To enter their home was to be exposed to other artists from other parts of the world, and also to experience something you wouldn't have been able to experience, without the assistance of Stanley and Elyse Grinstein. In other words, it was not just a party for Los Angeles-based artists. It was a portal to other worlds. They were consistently doing fascinating things or going to interesting places. My mom told me that she went over to their house with my dad to see Elyse's photographs of her trip to China, which I think was focused on that country's architecture. The only other person there beside the Grinsteins and my parents was David Hockney.

Parties are meant for relaxation but also for people to meet up. My memory is hazy, but I do remember being in the presence of the Dalai Lama, Robert Rauschenberg, Jasper Johns, Judy Chicago, the entire Los Angeles art community, a traveling sumo wrestling team from Japan, Bryan Ferry, The Tubes, Toni Basil and the Lockers, and every major curator/museum/gallery owner on the planet. Being in a room full of strangers can often be awkward, but for some reason, once you passed through the Grinsteins' doorway, it become home. They had an active jukebox full of dance music, and the dancing got crazy. I have a faint memory of Merce Cunningham dancing near the jukebox as well.

The common sports love was basketball and the Los Angeles Lakers. The Grinsteins had season tickets, and often invited artists, such as my dad and mom, to go with them, or else just handed out tickets if they couldn't make it for some reason. I can't speak for the other artists, but Lakers tickets were not something my dad could normally afford. So the games were an incredible luxury and treat. I distinctly remember Wallace incredibly buzzed about going to the game. In fact, he purchased the two life-size posters of Jerry West and Wilt Chamberlin that hung over my parent's bed. There were also pick-up games in the parking lot of Gemini G.E.L. as well. At times, artists would come over to the parking lot to take a rented van to the Lakers game.

Even now—and I'm feeling terribly sad about Elyse's passing—the memory of her life was, in essence, fun. Whether they were doing community political work, or just hanging out, it all had a very serious purpose—which was to have fun. I don't think I've ever seen a more joyful existence than that at the Grinstein's home. Everyone who was invited to participate was put in a world that was, in a word, perfect. The food they served was consistently low-brow but incredible: huge Italian sandwiches, made to feed hundreds. I remember a lot of finger food, which never seemed to run out, and of course, the bar never seemed to be empty. When one reads about Elyse and Stanley, it is usually about *the party*, which sounds like such a superficial type of subject matter, but not in their case. It would have been impossible not to have a great and memorable time at one of the get-togethers in their home.

And again, the combination of people who attended made their parties great. Their parties usually had a theme of some sort, a party for so-and-so from New York or Europe or even Asia. Or a party to watch something, a slide show, perhaps, or a short film. It was consistently a place to obtain information of all sorts. And everyone there was on a neutral ground of importance. In other words, even a child, who couldn't possibly have anything to offer to this world, was made to feel at home, and I could wander freely around their house. The artworks they had up were all exquisite and of course by well-known artists, but they were up for the sole purpose of being excellent works of art. The Grinstein's sophistication was how they lived their lives. They were not just patrons of the art world, but actual people who participated in that world as much as the artists and art institutions. And it wasn't just a money thing. It went beyond money and into a genuine relationship with the artists and the rest of the world.

Stanley and Elyse had a lot of artwork by my dad in their personal collection, including *Topanga Seed* (1974), which, to be exact, was a huge rock, weighing over a ton, that Wallace had hand-painted Hebrew lettering all over, a beautiful piece of sculpture that was also conceptual. Nevertheless, it made perfect sense for Elyse and Stanley to buy this work because Stanley owned and operated a forklift company. So there is film footage by Russ Tamblyn of them picking up the rock and transporting it back to their home, a distance of 11.9 miles, and the forklift was going three mph. Wallace and Russ followed the rock from the Berman house to the Grinsteins' as if following Jesus through Jerusalem.

It's a fact that the art community would have been a very different type of landscape without the presence of Stanley and Elyse. In terms of art history, one has to imagine that Louise and Walter Arensberg were the first serious collectors of modern art in Los Angeles, but I feel that Elyse and Stanley even went beyond the legendary Arensbergs, in that they focused on not only the visual arts but 20th-century culture. The Grinsteins' was the second home to people like William S. Burroughs, Allan Ginsberg, Phillip Glass, Gregory Corso, and others visiting from New York. It is almost as if that there were a secret underground tunnel from Soho, New York, to Brentwood. That pathway led to a significant number of things occurring in Los Angeles. I can't speak for every artist in Los Angeles, but I do know that my dad and mom treasured every second with this dynamic duo—separately or together—and I have a hunch a lot of artists feel that way. I guess, physically, Elyse and Stanley are no longer here, but their DNA, taste, and support will always be felt whenever one visits a museum here in Los Angeles.

The Doors / chapter 35

One of the many soundtracks to my early teenage years was the Doors. My dad took me to a matinee show at the Whisky a Go Go, when, for the first time, the iconic nightclub had all-ages shows. These sets took place at 2:00 p.m., which is an odd time to see a rock 'n' roll show. The concert I asked my Dad to take me to featured the Irish band Them with Van Morrison. I was a huge fan of "Mystic Eyes" and, of course, "Gloria." Opening for Them was a local L.A. band, the Doors. I never heard of them, but their lead singer Jim Morrison made a huge impression on me. He wore black leather pants, which oddly enough, I'd never seen before. The Doors' line-up was strange to me as well. It was a drummer, keyboards (mostly organ), guitarist, and singer. Where was the bass player? It didn't feel right to me for some reason. The sound they were making was brilliant, but I was stuck on the idea that every band must have a bass player. Even though the keyboard player was playing the bass parts on his instrument, it just seemed weird. Jim barely moved on the stage. He held the mike stand like it was a life support. The song that made me a fan that afternoon was their version of Kurt Weill and Bertolt Brecht's "Whisky Bar." The only other version I have heard of this song is by Lotte Lenya, which, as I wrote before, was probably the first recording I ever heard. So the Doors covering this song (and doing it so well) connected with me in a very direct manner.

On the other hand, Them struck me as a band in an atrocious mood that afternoon. Van Morrison's voice was perfectly sassy and dirty. He also had a pair of dark sunglasses on, which he didn't take off for the whole performance. I got the impression they would have preferred not to do the afternoon kiddy show. On the other hand, the Doors were magnificent. About a month later, their first album came out, and of course, it's a rock classic. The beauty of that album is that they didn't sound like any other band of that time and place. They've always been considered the ultimate Los Angeles band, but their music to me always represents another world, something more European than, say, Santa Monica Boulevard.

When I saw the Doors for the second time, it was in some field on a scorching sunny day in the San Fernando Valley and, shockingly, they were horrible. Every song they did was just an extended jam that went nowhere. Sunlight was not good theater for Jim Morrison. He wore the same leather pants, but under the direct sunlight they seemed dirty and worn. In a club setting they were a fetish-type object, but daylight turned the illusion off. There was a jazzy side to their sound, and when combined with their pop instincts, it was a marriage made in paradise. But when they relied on their instrumental skills, they were nothing special. I remember being very disappointed that late afternoon.

By this time, the Doors were huge. When the first album came out, I got the sense that they changed the music landscape with one big leap. Now, when I listen to their music, it's hard for me to get into, due to the Lizard King blah blah of their image. The mythic aspect of Jim Morrison is splendid for the young fan, but for an adult, it gets old fast. The music is exquisite, and Morrison is a remarkable vocalist, but it's teenage music. I also feel that way about Joy Division. As a youth, they spoke directly to me, but as I got older their music started to fade away from my world. Still, they did once rock my world, and I will always appreciate them for that.

Also, Jim became best buddies with Michael McClure. On one level that sounds great, but it couldn't have been good for their livers. They drank a lot together. Through Michael, Jim approached my dad to do the cover for *Strange Days* (1967), the Doors' second album. My father turned down the job, not because he didn't like the album or the band, but because he couldn't deal with doing art for a product that would be mass-produced, and therefore didn't allow him control over the project. Wallace would have hated the thought of someone putting a price sticker on the right side of the album or even having the album shrink-wrapped. So Wallace gave a quick "thank you, but no" to Jim and Michael.

As far as I know, neither Wallace nor my mom met Jim. On the other hand, I remember walking down Topanga Canyon Boulevard and seeing a man in a Volkswagen bug parked on the side of the road, drinking out of a brown paper bag. It was Jim Morrison.

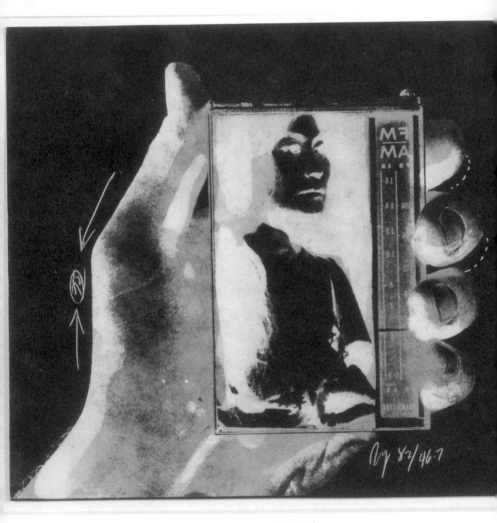

WALLACE BERMAN /
Untitled #84, Yoko Ono

Friends / chapter 36

In Topanga, before the suicide march to the teen years, I found myself with friends. Topanga was the first location where I made friends. Before then, I didn't have a serious relationship with other kids my age. One of my early friends from the canyon was Paul. He always reminded me of Jeff Beck. I think it was mostly due to the fact that he played an electric guitar and had a haircut that looked very much like Beck's on the cover of an early Yardbirds album. Paul and his family were living in this remarkable house near Topanga Creek. The surroundings were quite romantic in a "boy's adventure" sense: lots of rocks, flowing water, and probably some horrible wildlife lurking around the area. I remember I brought the first Jimi Hendrix Experience album, *Are You Experienced* (1967), for him to listen to; I thought he would find Hendrix interesting. I played "Purple Haze," the first track off the album, which for me was the first sound of the modern age. Once I heard that sound, I couldn't look back. Hendrix opened the door, and once you walked through that entrance, it slammed shut behind you, and there was no way back home.

Paul was impressed with Hendrix's skills with the guitar; he looked at Hendrix in a very technical way. I, on the other hand, was very much impressed by how he looked on the front and back cover of the album, as well as the look of his fellow band members. Hendrix was just an amazing dresser. I was so impressed by

211

WALLACE BERMAN /
Tosh and Wallace Berman and Allen Ginsberg, Topanga Canyon

Hendrix's look, and I loved that his group (Noel Redding and Mitch Mitchell) had matching Afros. The way he mixed and matched his clothing seemed to go beyond logic. I couldn't imagine how anyone could dress that way. I was so impressed with the sounds coming from his guitar, but I had no need to know how he did it; I was just glad he did it. *Are You Experienced* was my first real introduction to a sound that was much bigger than I. I felt quite small listening to it. The discovery of that album changed my perspective on pop music at the time. It became a tad more exotic to me. Then as now, I only cared about how I felt about something. I didn't care what others thought. Still I enjoy sharing something I love, like an excellent record. Playing *Are You Experienced* for Paul was the first time I played something I loved for a friend. I just wanted to share it with him, and I thought it was important to introduce him to the Jimi Hendrix Experience.

The other kids besides Paul I became friends with were David, a blond, sturdy, and good-looking lad; Devin, who had the

WALLACE BERMAN /
Tosh and Allen, Topanga Canyon

most beautiful mom; a beauty named Stormie; and, of course, my beloved friend, Lisa See. All of these people had beautiful homes in the rural landscape that signified Topanga. Devin's mom and stepdad had this terrific house full of sunshine, in walking distance from my house. It was surrounded by trees and very lush greenery. His home was the spot to go to during the dog days of summer. Devin also had a record collection as a kid, some of it provided by his mom and stepdad. His stepdad was the actor Michael Greene, who had an incredible presence. For a kid, grown-ups can be scary, uncomfortable, or just not fun to be around, but Michael had a genuine rapport with children, and he was easy to be around. I got the impression that he listened to children and treated them almost as equals.

For some reason, the household had the entire Monkees catalog. Devin and I spent a lot of time listening to the Monkees. I was crazy about the TV show, and I admired their music, though I wasn't nuts about it. I remember the producer of *The Monkees*

(1966–68) show, Bob Rafelson, came to our house. He brought with him the 45 rpm single "Going Down," which is Mickey Dolenz doing a James Brown-type of cut. At the time, I was just impressed that we got this record directly from the Monkees' world. Of course, I brought the single to Devin's house to play on his turntable, and to have a serious discussion about it. My show-and-tell needs must have been obvious. Like me, Devin met a lot of showbiz figures as a child, so he wasn't uncomfortable in that world.

His mother, Patty, was, in Eddie Cochran's terms, "something else." Not only was she sweet, but I found her to be sensual in her manner. It wasn't anything obvious, but she just had that "it" quality. Of course, as a child on the brink of becoming a teenager, I couldn't articulate my feelings about what was happening with my body, and I didn't have explicit erotic images of her in mind; it was just her presence. I have a faint memory of seeing her half-naked around the house. Maybe I got to their house early, and she was drifting through the rooms naked, but it made an impression on me. I admired her from a distance, and, like Michael, she struck me as a great parent to Devin and his little sister.

Around this time, Devin and I formed a band. Devin had a drum kit, and it was fun to bash his drums (surely his folks must have found it horribly noisy). We got our friend David as lead singer, mostly because he was good looking, and Bruce and Paul were on guitars. I don't think we had a bass player because finding an 11-year-old bass player was quite hard in our social circle. My job was to play the tambourine. I lasted for one band practice because it was evident I was a lousy tambourine player, and my dancing was even worse. The band had a short set of songs, all covers: "(I'm Not Your) Steppin' Stone," "Satisfaction," and I think "96 Tears." My new role in the band was to be part of their audience. That I could do with great skill. They played at Topanga Elementary School in the cafeteria during lunchtime, and I gather they did all right, because no food was thrown at them. At this point London was calling, and it would be my parents' and my first trip outside of the United States. My elementary school years were coming down to something even more interesting.

London / chapter 37

I didn't usually open my father's mail, but the package had *London, England,* as a return address. I tore the oversize envelope open, and what fell out was a black-and-white glossy photograph of four guys wearing turn-of-the-century marching band jackets with three rows of heads looking on behind them. As my eyes became accustomed to the images, I realized it was a funeral, and the heads were all there to attend the ceremony. I stared at it for a while and recognized one of the faces behind the four guys: my father! I also saw W.C. Fields. Why my dad, and why W.C. Fields? Together? Why at a funeral? There was a brief, business-like letter from Brian Epstein, who I recognized as the manager of the Beatles, my (and the whole world's) favorite band at the time. Epstein was requesting that my dad sign the contract for permission and send it back as soon as possible. The letter was so dry and kind of vague to me. I understood they needed Wallace's signature, but what the hell was this photo? And what did he have to do with W.C. Fields, who was a perfectly great American comic and humorist, but what was the connection? For around 10 minutes or so, I went back and forth from Epstein's letter, to the picture, then back to the letter, then . . . Bingo!

The four guys in the front wearing the band outfits were the Beatles! I didn't recognize them, not only because of the outfits that they were wearing, but also because they had facial hair, which made them look so much older than they did on the cover of their last album, *Revolver* (1966). Within 12 months, they'd changed from lovable mop tops to prototype turn-of-the-century dandies with mustaches and even, in John Lennon's case, a pair of glasses. McCartney, being McCartney, had sort of a conservative mustache. But why was my dad in this photograph?

Rereading the letter, I realized that Epstein was asking permission to use my dad's face on the cover of the next Beatles album, *Sgt. Pepper's Lonely Hearts Club Band* (1967). I called my dad, who was at Dean Stockwell's house, and told him all about the package and its contents. Over the telephone, he didn't seem to be that interested. And he wanted to get back to the gin rummy game he was playing with Dean. It was a couple of days later before he finally looked at the package from London. By that time, Epstein had sent a second telegram begging my father to sign the release. My dad ignored that telegram because he was in the middle of doing art, cooking me lunch, smoking pot, and focusing on other important things at hand. It took at least three telegrams to get my dad to sign the release and send it back. I think the payment was 30 pence. Big money in early Tosh days—maybe $1.50?

It took me a long time to figure out why my dad was on the cover. He never asked anyone on that side of the world and, in all honesty, he wasn't that curious about it. But years later, I realized that London art dealer Robert Fraser had a lot to do with the cover and chose certain faces, including Larry Bell and most likely Terry Southern. The Beatles wanted Laurel and Hardy and Sonny Liston. At the time, I had no knowledge the Beatles had even heard of Wallace Berman. The British personalities made sense, and so did Burroughs, who was living in London at that time. But there's also a strong Los Angeles presence on that cover, which has to have come from Fraser, one of the few people from the established London art world to make a trek from the British capital to

L.A. to see the artists who worked and lived there. The only other connection was Yoko Ono, who once sent my dad a miniature artwork, but that was during the Fluxus period, way before she met and hooked up with Lennon.

Approximately 32 million people bought *Sgt. Pepper's*, and I can't even fathom that many faces looking at Wallace's face. It's paradoxical: he liked to be invisible in a crowd, and yet there he was, totally unfamiliar to the masses who bought the album. Over the years, he never actually commented on being on the cover to me, or to anyone else for that matter. On one level, it was the highest honor to appear in such an iconic image of the 1960s, but it didn't change Wallace's life in any shape or form. For many years, someone who labeled each personality on the cover credited him as being an actor. That wasn't corrected till a recent reissue. There's only been a few people who sat down to think about that cover; most skim over it, even if they've purchased a poster or a coffee cup of it. What the people on the cover mean in relation to the music didn't register for most listeners. In an odd way, it's a coded message. If you want the surface of just an "album cover," it works on that level. Oh the other hand, I like to think, what is the relationship between boxer Sonny Listen and Shirley Temple, or Burroughs and the Bowery Boys, Poe and Jung, and so forth? No doubt, my dad is in excellent company. I believe that Wallace was honored to a certain extent, but it wasn't the first thing that came to his mind when he woke up that Summer of Love in 1967. As I now write, *Sgt. Pepper's* came out 50 years ago, June 1, 1967. But a mere turn of a page for me.

Wallace received a grant, or rather a gift, since he didn't apply for it. He was surprised to receive some funds from the Avon Foundation, at the behest of filmmaker Jonas Mekas. The money was marked for Wallace to finish his film *Aleph*, but instead he used that money for plane tickets to London for the whole family. It was an enormous adventure for my dad and mom. They never traveled outside of California at that time, so taking a trip like that was like jumping into the unknown. But I think Wallace was curious about London culture, as well as Robert Fraser's support of Los Angeles artists in the British world. Alas, on our first day in London, we saw Fraser in another car going to Wormwood Scrubs prison due to his arrest and conviction from the Rolling Stones' drug bust at Redlands, where Keith Richards lived at the time. We were initially going to stay in British artist David Hockney's flat in London, but once we got there, someone else was taking care of the place while Hockney was in Los Angeles. Luckily, even though Fraser was on his way to prison, he made arrangements for us to stay at his flat while he was locked up.

We visited the studio where the cover of *Sgt. Pepper's* was shot. Michael Cooper took the photograph at his studio, and when we visited him, I could see some of the discarded cardboard sets from the photo shoot thrown about in his workspace. I didn't see my father's cardboard image, but I did see some others there.

You would think that Wallace would seek to obtain the cardboard figure of himself, but the subject never came up. And he never showed any interest in owning such a collectible object. The whole thing was just so casual, except for the contract with Brian Epstein. I have a faint memory of Cooper. In my mind, it is like a developed image in which some of the figures are present and some are ghostlike; Michael Cooper was one of the faint images on the photograph in my mind. Wallace met him in Los Angeles, most likely through Fraser. I think Cooper traveled with Robert when he came to the West Coast. He eventually hung out with the Stones and became their official photographer, which, looking back, might not have been the wisest move for him, healthwise. On the other hand, he took amazing behind-the-scenes photographs of the band. The odd thing about photographers is that their presence is much needed. They are ghosts in the scene. I remember that Cooper did have a son, a small child. I think there was a young boy in the studio when we were there.

As a child, I imagined London was ground zero for everything that was cool in this world. From my first purchase of a Beatles album to the first episode of *Secret Agent* (1960–68) (UK title: *Danger Man*), I was intrigued with the idea of London. To me, Londoners seemed to be a race of superior humans who spoke our language, but in a very funny way. To be in that part of the world with my parents was beyond belief at that point in my life. Oddly enough, I remember the sunlight there, which surprised me because I always heard that London was cold and gray; in actuality, that summer it was warm on some days. Then again, the weather was unpredictable. The image of gray days didn't fit the reality I experienced while there. It was chilly sometimes, yes, but there were days when I felt like I was overdressed for the weather. Walking down Oxford Street and being sweaty stays in my mind. One thing that made an impression on me weather-wise was the speed with which it changed from warm to cold or cloudy to sunny. Weather in Los Angeles tends to stay the same throughout the day. In that sense, I felt I was on foreign land.

The first time I can remember shopping for my clothes was on London's Carnaby Street. The experience went beyond being essential clothing, into another, peculiar reality. I remember purchasing a pair of striped pants and a T-shirt with the *Sgt. Pepper's* logo on the front. I also had a black cowboy hat and several scarves. Seeing Steven Stills when he was with Buffalo Springfield wearing a cowboy hat was a weird juxtaposition for me, so I took part of his style but added my twists as well: a black cowboy hat, a *Sgt. Pepper's* T-shirt, black and red striped pants, and desert boots. Now I was ready to explore the London landscape.

British food was strange. For instance, when I ordered a glass of soda and asked for ice, they only gave me one ice cube. The cube looked like it came from somewhere else. A lot of people in London (and I presume in the UK) didn't own an icebox or a refrigerator. We went to friend's flat, and the toilet was outside in a little wooden structure in the yard.

The great connector in my life, Toni Basil, enabled us to meet John Dunbar. One of the significant figures in 1960s London, Dunbar, along with Peter Asher (of Peter & Gordon fame) and Barry Miles, started the first underground bookstore, called Indica, where they also had a gallery. It was here that Yoko Ono had her show where she met John Lennon. Dunbar was a great pal of the Beatles' camp, as well as Robert Fraser. At that time, Dunbar had just split up with his wife, Marianne Faithful, who was living with Mick Jagger. But I wasn't aware of any tension within that camp. As a kid, unless you see something in front of you, or it's discussed in your presence, it's not there. In the same sense that one just accepts the belief that Santa Claus exists, I just accepted that things in that social world were perfectly all right. Keep in mind that we never saw Jagger or any of the Fab Four on this trip, even though their presence was everywhere. Where we stayed,

Fraser's place, there was an actual piece of artwork on the wall by John Lennon. Dunbar told us that Lennon drew on the wall one night while he was tripping on acid.

One of the things that impressed me as a kid in London was watching how men carried themselves in terms of their clothing and manner. I was quite taken with the foppish, slightly camp style of men that we met there. It didn't strike me as gay, but more of a style as a "front" for the world to see. A particular type of British accent had a melody to it that seemed to be a mixture of disdain, distance, and wit at the same time. It never turned me off. In fact, I loved it. I wanted that style of speech for myself but while I couldn't for the life of me imitate the accent, I thought I could do my version of that style. I realize now that form of speech has influenced me as a conversationalist as well as a writer. British humor, for me, didn't start with *Monty Python*; it was P.G. Wodehouse. When I read him now, it takes me back to when I was young, and for me, the typical British male is represented by a Wooster type of character. It was the first time I understood language being playful, yet conveying so many layers of meaning. I was brought up in an environment where language was kind of cool and said very little. In London, I felt the vocabulary was rich, and it brought ideas to my head. I'm convinced it was around this time that I wanted to set that language on a page. I wasn't aware what that meant, but the British accent, the wording, and the perception of the British became imperative to me, especially as a teenager, wanting to distance myself from various influences in Topanga Canyon.

More than anything else in my little world, I was shocked how small the London social scene was. Knowing one person led us to another person, who in turn introduced us to a larger group of individuals. If you share a common interest with others, it doesn't matter if you are famous or not. That interest will eventually get people together with each other. The interest is culture; travel, music, the visual arts—it was like everyone was watching the same TV channel or listening to the radio station and getting the same information, and there was a need to share that information.

One of the first people my father looked up in London was Alexander Trocchi, a true legend in the world of literature and a beat don, as well as one of the biggest drug addicts on the planet at the time. Wallace knew him in San Francisco and put a piece of his writing in *Semina*. We visited him at his flat, and it was a shocking moment for me. For one, he shot up heroin in front of me, and at that point in my life, I don't think I had ever seen a needle before—not even a doctor's needle—and therefore had never seen such an object inserted into an arm, except maybe on a medical show like *Dr. Kildare* (1961–66) or *Ben Casey* (1961–66). Alex had a lot of scars and scabs on his arm, and he took his time in preparing the heroin while carrying on a conversation with us. Also, he had a small child in the apartment with him, on his lap or crawling around the area; it seemed to me, young as I was, that there was something wrong with the picture in front of me. I don't remember my parents even commenting on that visit. I think most people who presume to know the world I live in would think I would have been exposed to that type of drug taking, but my father hated heroin and had a very strong anti-drug stance, even though he was for legalizing all drugs. My mom and dad never made judgments towards people they knew and even people they didn't like. "Live and let live" seemed to be their motto or their way of thinking, especially when it came to a character like Alex. He was not the type of chap that one would call a sweetheart. In a funny way, he was very much like my father, in that he always turned up in great or exciting company. I don't think a life like that can be planned out; it's written in the stars.

One of the big events I went to was the International Congress of Dialectics of Liberation that took place at the Roundhouse in Chalk Farm. We went there specifically to see and hear

Alexander Trocchi, 1967

Allen Ginsberg read his poetry (or perhaps he just gave a talk). It seemed to be a meeting of minds, including Julian Beck of the Living Theater; Stokely Carmichael, a leading American Black Power figure; Paul Goodman; Emmett Grogan, the founder of the San Francisco Diggers; R.D. Laing; philosopher Herbert Marcuse; the auto-destructive artist Gustave Metzler; performance artist Carolee Schneemann; Vietnamese Buddhist monk Thich Nhat Hanh; and of course, Allen. If I'd been 18 or in my early 20s, I would have been thrilled to be there, but being 12 meant I was not that interested. Right place, right time, but wrong age.

After the event, Wallace found the sole taxi lurking around the street near the Roundhouse. We got it, and Wallace noticed that an older, conservatively dressed gentleman was trying to get the same cab, but he was on the opposite side of the road. Wallace yelled out to him that we could share the cab, because the neighborhood was highly quiet at that time of night, and it was hard to locate a taxi. He accepted this offer and came across the street.

We all fit in the back. I remember my mom, myself, and Wallace in the back seat, and our guest pulled a seat down directly across from us. He introduced himself as William Burroughs. The irony of this meeting was that Wallace was one of the first (if not THE first) to publish an excerpt of *Naked Lunch* (1959), in *Semina*. There was no mention of this in the taxi, and the conversation was small talk, except when my dad told the driver the address we wanted to go to. Burroughs commented that he knew that address because he'd been to Fraser's flat numerous times. It was just an interesting meeting of minds that had a solid connection but were like two ships passing each other in the night.

We saw Burroughs again a week later at a party that Ginsberg helped put together for my parents. Once in a great while, the fame thing would come up and startle my perception. Ginsberg was in the news consistently. Not only that, but I remember eating with my parents in a neighborhood Indian restaurant, where we had to share a table with two other people who we didn't know. Both of them were Indians and were talking in their language. Once in a while, we'd hear the name Ginsberg between the foreign words in their conversation. It was kind of amazing to know someone that famous in London. How did that happen? The hostess of the party for my parents, Panna Grady, was an American who lived in London and quite fond of beat or counterculture artists. The party for my father took place in her house, and Burroughs, Ginsberg, and Alexander Trocchi were there. I was told much later that her home was once the Chinese Embassy in London. The party was unusual for me, in that I got the impression that the people there didn't know each other. It wasn't exactly awkward, but it was the only time I experienced the feeling of being in a mixture of the upper crust and the underclass. But even in the underclass, there are levels of social class: the criminal, the drug addict, and the artist.

What shocked me was reading the headlines of a British

paper that morning announcing the arrest of Black Power advocate Michael X under the Race Relations Act, which was technically put into law to protect minorities in the U.K. He had been quoted saying any white man who is seen "laying hands" on a black woman should be immediately killed. He was sentenced to 12 months for that offense. On the day of his arrest, he showed up at the party for my dad. Never in a million years did I think I would see Michael X in person, but there he was at the party, and he looked like he just stepped off of the front page of a London newspaper. Eventually, Michael X was charged and hung for a murder that took place in the 1970s.

The thing about the London trip with my parents was that it was the first time I had ever been to a place that I had worshiped from afar. It was like watching *The Wizard of Oz* (1939) on TV and being in a position to go there. My dad was on the cover of *Sgt. Pepper's* and we were meeting all sorts of engaging people from that world. We were invited to the recording studio to see Donovan mixing his album, most likely with John Dunbar. London to me seemed like a series of platforms, and John had a key or a pass to each level of cultural life. It was the beauty of the London '60s era, when, for a brief moment in time, if you were interesting, you could merge with others who shared the currency of a particular drug, or taste in music, clothing, and art. Wallace had the innate ability to be always interesting on many fronts.

Donovan's legendary producer, Mickie Most, must have been somewhere in that studio, but I can't remember meeting him. The recording studio itself was huge, and I was impressed with what Donovan was wearing. I remember a white silk shirt with lace, faded blue Levi's, and beautiful leather lace-up shoes. He was listening to the playback of "Wear Your Love Like Heaven." There wasn't much interaction between my parents and him. He was entirely focused on the music.

John Dunbar and someone named Jenny, who I only

remember as being beautiful, took me and my parents to the 14-hour Technicolor Dream that took place at the Alexandra Palace. I think we got there really late, maybe around midnight. I remember a lot of people; music played live in the background. Much later I realized that concert was one of the ground zero moments of London '60s culture. Famously, Syd Barrett's Pink Floyd played there, as well as Graham Bond, The Creation, John's Children, and The Move. Yoko Ono may have done a performance there as well, and John Lennon was reportedly in the audience, watching. It was without a doubt the ultimate counterculture event, but I have very little memory of it; I mostly remember Jenny because she was gorgeous, and she was responsible for us leaving the hall. I think she was ill due to something she took earlier that evening, and therefore, I didn't get my mind fully blown. Sadly, that has never happened. As of this writing, my brain cells are still here, yet I do desire to have my mind blown.

The beautiful dream ended for me when my Dad received a postcard from our neighbor George Herms, showing our house in Topanga from the Herms's perspective across the way. Wallace got homesick and immediately booked a flight back to Los Angeles. He wanted to go back to his studio to work. The only thing I remember him doing in London was making rubbings of manholes throughout the capital, usually in the middle of the night. Getting back to Los Angeles was a culture shock to me. I had my *Sgt. Pepper's* band jacket, *Sgt. Pepper's* T-shirt, paisley scarf, Steven Stills cowboy hat, and striped pants. I was a little mod going back to the hell that was and always will be Topanga. Back to isolation, back to stupid hippie culture, back to being stranded in an area I hated. In other words, back to school. Even worse: junior high school.

But the Beatles acknowledging the existence of my father was a top supreme number one for a young, obsessed pop music fan like yours truly. To this day, I brag about it to my heart's content, and no one can say anything bad about that. The fact that my dad's face is on every item possible via the *Pepper* cover is pretty amazing. The funny thing is that I don't own the album or any other image of the cover except for the original black-and-white print Epstein sent my dad. As I write this, it's on the wall in my hallway, along with pictures of Kenneth Anger and Russ Meyer. So even in my household, it belongs to the hall of fame.

Junior High / chapter 38

I pretty much dreaded the thought of going to junior high school. What I was afraid of were the military aspects of the Physical Education department and its mean, sadistic teachers. Parkman Junior High School in Woodland Hills was a series of ugly buildings with lockers that continually frustrated me. Once I got the knack of opening them within three minutes—though I always forgot the locker combination—I appreciated having my own space on the school grounds. I wished that I could just stay inside my locker, but due to space limitations and the fact that lockers smell—well, it was a false sense of home. The real terror was the gym locker. I had to remember two combinations, and that was an impossible feat for me. A typical day at P.E. would find me rushing to change into my gym clothes because, of course, I'd be late due to figuring out how to open my locker. Once late to the line-up, I'd be singled out as someone weird and forced to do push-ups over muddy, dirty water while the gym teacher flirted with the teenage girls on the other side of the yard.

There were three gym teachers: Mr. Brown (white, with a thin mustache and the nicest of the three creeps), Mr. Fruita (Japanese American and mean), and Mr. Cord (very white and mean, psychotic even). I prayed to be assigned to Mr. Brown's class, just to survive the ordeal, but I ended up in Mr. Cord's class. To say he hated me is simply to state a fact, like "the sun is out," or "it's nighttime." I couldn't question this fact, because I never saw him smile unless he was torturing me for some odd reason. I remember times when I couldn't do something physical, like climb a rope, which was never going to happen in the first place due to my fear of heights. Mr. Cord forced me to stand by the rope till I climbed, but I never did climb out of fear and, of course, for moral reasons. So I spent a lot of time in his class doing stuff like push-ups or running extra laps around the playground because I was too slow, compared to the rest of the class. Sometimes he would make the whole class suffer. He would tell the gym class in front of me that we'd have to run an extra lap around the yard, due to me not climbing a rope or not being able to do enough pull-ups on the monkey bar. I felt lots of shame and embarrassment from causing the entire class to run extra laps. I felt there was a conscious attempt on the part of the P.E. teachers to turn my classmates against me, but in actuality most of them liked me.

One time, after I showered after class, Mr. Cord called me into the office. The other two P.E. teachers were there as well. The knot in my stomach told me this is not going to go well. All three of them called me a "fag" over and over again. All three gym teachers took me into the shower, and they made me take another shower while they watched. Once I finished, they forced me to go in again to wash my hair, which was a little longish; I usually avoided doing that because it took a long time for my hair to dry. The oddness of being attacked by my gym teachers seemed like I was watching a movie of myself. It didn't seem real, and to this day, I don't fully understand their disgust with or perhaps hatred for me. I was even more surprised by Mr. Brown joining the others in taunting me. He struck me as an older guy who should know better. Of them all, I was disappointed with him the most.

That, I have to admit, was a horrifying afternoon. I did complain to my parents, but it was my word against the entire P.E. Department. To this day, I don't remember the response from either

WALLACE BERMAN /
Junior High School, Graduation, Topanga Canyon, 1970

my dad or mom. They may have felt it was one of those life-learning experiences, knowing that the school system wasn't exactly paradise, or they just didn't know how to deal with something like that. Come to think of it, my entire school life was probably something odd and fishy, and for whatever reason, my parents as far as I know never fought against the educational system. It was an era where I think one just accepted the evil, and tried to get on with life. On the other hand, it seems odd to me that a bunch of grown-up guys who chased balls around the schoolyard or made students chase balls were so focused on me being a "fag." It was scary because I was alone with these grown-up guys. Fellow students bullying me was bad enough, but my teachers doing it was horrifying.

Since I wasn't big on the sports thing (that session alone

destroyed any interest in that world), the teachers never invited me to play for a school team, which was probably for the best. My dad would never have come to school to watch me play baseball. I didn't go to the prom, either. In fact, I didn't even take a class photograph like the other students. I don't think my parents cared if I had a photo in the yearbook or not. They rarely, if ever, participated in school projects. Our dear family friend George Herms was president of the Topanga PTA, but my dad never once came close to the school. In fact, when I graduated from high school, he waited outside in his car, reading the newspaper. My mom and grandmother Martha went to the event, but my dad either refused to go or didn't care. Considering the length of a graduation ceremony, he was very patient, but there was no sense of relief or even congratulations on my father's part. He was totally disconnected from that world. For my part, I wasn't offended or disturbed by Wallace's reactions to my school years. Over the years, I realized that his experiences in the education system pretty much shaped him as an adult. And school was not a significant or positive thing in his life.

Due to a lack of paper or photo evidence, my school years are just memories for me. And my major memories are of the females that I went to school with: girls I wanted to sleep with, girls I wanted to talk to, so they would talk to me, and girls just being girls. I was very shy, and I wouldn't say I was popular with the girls, but I was well liked, if not loved, by the female world in the San Fernando Valley. That said, like my other friends in junior high, I didn't have a girlfriend. I think it would have been impossible for me to tell a girl that I loved her. I had no way to develop a language or gesture to show a girl I liked her. I liked plenty of them, and some liked me back, but I was distant due to my shyness. I just wanted to have the attention of the cute girl in the classroom. Or the one in the cafeteria. Or the beautiful girls on the quad, showing off their last fashions and exposing their beauty to their fellow students. In all honesty, by the time I was in high school, I couldn't have cared less about classes, but I was really into girls. High school is step one toward the adult world that's out there, and I had a hard time adjusting to it.

I took the standard classes in junior high: English (I was an appalling student), Math (insanely bad), and, of course, P.E. But they had extra classes like woodshop, which I enjoyed. The fresh wood scent of the class was relaxing to me. Also in woodshop, I felt I could enjoy something very male-oriented. At the time there were no females in the class. The very first project on hand was the sanding block. The sanding block is ground zero for anyone who works with wood. It was virtually a fetish object for those of us who entered the class. Probably the best thing about the woodshop was the pride of making an object that could be utilized later in life. The feeling of accomplishment from working with your hands on a particular project cannot be overestimated, and can't help but build confidence for the present and the future. Sadly, as in my other classes, I was crap in woodshop.

My main difficulty was, when I started sanding one side of the block, the other side became uneven. With a square ruler, I measured how much I was off, but of course, I just pretended to know how to use a square ruler. I just made it worse, and even more lopsided. To add insult to my injured self-esteem, the fellow student with whom I was sharing the table finished his sanding block on the first day of class, and by the end of the semester, he had made an impressive bookshelf, as well as a hummingbird house with a dipper attached. For yours truly, the sanding block gave me splinters—especially under my nails for some reason—and I was a complete waste of the taxpayers' money. I remember we had to pay for the wood out of pocket or, I should say, my mom and dad had to pay for that one piece I worked on for the entire semester. I have to imagine it pained Wallace no end to pay for that sanding block, where frequently he would steal wood from the lumberyard.

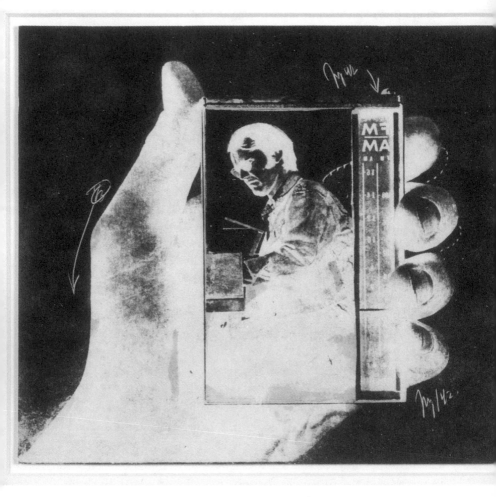

WALLACE BERMAN /
Untitled #36, Jack Nicholson

Easy Rider / chapter 39

My so-called film career started off great, being in Andy Warhol's *Tarzan and Jane Regained . . . Sort Of*, but my co-star in that film, Dennis Hopper, offered me a brief role in his film, *Easy Rider* (1969). We saw a lot of Dennis during the making of this movie. Through luck and the charm of *The Monkees* TV show, producers Bob Rafelson and Bert Schneider were in the position to finance independent films through their company Raybert Productions. *Easy Rider*, directed by Dennis and written by Dennis, co-star Perter Fonda, and Terry Southern, was Dennis's obsession for a long time. I remember him wearing the clothes of his character, Billy, day in and day out. He insisted that my parents be in the background in one of the scenes in the movie. At first, they refused, but Dennis sent a car to pick them up, and therefore they became extras in the commune scene that was shot in the Malibu hills.

I went along to watch a film being shot and thought it was fascinating. The only other time I had visited a movie set (besides Warhol's) was when Dean took my dad and me to the set of *Combat!* (1962–67), which was a favorite TV show of mine at the time. *Combat!* had a full crew, lots of lights, and, of course, the set itself was fake. *Easy Rider*, on the other hand, was shot on location with a small crew of people around Dennis. I remember being impressed with the catering, because there was plenty of food, and I could get a plate of food anytime I wanted to. After the day's shooting, Dennis approached me and asked if I wanted to be part of the film. I thought it would be like my parent's job in the movie, just sitting around while he shot me, and when he wasn't shooting me, I'd be eating from the catering table. So I said yes.

Dennis took the script, ripped a page out, and gave it to me. I was to remember the lines on the page and show up the next morning. After reading the one page over and over again, I knew it would be impossible for me to do. What I had to do was run up to Peter Fonda when he and Dennis first come to the commune and hug him, with some dialogue between him and me. As I read this one-page script, I couldn't for the life of me remember even a single word. I became nervous and, that night, I told my parents I didn't want to do it. As they had to go back the next day for more shooting, they conveyed to Dennis that I wouldn't or couldn't do it, and he said OK. What I remember is that he wasn't upset with me, and he just dropped that whole scene. Looking on the positive side, perhaps I improved the actual film!

High School / *chapter 40*

Taft High School at that time consisted of white people in three groupings: glam kids (the gang I was in), greasers (who I liked), and the nerdy, school-event-going geeks (by far, the majority in the school, and who were not even on my radar, oddly enough). The greasers and the glam kids were entirely minority groups that completely ignored the status quo. There were no hostilities between the groups, but jocks just didn't exist in our world. We didn't know how they felt about us, and we didn't care. A lot of the greaser kids came from Topanga. Culturally, there was a significant difference between teenagers in Woodland Hills and teenagers from Topanga. There was a stable family structure in the Valley, with a father and mother in each household. Topanga was mostly single moms taking care of children. The Topanga kids were similar to the iconic image of James Dean: hungry for attention and in internal pain.

The greaser uniform was pretty good in my opinion: Levi's worn low (almost hip-hop style) with boxer shorts exposed as the ass, matched with a starched white T-shirt or, if feeling dressy, a button-up, checkered, short-sleeved shirt. Levi's jackets and 1950s hairstyles. To be honest, it wasn't a full-on '50s hairstyle, because their haircuts weren't geared for the classic duck's-ass in the back and long on the top. Their hair was very long and combed into a pompadour with the sides greased back. To be proper, they would

WALLACE BERMAN /
Allen Ginsberg and Tosh Berman, Topanga Canyon, 1972

need to cut the sides and keep the top half longer. Nevertheless, they were gruff but quite sweet at the same time. They also smoked cigarettes in a manner where they held the butt of the smoke with their index finger and thumb. I didn't see a huge difference between glam rock and '50s rock on recordings. But certain strains of glam liked prog rock, and that for sure was a no-no (as it should be) for the greasers; I hated prog rock, as well.

Taft High School was a lot easier to deal with than Parkman. I'm not sure why. To me, Parkman felt like it was in another

WALLACE BERMAN /
Tosh Berman in High School, Topanga Canyon, 1972

country or century; I felt like an alien at that school. At Taft, I
didn't feel alienated either by the teaching staff or my fellow students. Perhaps everyone just grew up! One thing for sure was that
my grades were so average, I'm sure the teachers at Taft overlooked
me. I was a C– student in everything. The only classes I enjoyed
were the ones where I had to read a book or a short story. We
had a teacher named Michael Jackson, who reminded me of Dick
Cavett in his TV prime. He was literate and easygoing, a perfect combination for a teacher. In his class I read two books that

had an effect on me: Emily Brontë's *Wuthering Heights* (1847) and Baroness Orczy's *The Scarlet Pimpernel* (1905). At the time, I didn't realize that *Wuthering Heights* was such an erotic, dream-like novel. The everlasting love (or is it undying hatred?) in the book made for a very subversive narrative. Its violence of feeling struck me, and the Gothic eroticism also appealed to my teenage aesthetic at the time. *The Scarlet Pimpernel* was a European version of Zorro, and I loved that. Whenever a character acts fey to disguise his more violent nature, I'm all for it. My future and the future of my fellow students were in doubt due to the Vietnam War. In high school, the threat of the draft was still upon us. So I look at those two books as having exposed me to a different inner life. *The Scarlet Pimpernel*, due to that character living in two worlds, reminded me not only of the potential future danger of the draft but also of day-to-day survival in the school system. One had to play the system to survive.

Going to school was entirely a social affair, and I rarely concerned myself with how well I was doing in class. I was always respectful to my teachers, but I was never worried about grades, as long as I didn't fail. My failure in my kindergarten still lingered in my thoughts, and I didn't want to stay an extra semester to compensate for my failure. I also enjoyed being in a room full of my peers. I discovered that I liked people. Still, my parents never participated in the school scene, and my father especially just didn't have a feel for it. The little things about school made it enjoyable. For instance, ever since first grade, I loved the school bus. I remember in elementary school we had a strict driver who wouldn't even allow us to talk on the bus, which was weird, but overall I didn't mind. I liked taking a nap or watching the cinema in my head as we drove down or up the canyon.

A lot of celebrities went to Taft, but one was an actual working TV star. Maureen McCormick played Marsha, the oldest daughter on *The Brady Bunch* (1969–74). I never, in fact, spoke to

Maureen, but I remember seeing her during school lunch breaks or going towards a class. She seemed to be the same person as the character in the TV show. Again, television and real life were a blur to me. As with my parents' friends like Billy Gray, I couldn't separate my sense of reality and the "reality" projected by the TV, the difference between the roles actors played on TV and their actual life when the camera shuts off. Also, as a teenager, I started projecting myself as a character in the movie I made up in my head. I have a tendency to place my friends or people I see on the street as the characters in the peculiar narrative that is brewing between my ears.

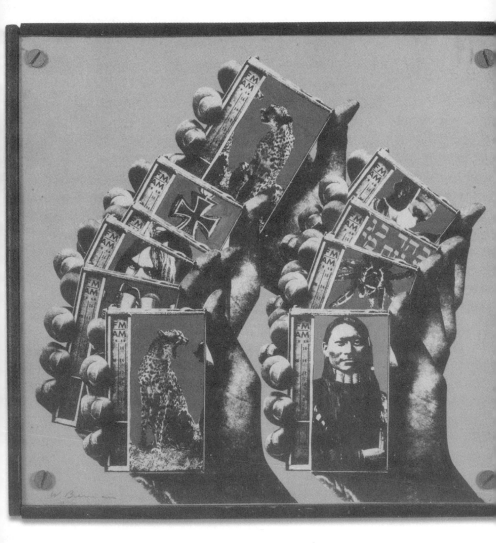

WALLACE BERMAN /
Untitled (Multi-color Shuffle, A-4 Neil Young), 1969

Neil Young / *chapter 41*

Without a doubt, Neil Young was *the* artist of Topanga. One could argue my dad is the icon of Topanga, but the truth is, it's Neil. The short amount of time that he spent in Topanga was very fruitful for him. As far as I know, he lived in the canyon during the making of his first three solo albums. As a young teenager, I always thought that Neil was the king and the canyon was his kingdom. Topanga, in other words, was Neil-Land.

He had his entourage that stayed with him, and in ways, it reminds me of Elvis and the Memphis Mafia, or perhaps more like Frank Sinatra and his Rat Pack. I always felt it was no coincidence that Neil was on the same label as Frank, Reprise Records, which Frank also owned. My dad ran into Neil quite often, because both Dean and Russell became close to Neil. Wallace was a pal, but not someone Neil would call up on a regular basis. In fact, they only hung out if Dean and the others were around. Neil surrounded himself with guys who worked for him or just hung out. I knew some of his buddies as a teenager but was never sure exactly what they did for a living or what they did for Neil.

Dean, along with another friend, Herb Bermann, wrote a screenplay together called *After the Gold Rush*. Bermann also wrote the lyrics to Captian Beefheart's album *Safe as Milk* (1967), an early and enduring favorite of mine. Herb lived in the creek area very close to Topanga Beach. Besides writing poetry and lyrics,

Herb was a writer who worked on TV shows as well. Neil read the script and offered his services to do the soundtrack. The film never got made, but Neil did write and record the music and, of course, the album did come out. We were all invited to a listening party at Neil's house for the record. *After the Gold Rush* (1970), I thought at the time, was super great. I was never a Neil fan, but I liked this album. When the LP came out, I noticed there were significant differences between it and the version I heard at his house. Some songs were dropped, and the sound seemed changed as well. This may be due to Neil's sound system that day, but for sure he changed the order of the songs, and I believe he eliminated some tunes and added new ones for the final version. Wallace and Neil also had a long discussion at the listening party regarding the first Paul McCartney solo album. Both liked *McCartney* (1970) a lot; though history doesn't show this, that album was quite influential at the time of its release. An artist playing and writing everything on an album was an unusual practice at the time, although Paul wasn't the first to do so. I believe Les Paul came first with the art of multi-tracking.

Neil invited Wallace, Shirley, and me to nearly all of his shows in L.A. I remember going to three of them. One was with his band Crazy Horse at the Troubadour, where Neil had some attack and passed out on the way to the stage. I remember he recovered and did a regular set. Then there was another Crazy Horse show at the Santa Monica Civic, and then Crosby, Stills, Nash, & Young at the Greek Theater. CSNY was a major spectacle. To me, the music was so-so. But what impressed me was that CSNY came out on stage for an acoustic set in front of a big curtain. Once they finished the set, the curtains opened up to a wall of Marshall amps, electric guitars, and full drum kit. On paper that doesn't sound that unusual, but the difference between the two set-ups made the amps into a spectacular visual treat. There was a sense of theater about it all that I loved. We went backstage to see

Neil, and as we went through the entrance to the dressing rooms, we saw Jim Morrison getting thrown out. As Jim was being forced out by security, Steven Stills came out and said, "Jim!" It was an impressive few moments.

The Berman Family in Taos, NM

Taos / chapter 42

We took two trips out to Taos, New Mexico. The first was by train, which was fantastic. The other was a car trip with Dean. The destination, on both trips, was Dennis Hopper's home in Taos. He lived on a 12-acre compound once owned by Mabel Dodge, who was a great early 20th-century bohemian. In her house, Dodge entertained artists and writers such as Marsden Hartley, Ansel Adams, Willa Cather, Robinson Jeffers, Georgia O'Keeffe, and D.H. Lawrence. Both trips were quite different from each other. The first trip was right after Dennis made *Easy Rider*, and he was working on his next film, *The Last Movie* (1971). In fact, he was editing *The Last Movie* at the Dodge house, where he set himself up in a small studio. He was away when we arrived, but Dennis arranged for us to stay at the house. Besides Dennis, there was a whole gang of employees, or what one would call an entourage.

The entourage was very kind to us, and seemed to be hippie-orientated, with various skills related to the film business. As we got to Taos late afternoon, after settling into our rooms at the Dodge/Dennis house, we all decided to go out to dinner in Taos. This we found to be problematic. It seemed that Dennis and his entourage had been kicked out of every restaurant in town. We were refused service everywhere, except one restaurant that showed pity towards us. Still, I sensed hostility between the server and everyone else in our dining party. Unknown to us at the time, the local population of Taos hated Dennis with a passion. In fact, Dennis had a movie theater in Taos, where he showed films by Luis Buñuel. As we drove by the theater, we could see it was shot up, either by a couple of rifles or a bunch of handguns. It became apparent to us that the Hopper entourage was armed, at all times. Common sense told me that the citizens of Taos were probably in the right, with respect to their hatred of Dennis and his world. Dennis and company were hard drinkers and drug addicts, and they had a sense of "play" when they went out on the town. The Native American community, the Spanish American people, struck me as socially conservative. This was not a community that would be open to Dennis and company, which is entirely understandable.

Taos is incredibly beautiful, the landscape around the town as well as its architecture. The structures were made out of the mud. It didn't seem possible to me, yet my senses told me I was in a structure that came from the ground up. Mud, rather than wood, was the ingredient that people depended on. For me, besides the hostility between the Hopper clan and everyone else who lived in Taos, there was a sense of dread as well. I had a haunted feeling, and my overall reaction to Taos was fear and sadness. I didn't like visiting the Indian reservations, because I felt, rightfully or wrongly, that it was set up for visiting tourists. The Native American people were treated so horribly throughout the United States history that I found reservations depressing. Taos, which seemed to be a paradise for so many, stuck me as a desolate and spiritually vacant area of the world—in that sense, a perfect location for Dennis.

I didn't sleep well on that trip, due to the fear that the citizens of Taos would attack the compound. At least, we got that impression from the entourage that lived on the property of Dennis's dream pad. Personally, I couldn't wait to leave the house and the area. A year later we made another trip out to Dennis-Hell with

Dean, driving from Los Angeles to Taos. The car trip was fun, and this time Dennis was at home. He had just married the actress Daria Halprin, and it seemed like he was trying his hardest to be a homebody. At nighttime, he would wear matching pajamas, which seemed like really unique clothing for him. On this second trip, I didn't feel fear or paranoia of being in Taos with him on his property. Dennis was always intense, but he seemed jubilant and content being in Taos with his new wife; I think, at the time, they were expecting a child.

On this particular trip, we went to the Hotel La Fonda, which was the primary residence for anyone who visited Taos. There were a lot of strange New York City people there to film *Greasers' Palace* (1972), a film by Robert Downey Sr. Toni Basil had a small role in the movie, and I think the main purpose of us going to Taos was so Dean could spend time with her. The only other person I have a strong memory of seeing is the actor Hervé Villechaize. I have no memory of meeting Robert Sr., but there was a small boy floating around the set, who I have to imagine was Robert Jr. Oddly enough, I have never seen the film.

Concerts / chapter 43

Wallace and I never really talked. He communicated more in silences than chit-chat. It sounds rather cold, but that wasn't the case whatsoever. He was a pretty funny and supportive father nearly all the time. One thing we shared was our love of music. I remember my mother playing me folk songs on the guitar and singing to me, perhaps to get me to sleep at bedtime. I remember her having a pretty singing voice, and it was quite pleasant when she picked up the guitar. Wallace was the explorer of the household music scene. He had more cutting-edge taste in music than I did, even up to the age of 18. For instance, he brought into the household the first Velvet Underground album, The Fugs on Folkway Records, Paul Bowles's recordings of Moroccan native music, Captain Beefheart's *Trout Mask Replica* (1969), Miles Davis's *Bitches Brew* (1970), and other stuff that a 10-year-old or even a 17-year-old wouldn't have picked up by himself. I have never met another person, to this day, who has such magnificent antennae tuned to the outside world, picking out the best or most interesting sounds and bringing them back to the lair. He never sat me down and forced me to listen to music; it was just part of the household.

He knew a lot of musicians, from Jimmy Witherspoon (when Wallace was a teenager) to Brian Jones, and I think they admired his sense of hearing and sensitivity to sound. I remember once playing a John Lennon solo album, *Mind Games* (1973). At the time, no one would criticize any Beatle's work, but Wallace gave the album a listen and said Lennon had lost it. It was shocking to hear someone give such a negative comment to Lennon's work, but he was entirely correct. John Lennon, at that point, had turned off his genius and was just going with the times. His biggest musical crime was coasting on his talents, which is something Wallace always caught in a musician or fellow visual artist, if they were just doing their work, without pushing some boundary. I think for Wallace there was always the need to see what more could be done, or how better expressed that work could become, through study, and through just doing the job. To just put out product was a real no-no in my dad's world.

Although he loved jazz, my father had a good ear for what was happening around him. He wasn't stuck on the music heroes of his era: Charlie Parker, Billie Holiday, etc. He also admired David Bowie, Patti Smith (particularly *Horses* [1975]), early Santana, and Roxy Music, and once he insisted on listening to my complete Syd Barrett catalog (all two albums) in one sitting. At the time, EMI had put out a set of his two solo albums. Wallace put the records on in order, adjusted the headphones, and didn't move for 80 minutes. Once the records were over, he flipped the headphones off his head and said, "Pretty good." I don't think any of his friends were into this type of music. They were into the Beatles (who wasn't, at the time?), but probably were not aware of the punk scene that began brewing just before my dad's death. He had a natural appreciation for what was happening, as well as for what had happened in the past. There wasn't a sentimental bone in his body. Others of his generation, I think, were stuck in a time warp.

Another great pleasure we shared was going to concerts. In 1969, the Rolling Stones went on their first official tour after the death of my dad's friend Brian Jones. The tour itself was big news and quite important to teenagers like me at the time. The Stones' status, not only in the rock 'n' roll world, but as an iconic musical force, was at its height at the time. Somehow I bagged a couple of tickets in the very last row of the gigantic Inglewood Forum for myself and a girlfriend. My dad drove us to the concert and then asked if he could come to the show with us. I told him that tickets were impossible to get and all good seats were taken, which was why I'd be suffering vertigo in the last row at the Forum. My father paused and said, "Well, we will see." Our seats were truly horrible. With my 20/20 vision, it was like looking at ants on a massive stage. I hate being up high, and I remember the feeling of my stomach in knots, due to the height and distance from the stage and show. My date did bring a pair of opera glasses. Just before the show started, I scanned the stadium with her opera glasses to assess whether I knew anyone in the audience. Focusing on the center of the stage to see if I could even see the Stones at that distance, I looked at the front row center, and there sat my father, looking very bored, yet very comfortable and pleased at the same time. I was speechless. I don't think I even told my date about it. Throughout the concert, I was thinking to myself: How? Why? True to his character, he never brought up the issue of him getting a ticket, especially one directly in the front row. He never told me how he got that seat. It was one of the many mysteries of life with my father.

At the other end of the spectrum, Wallace took me to see John Cage, who I think was at UCLA. Cage came on the stage and he was totally wired for sound. He would drink something down, and one could hear the liquid going down his throat into his digestive system. And Cage would cut up vegetables, I think carrots, and that too was wired for sound. The performance was very much a theatrical show, in that watching Cage do this was even more interesting than the "sounds" he was producing. Cage was a very famous person in my circle, and I knew of him even as a child. Either my parents had recordings of his work, or other people in our circle did. He was THE composer of my time.

The big concert for me was mostly David Bowie, who was, and is, probably the most prominent rock figure in my lifetime. I caught onto Bowie kind of early with his *Hunky Dory* (1971) album, which was a huge hit with my social group at Taft High School. I was intrigued by the album cover because he looked like a German female movie star, and I loved his baggy Oxford pants on the back cover. I remember Gerard Malanga staying with us, I think for two weeks, while he was shooting images of poets for a book of his poetry. I found him fascinating because of his connection with the Warhol world, but I was also impressed that he was a poet, and he was the first one that I sort of related to, being around my age. Although we must be ten years apart, we were almost the same generation. I was playing *Hunky Dory* in the living room, and Gerard mentioned to us that he met Bowie with Andy at the Factory, but Bowie didn't make that much of an impression on him. The album became enormous in my life due to the song "Queen Bitch," which sounded like the Velvet Underground; it was an obvious nod to that band. I missed out on the Velvets when the first album came out, even though Wallace had it; I was too young to get into it.

However, when glam hit, an appreciation of the Velvets ran through the make-up crowd. Listening to Bowie was acknowledging that we were in the same club of sorts. It wasn't a mainstream world at all. We were the select few—in our minds. Then Ziggy came and changed a lot of things. My dad, mom, and I went to see David Bowie's Ziggy Stardust and the Spiders from Mars show at the Santa Monica Civic in October 1972. I remember the month, day, and year because there was both an official and bootleg recording of that specific show. It was revolutionary. It was probably the last imaginative gesture in pop music's history. Well, allow me to take that back; I think hip-hop is much more out there than rock and pop, but it's a form of music I'm not close to. For a rock and pop head like me, Ziggy spoke the poetry I had been dying to hear. Every other thing before Ziggy was a tease, even a promise of some sort, but at that concert, we saw the future. The future consisted of a no-gender figure with bright red hair, with a band dressed in similar science fiction outfits, though none outshone their leader. It was simply a series of superb moments in my life, being in that audience, without a doubt one of the greatest rock 'n' roll shows I have ever been to. The radio broadcast still gives me goosebumps through sound waves, due to the memory of that blissful evening. I have seen Bowie in concert at least two more times, but the first kiss is always the best. It was probably the first rock show that was a theater experience for me. There was nothing left to chance. It was designed to have a pace, which hypnotized the audience. Then it was gone. The whole concert was an illusion.

Toni Basil started to work with David Bowie and choreographed his *Diamond Dogs* (1974) show, so we got tickets to see the concert. We sat next to Steve Allen and his wife, Jayne Meadows. They were (and continue to be in my mind) the ultimate mainstream showbiz couple, even despite Allen's weird dip into the world of Jack Kerouac, with the album they did together in the late 1950s. The juxtaposition of seeing Bowie with Steve and Jayne was weird. The show was fantastic, and at the time it was shocking because Bowie had become this 1940s zoot suit character with futurist flourishes, and totally left the Ziggy identity behind. Around that time, Wallace dragged me to a show at the Troubadour, to see a new artist he had heard about: Jobriath. Jobriath would have been a sensation if he came out in 1972, but by this time, he was more of a question mark, rather than taken seriously on a musical level. There was an enormous hype behind him at the time that most people found distasteful. But my dad was intrigued by Jobriath. Jobriath had released two solo albums through Elektra, and this was his first proper appearance on the West Coast. Opening was Zolar X, a local band that came from some other planet (according to them) and they all looked like Mr. Spock's younger brothers or perhaps his nephews. Zolar X was classic glam and, like Jobriath, had a sales date attached to the image and music. Still, they were a lot of fun. We knew their manager, Charlie, who was an old friend of the family. Jobriath was very campy and did costume changes behind a portable dressing area on the very stage he was performing on. The show was great. I totally forgot about him, till many years later, when Morrissey brought him back to the world's attention.

In late '74, Wallace took me to see the New York Dolls with Iggy Pop at the Palladium. That was an interesting show called "The Death of Glitter." Punk was starting to bubble up slowly that year. "The Death of Glitter" was a sad show because I couldn't see any future, only the past—not a distant past, but a recent one dying young. The Dolls, especially, seemed to be doomed. Iggy was an insect or a fascinating reptile. I find it amusing that he was a Jim Morrison fan, because the truth is he was way beyond the Lizard King. For one, Iggy was (and is) a better writer, perhaps even a genius. Certainly Morrison never wrote anything as brilliant as "No Fun."

Another great evening was when the whole family went to the Santa Monica Civic to see Roxy Music. Roxy Music hadn't done a tour in the United States since their first album with Eno. Afterward, we went to Stanley and Elyse Grinstein's house for a party for Jasper Johns. It was great seeing Bryan Ferry, the mastermind behind Roxy Music, at the party. I couldn't keep my eyes off him. What I liked about him was his discomfort at being at a party. He was with a woman who looked like one of the models from the Roxy Music album covers, but he was totally not comfortable in a party setting. He seemed jittery. This surprised me because the image I have of him is as someone totally at one with any party—especially a party for Jasper Johns.

It amazed me how close the visual art world was to the music world. Roxy Music had a strong fan base among artists, including Wallace. He loved their second album, *For Your Pleasure* (1973): "The Bogus Man," the extended opening cut on side two, was a song he listened to over and over again, often with the headphones glued on to his ears. Not every musician was tied to the visual arts, but the ones who were I found fascinating. Musicians seemed to be drawn to his artwork, due, I think, to his images of the transistor radio. My father also used pictures of the Rolling Stones, the Beatles, Phil Spector, James Brown, and other musicians in his art. In that sense, there is a bridge in the artwork between music and the visual image.

WALLACE BERMAN /

Mermaid Tavern Poster

Mermaid Tavern / chapter 44

It was in Topanga that my father developed his famous recluse identity, which was, in reality, a projection put on him by people who didn't know better. He was a very social person in Topanga. I don't think my parents turned down one picnic, beer party, Topanga fair, Topanga concert, or benefit for drug dealers who got busted or musicians who couldn't pay their rent or lost their instruments. He also frequented the unique and beautiful Mermaid Tavern.

Though on the surface Wallace was subdued, he was, if truth be told, very much a part of the world, and he went out of his way to promote people he liked or art he admired. He once presented the performance artist Harry Kipper, who had been a member of the Kipper Kids, but at the time was going solo. My dad arranged for Harry to do a performance at the Mermaid Tavern, and also designed a flyer to announce the show. He put the flyer up in Topanga everywhere he could in the middle of the night. He was very much a DIY type of character. The punk movement would have been entirely suitable for Wallace's sense of presentation and art. Wallace also frequently visited art dealers in the hopes they would be interested in an artist he championed. In many ways, he resembled Marcel Duchamp, with his interest in promoting artists he liked. Artie Richard, Russ Tamblyn, and others had superb talents as visual artists, and my dad very much worked on their behalf, as an agent of sorts. He had no interest in their finances or obtaining money for himself; he just wanted to get the word out about various friends who were artists. He attempted to look out for his fellow artists as much as possible.

Wallace also produced and promoted a concert by Christopher Tree, a composer/performer who played with giant gongs. The music was very ambient and beautiful. Wallace was a fan, and he arranged for Christopher to do his "Spontaneous Sound" show at the Topanga Community Center, which was a theater not far from our home. Wallace championed the most avant-garde artists in what was a very conservative community, in terms of popular hippie tastes, anyway. Wallace was one of the ones who were out there and not accepted by the masses or even by the brain-dead hippies of the Canyon. I always got the feeling that most of the citizens of Topanga were into the status quo of that time and place. Wallace was always interested in the new and had a great curiosity about what was out there at the time. For him to put on a show, either at the Mermaid Tavern or the community house, was a cool thing to do.

The Mermaid Tavern was for a sophisticated class of Topanga life. The actual structure had been a gay club in the early '60s, a whorehouse and gambling club run by Mickey Cohen in the '40s, and way before that a country club where, rumor has it, Teddy Roosevelt used to hang out. Mickey Nadel and his wife Ann, who came from the classical music world, moved into the lodge in the '70s and restored the building to its natural glory. Mickey was a classical bassist, and at one time I believe the head of the Musicians Union in Los Angeles, as well as being the concertmaster for the L.A. Philharmonic. By night, he and his wife organized amazing concerts. Their concept was for the Mermaid Tavern to become a cultivated classical music nightclub, and it was a unique experience. Where else could you go to see and hear string quartets playing Beethoven, while having dinner and wine served at your table? Even the *Los Angeles Times* covered their concerts. Classical musicians could drop in and play as if they were blues musicians dropping in at a nightclub. Not only that, but they could also perform music not typically heard in an established concert hall. It was very casual, but the playing standards were quite high. The programming was always unique, and without a doubt, it was the best place in the Los Angeles area to watch or listen to music. The string quartets mostly played music from the Baroque era, but they sometimes did 20th-century pieces like Stravinsky's *L'Histoire du soldat (The Soldier's Tale)* (1918).

Mickey eventually broadened the programming by having The Mystic Knights of the Oingo Boingo play at the Tavern. I saw them and fell in love with the two girls in the band. It was still led by future film composer Danny Elfman, but at the time Elfman and others were entirely focused on early New Orleans jazz, and Bertolt Brecht and Edith Piaf songs, and they were very theatrical. They were highbrow artists with lowbrow humor, one of the greatest live acts I have ever seen. There was something very Felliniesque in their presentation, and the fact that every member of the band could play numerous instruments was impressive. Beyond their musical talents, they had a remarkable vision. In many ways, it was sad when they turned into the New Wave band Oingo Boingo, because anyone who knew their past didn't see it in their new framework. Although it shared the same name, the band wasn't the same anymore. They were very successful, but equally annoying as well. But when they were the Mystic Knights . . . well, they were fantastic.

Many years later I found myself at a large dinner party with one of the Oingo Boingo girls—Marie-Pascale Elfman—and it was terrible. I was drunk and started a conversation with her. We were sitting at a huge banquet table, and as I was talking with her, I hit my glasses off my face, and they landed right in the middle of someone's plate. I think I blacked out, not due to drunkenness, but out of sheer embarrassment. To this day, I shudder and hope that Ms. Elfman has either forgotten that moment or kindly re-members that I was a fan of the original band and that her work will always bring a sense of warmth and wonder to me. It is more likely she will remember that I was a total drunk idiot. Neverthe-less, she was great in their show, and I made a point to see them as much as possible. One of the beautiful things about Marie-Pascale was that she brought a sense of the outer world to my life in To-panga. There were no French girls in my elementary, junior high, or high school. She represented the world that to me was sensual, but I never spoke to her at the time. She was an adult and married to the head knight in the band, and I was still a teenager. Thinking back, it must have been an absolute horror to have me as a fan. Oh well. . . .

Topanga / *chapter 45*

Before I had a car or learned how to drive, I had to settle for being stranded in Topanga. Wallace was the only one who knew how to drive. I'm not sure why my mom didn't drive at the time but, nevertheless, we didn't leave the house unless Wallace got behind the wheel and took us somewhere. He didn't like to waste energy or money, so if we did go out it would have to be to three or four places on the one trip, which usually meant going to the market, the lumberyard, and Topanga Plaza in Woodland Hills. I had to wait patiently to go to the Valley to my local record store, Warehouse Records, which was on Topanga Canyon Blvd, just before Ventura Blvd. I bought a lot of the original Bowie vinyl there, as well as some 8-track tapes. It was a great little store, and well stocked for such a neighborhood business.

Looking back, I don't fully understand why my mom didn't drive or why my dad didn't push her to. It would have given her more independence, and I suspect that's the reason why he didn't. Wallace, on the surface, wasn't a mean man at all, but I think not giving her access to an automobile in the middle of nowhere was a stupid plan. Suppose there were an emergency of some sort, and he were somewhere else? Believe me there are numerous emergencies living in a canyon, earthquakes, for example, but more frequently floods and the occasional fire. Without a car, you are stuck in the canyon. There's no bus system there. I don't think Wallace ever thought about it. Things like that never entered into his world. One can nitpick looking at the past, but the truth is a parent is a human being, with all the faults and trials one goes through as a member of the human race. I say this without regret or blame.

We would go to see films near the Topanga Plaza. Both of my parents were acutely aware of the cinema world, both underground and mainstream films. They were never huge fans of Hollywood movies, but Wallace was quite fond of the first *Dirty Harry* (1971) film. As I mentioned, he took me to see all the James Bond movies, usually on the day of release. He also liked *Pink Flamingos* (1972). We went to the West Coast premiere for *Pink Flamingos* with Russ Tamblyn at the Nuart Movie Theater in West Los Angeles. Russ was amazed to see George Maharis, who was the star of the TV series *Route 66* (1960–64), in the lobby. Maharis told him that he was responsible for bringing the freaks out for the opening. For whatever reason, Russ was shocked to hear that George was connected to the world of *Pink Flamingos*. In other words, he didn't have the slightest idea that George was gay. In Russ's eyes, George was this straight TV actor, who had a large female following at the peak of his TV series. Around the time of the screening at the Nuart Theater, Maharis was the first nude centerfold model for *Playgirl* magazine. About a week after the *Pink Flamingos* showing, Wallace purchased the magazine and carefully cut out the Maharis fold-out, signed it to say, "Thanks, Russ, for the wonderful night. Love, George," and had it framed. Wallace somehow broke into Russ and Liz's house and replaced one of the artworks on the living room wall with the framed photo of George. I believe it took Russ about a week to discover the Maharis photo in his house.

Living in Topanga was a strange time for me. I think just becoming a teenager alone makes things awkward, but being surrounded by the rural life made it even more challenging. I didn't like the isolation of being right in the middle of the canyon. It took 40 minutes to reach the ocean, and getting to the Valley took 20 or so. Going to the local market was a 10-minute drive. I can close my eyes and imagine myself walking up Artique Road from Topanga Canyon Boulevard, and I just remember the dust and heat of that place. There was a dog that shouldn't have been loose, but was, and it seemed always to be waiting for me to pass its owner's house. It never bit me but would get close to me and bark like crazy. One morning on my way to the school bus stop, down the hill, I tiptoed past the house in question. I thought, "Wow, I made it." But then I heard paw steps behind me and, looking back, I saw the dog silently following me. Once we made eye contact, it barked like crazy. I hated that dog with great passion.

In the sad but charming Topanga Canyon shopping center, there were plans to open both a bookstore and a record store, but potheads or pot dealers must have managed them because they never fully opened. They began with maybe a handful of records and books. It was like each place only had credit with the wholesaler for five items, and with those five items, the owners opened up the stores. I was just so bored in Topanga I would go to these two stores and hang out among the five items each. I remember buying Abbie Hoffman's *Steal This Book* (1971) and the clerk didn't bother with the sales tax. The store, I believe, went out of business that very day. At the record store, I would see the same album covers over and over again. For some reason, all I can remember are the Jo Jo Gunne albums; Jo Jo Gunne was a "Topanga band." But most of the time the store was closed. Through the shop window, I could see the fixtures and probably a rock poster or two. More than likely one of the two posters was for the new Jo Jo Gunne album. I think the owner or whoever totally ignored the posted hours on the door and couldn't care less if the store opened or not. Clearly, this was the first conceptual record store, which had no records and never actually opened for business. I think I did buy one album there, and most likely it was a Jo Jo Gunne album.

There was this beautiful woman who ran a used clothing store in the shopping center next door to that record store, and I think she went out with the blonde member of Jo Jo Gunne. In my innocent way, I was in love with her, but I didn't know her name or much of anything else about her. I remember buying or having my parents buy a patchwork quilt jacket from her store. That type of clothing doesn't appeal to me at all. I'm sure the main reason I wanted it was the fact that it came from her store. I was totally infatuated with her. My approach was to look like I was shopping, and hope that she would ask if I was looking for anything special, but she never asked or acknowledged me.

Topanga reminds me of *The Rifleman*, which was a favorite childhood TV show of mine. Chuck Connors played a widowed farmer who lived some distance from the neighboring town. He lived with his son, who worked on the farm with him. I could never tell what kind of farm it was; nothing huge, just a small family farm, probably with six chickens who laid eggs and maybe that was it. But they spent lots of time in the harsh daylight rebuilding the farm or getting the well to work, or anything that made Chuck Connors sweat and his shirt stick to his torso. The poor son, played by Johnny Crawford, had to wait till dad was ready to go to a store. I felt the same way. I suspected that, like my father, the Rifleman only liked to go to town when there were a lot of stops involved.

It wasn't till the mid-1970s that a series of record stores opened in the Valley. That was the major saving grace for the Valley at the time, its superb record stores. In the punk era, there was Moby Disc, which at heart was a prog-rock sort of store, but it was open to the punk rock scene, selling a lot of punk imports from the UK and other faraway places. The twist was that Moby Disc was owned, I think, by a born-again Christian, who didn't allow certain records in his store, though I can't remember if he ever actually banned a record or not. Still, it was a superb shop with an excellent staff.

My favorite record store of them all was Bomp! Records. Greg Shaw, the owner of the store as well as editor of its zine and head of its record label, was a man of great taste. I purchased countless great 7" singles at that store. It was small, but everything in it was naturally cool: not only the local bands but also the music coming out of London and New York City. Bomp was the one place to go to locate the hard-to-find punk recordings from New York's independent labels. It also had all the Stiff Records released from London as well. Especially in my teenage youth, it felt very sophisticated to go there. Moby Disc served the music nerd, but Bomp had a particular taste, and it didn't carry everything—just the essential music coming out of the punk scene. Bomp focused on the regions that were important at the time: San Francisco, Los Angeles, New York City, and London. I still remember the records I bought there, like Richard Hell's Oak Records single and the 7" EP by The Sneakers. Other than the record stores, there was no place to go in the Valley.

Driving / *chapter 46*

With the financial assistance of my father and mother—i.e., they paid for it fully—I bought my first car, which was a white Datsun. The nerve-wracking process of getting a car was something. The car salesman was untrustworthy. I remember one time a clerk hid my dad's car keys, so he couldn't leave the used car lot without purchasing a car. The hustle was non-stop. I think Wallace enjoyed it, but it made me nervous. Having a car, or even wanting a car, was never a huge passion for me. In fact, I don't remember ever asking to have a car or to learn how to drive. At Taft, there was Driver's Ed, which was fun because you went into this trailer where they had a driving game set-up with a gigantic screen. There was a steering wheel, with gas and brake pedals. I recall that my initial fear was getting the pedals mixed up. When you started the game, you moved the steering wheel and the filmstrip would move. If you hit something on the road or the side of the street, it made a loud beep. Also, the class screened a 16mm film of graphic traffic accidents, which made me even more conscious of what side the brake pedal was on. In a fun way, the class reminded me of the scene in *A Clockwork Orange* where Alex is forced to watch horrible things on the screen.

I think it was more my parents' desire that I have my own car, rather than dealing with me begging for a ride out of the canyon. I went to a professional driving school, and I remember the sessions fondly. I liked the instructor, and he pretty much taught me everything in a typical time frame. I was used to failing when someone tried to show me something, so the fact that an instructor took me driving and successfully taught me how to brake, park, reverse, turn the steering wheel, and go forward—well, that's remarkable in my world. Mostly we took the car from Topanga and headed towards the Valley, and he made sure I was aware of the neighborhood, to make me feel comfortable. I remember feeling seasick driving the canyon highway, because of the broad and consistent curves. Rarely was the road straight ahead; there was always an invisible bend or a sharp turn, and who knew what was around it? To this day, I have a fear of encountering an object around the corner and not being able to avoid it. Topanga was full of drunk drivers, so it wasn't unusual to see or hear a car accident. From where we lived on Artique Road, we could usually hear a siren or two per day.

My instructor spent lots of time with me in parking lots as well as driving in traffic and practicing parking. I enjoyed the process. I needed a car, not only because I was a teenager, but also because I lived in the fucking middle of nowhere. Didn't the great Neil Young have an album that was recorded in Topanga called *Everybody Knows This Is Nowhere* (1969)? Believe me, contrary to popular historical insight, Topanga was nowhere.

As soon as I learned how to drive, I went to a lot of concerts by myself at the Santa Monica Civic. I saw the Kinks (numerous times), Procol Harum, the Incredible String Band, Neil Young with Crazy Horse, Emerson, Lake & Palmer (I know! I was a teenager), and others I can't remember now. I liked going to shows by myself, because I felt a sense of purpose between the artist and myself, with no date or anyone else to get in the way. The shows I went to with girlfriends were always a drag for some reason or another. It wasn't because of the date, but I never liked being pulled away by another person. Music to me is an intense relationship, and I don't need other people besides the artist to be involved. It's great to be in a crowd, but to have someone attached to me was a little bit annoying, except for my dad, who was always fun to go to shows with. He had incredible taste, and he knew which shows would be great or, at the very least, engrossing.

For the longest time, the one 8-track tape I had and played on a regular basis in my car was *David Live* (1974). "Cracked Actor" made a very genteel soundtrack while driving to the Valley. I remember driving back and forth, taking my lovely classmates wherever they wanted to go. I was the designated driver for the beauties. One thing is for sure: girls like guys that have cars. A must. But I think the 8-track had a lot to do with it, as well. *David Live* on full volume while driving the winding Topanga Canyon Blvd with a series of cute girls on my right as well as in the backseat—well, it's an aesthetic high, if nothing else. And my collection of Sparks recordings on 8-track was like a dream of sorts. *Halfnelson* (1971)—better known as *Sparks* (1972)—and *A Woofer in Tweeter's Clothing* (1973), the first two albums, were no less amazing than their acknowledged classic *Kimono My House* (1974). Their viewpoint and sound were so off-kilter and just plain odd that you had to either hate them or love them. They took no prisoners. For me, it was love, and I clearly identified with songs like "Girl From Germany" and "Batteries Not Included." Their songs were like little Technicolor movies for my head. Driving in my white Datsun with a girl or two to the sound of Sparks was my version of heaven.

I would drive four or five girls around town. Usually, I would have to deal with their parents, and sit with them a bit and be charming while waiting for the girl or girls to come down from their bedroom in very proper clothing. Then, once in my car, they would change into clothing more suggestive and sexy, and I would drive them to the arms of their boyfriends, who were usually waiting at places like Rodney's. So yes, I was a patsy. Not one of those girls was my girlfriend, and nothing sexual happened between us. I was the chauffeur, and I had to pay for the gas as well. The "no ass, no cash, no gas" rule didn't hold within my world at the time.

Sex / *chapter 47*

I never got the sex education talk from my dad. I had to learn sex from girls much more experienced than I. My first actual sexual experience with a girl, I think, was at the very least at the age of 16. Sex represents a dream world of sorts, so to this day, I have a hard time pinpointing when it happened. But I can always remember the place. Locations have always had a sense of eros for me. The darkness of a movie theater was another spot to explore my sexuality with a girl. Not a porn theater, mind you, but a screening of Walt Disney's *Fantasia* (1940) was an erotic highpoint for me. If you go to the right showing, usually the last of the day, on a weekday, you have a sparse crowd. So it's not too difficult to find seats towards the back, while most are in the middle or even closer to the screen. I was never caught, because people either knew what we were doing and pretended not to notice or, more likely, were totally into the images and sounds projected on the big screen.

I was fortunate enough not to have a serious girlfriend, but I knew a few girls who liked having sex with me, or some form of practice, and being able to express that desire without the boundaries of having an actual relationship. At this time in my life, I was very fortunate to attract girls, due not to my looks, but I think to my communication skills. I'm naturally polite, and I don't believe there's one person who hates me. Not due to what I do, but to how I express what I do. At this time in my life, I wanted to be in love, but the fact was, I liked the thought of love more than love itself. In an odd way, it was like projecting my image on the screen and sharing that projected light with a girl. Some were pure fantasy. Some became true. If you wish hard enough, things do happen in your favor.

Once I was with a girl, I would explore her out of desire, but with lots of curiosity as well. I felt like I was floating above, in a sense, like a voyeur, when in fact, I'm watching myself in an imaginary state of mind. There was something theatrical about it all. In many ways, I find the sexual act to be a theater piece, as well as a release or a way of showing love for someone. The ability to express love is easy for me, but there is something hyper-real with making love. It's animalistic as well as artificial. I like the tension between the performance of the sexual act and real feelings. Once you get bitten by the possibilities of love and all its desirable effects, you can be addicted to it for life. There's always sexual tension in the air, and it can either frustrate or simply amuse. I tend to be amused by it.

At our house in Topanga, my father had the garage, which was his studio, rebuilt into a single apartment for me. I had to go through three sets of stairs to the bathroom and everything else, but I had private quarters in which to dwell on my hobby of trying to seduce the local girls. Sometimes I was successful. Nevertheless, the task of going on the road of heightened awareness is sometimes as enthralling as the end results, if you know what I mean.

In my room, I had a proper work table built into the wall that was perfect for lining up empty wine bottles and for a girl to sit on while I had sex with her standing up. My height and the height of the table were perfectly matched. There was also thick, chocolate brown carpeting on the floor that was perfect for erotic fun. To be honest, there was no bad spot in the entire room for having sex. If you put side two of Fripp and Eno's *Evening Star* (1975) on the turntable and had mood lighting, good times with a girl would be had. Side two of the album is my recommendation because the music goes up in pitch and I find it ideal for intercourse. Eno and Fripp were known as ladies' men, so I'm sure they planned this album as the ultimate sex record. Some called this ambient music, but I knew what that really meant. So generally, high school sex, if memory serves correctly, was great. There is something not right about it, and that allowed a certain sense of adventure to play into the practice of love.

The best part was planning the get-together. When my parents went out to a party or opening, I would stay home. It usually took a couple of days for me to arrange for the girl to come over the house. The invitation was very clear in its intention. I never spoke of the act; it was just common knowledge. Being with her was great, but what I liked most was looking forward to being with her. Thinking about it was often more satisfying than the actual sex. I would go over what I thought would happen in my head over and over again. In a way, it was like writing. The experience of seeing an empty page, and filling it with words, is seductive in itself. Therefore, I've always felt the act of writing to be quite erotic, as I press my pen onto paper.

The interesting thing to me about sex is that it's a zone or a landscape where one can play. We live in a world that's full of rules and proper procedures to do things just to survive. As a teenager, I liked disappearing into my thoughts and come up with something sensual and pleasing to my taste. The shock and pleasure in going into such a world remain, to this day, a constant presence in my life. I often felt jealous when a girl I liked was meeting an older man, usually at Rodney's or some other club. An intense feeling of jealousy would overtake me, and I couldn't even think straight. I actually enjoyed the sting of disappointment and the cruelty of the girl's attitude towards me. I would be hurt but, the truth is, I desired a sense of pain. It became very much Eros in action for me. I was consistently turned on by every betrayal and disappointment. That eventually stopped in my twenties, but I still look back on those days with wonder, remembering the sense of desire mixed in with that pain.

I knew a girl who was my favorite of all the girls. She was the first one to whom I felt I could say, "I love you." The truth is, I didn't love her but, nevertheless, I was genuinely fascinated with her. I never met her real dad, but her stepdad was a film and TV producer and, at the time, a quite successful one. I rarely talked to him, because, as a teenager suitor, I was a bit afraid of him. On the other hand, I liked the girl's mother, who was always very kind to me. This girl also had a sister who was maybe two years younger. As I suffered a degree of lovesickness towards the girl, I was, at the same time, attracted sexually to the sister. She was beautiful and had a lively personality. The girl that I "loved" wasn't nearly as much fun as her sister. The question is, why did I have such a strong pull for the girl, even though I had a sexual interest in the sister? On the other hand, the girl was beautiful as well. She had freckles, lips that naturally pouted, and brown hair that sometimes looked reddish in the sunlight. Her clothing (always important to me) was stylish, and she had a beautiful slim body.

We met for the first time in the quad area of the Taft High School campus. She was one of the girls that hung out with the guys with glam rock albums under their arms. I think at the time I was in 11th grade, and she may have been in the 10th. I was pretty much under her spell from the very first moment. Also, the fact that she approached me was something for me. At the time, I was still a very shy teenager. I would spend the following days just waiting for the recess or lunchtime so that I could hang out with her. Also, over time, I felt very comfortable being in her presence. By the next semester, she had moved on to a private Catholic school nearby Taft. This is when I started to feel the pain of rejection and loss. The eros in the air in the parking lot of the Catholic school was always turned up quite high, due to the girls' uniforms, which were a pleated skirt, white blouse, and usually brown or white knee socks. The tension in the parking lot was due to all the boys waiting for the girls to get out of school. Often older men were there as well. Another major hangout was Sambo's on Ventura Boulevard. We would drink endless cups of coffee and eat something sweet or else a plate of French fries. We never had much money, so there was a lot of sharing of food among us. We had countless cups of coffee; that was only 10¢ a cup. Thinking of it now, it's hard to imagine why Sambo's would let us hang out for hours on a Saturday night, yet that was very much part of the culture those days.

One thing that disturbed me was both sisters' love for the band Queen. I remember going to their bedroom to listen to their Queen albums, and even then, I knew something was rotten. To be honest with myself, I'm a snob. To this day, I have trouble being civil with people who have horrendous taste in pop music. I understood the appeal of Queen, yet I felt they were a major mistake, and I couldn't fully figure out why these two beautiful girls could find anything worthwhile in this band. That was the first disappointment. Other bands I had trouble with, and who were very popular with my girlfriends, were Emerson, Lake & Palmer (I did see them, but caught on quickly that they were shit), Yes, Todd Rundgren (who in fact lived with one of my classmates), and Led Zeppelin. We all met on the quad steps and brought our record albums to show each other. It was a bit pointless, because we had no turntable on campus to play them on, yet there was a great need to show off the album covers, especially imports from the UK.

The guys in my social group were Mark, Steve, Dana, and Greg. Greg, I think, was just visiting the school. I think he was a year ahead of us and he played the flute. I never really knew him, and in actuality don't remember having a direct one-on-one conversation with him. But that was not unusual; we just sat on the quad stairs with our shag haircuts. I mostly talked to the girls there, only rarely with the guys. Sometimes Mark and I had in-depth chats about the merits of Bowie versus Marc Bolan of T-Rex. Although we had different opinions about our fave albums, I greatly admired Mark for his musical knowledge and intelligence. I trusted his taste. All of this reminds me of Fassbinder's film *Katzelmacher* (1969); we just sat on the steps and commented on albums and people walking by us. The one thing we had in common was our love of the British music scene, but again, I had my doubts about their music taste in that scene. We embraced glam rock, but their taste in glam was questionable to me. In a word: Queen. How could anyone take that band seriously? The girl I wanted had all the Queen albums, and I clearly see myself sitting in her bedroom listening to *Sheer Heart Attack* (1974). The fact that I stayed and listened to the whole album shows you how in love or how horny I was. There can be no other excuse.

There was a figure who visited the campus from time to time and had the inside information on the artists. His name was Rodney Bingenheimer. To this day, I don't think I ever met him, but I have been in the same room or airspace as him. And for sure I shared the quad steps with him. If you found yourself in a room full of teenage beauties, more than likely Rodney was in the center. If you were lost and wanted to be in a world of young beauties, all you had to do was find Rodney, and you would be in a paradise. Someone in his circle probably figured out that this could be a business, and therefore invented a nightclub called Rodney Bingenheimer's English Disco. Rodney's was a little club located at 7561 Sunset Boulevard. The club was full of beautiful girls my age who seemed to attract a much older male clientele, so there were three categories of customer: the teenage girl, the much older man, and the ageless rock star—and, of course, me, the driver for many high school beauties. So I guess that makes four categories. There must have been more people in my group at the club as well. I can't count how many times I was abandoned there by my "date" for a much older gentleman. The things that kept me entertained in the club were the warm beer (I believe that this was the only alcohol served there) and watching the image of myself in the floor-to-ceiling mirrors on the dance floor. I watched myself watching the girls watching whoever came into the club.

I missed all the legendary shows at Rodney's: famous guests like Led Zeppelin and, rumor has it, Elvis Presley turned up at one point. The Los Angeles glam scene was basically about lovely youth. There was the tinge of darkness cast by the older men attached to the social group. On the other hand, the music played at Rodney's suited my taste to a T: lots of Bowie, T-Rex, Slade, Sweet, Gary Glitter, Suzi Quatro, and other glam-era greats. There was something so fake about it all that it held a huge attraction for me. I didn't like serious music at the time, and like Noel Coward, I found something deep in the cheap aspects of popular music. Rodney's was a very small place with a tiny dance floor that had mirrors to expand the space and for the girls to look at themselves while they were dancing. I never spent so much time with such a narcissistic bunch of teens. The guys would check themselves out, but it was nothing like my girlfriends. In fact, there was an erotic pull for them watching themselves. I don't think they needed anything except the music, the mirrors, and maybe a drink or two.

Rodney's, looking back at it now, was a very strange place. On one level, it was a club specializing in music that wasn't accepted by the mainstream of the time. It was one of the few places you could go for a taste of that particular lifestyle known as glam. But it was also a perfect spot to pick up groupies, who were mostly underage girls. There was a certain innocence being played out in the club, despite the older men from the music world who wanted to taste the young beauties in love with that world and going wild for various reasons. I think money was coming into the teenager world more easily than before, and families were having problems, which made it easier for teens to get out of the poison home and enter the gates of hell. But hell looked pretty good from my corner.

I once had a horrible series of moments with the girl. I took her and her sister to the club one time, and the worst thing that could happen, happened. I didn't know it at the time, but she had arranged to meet her boyfriend there, who I didn't know about whatsoever. I wasn't aware that he existed. He was considerably older than her, and I was shocked when I entered the club with her, and she went right up to him. It was evident they were an item. I was crushed. Without saying goodbye to me, she left the club with her gent. I ran out with the sister to see them getting into his car. I got the sister in the car, and we began to follow them. Eventually, it became a car chase. We ended up somewhere in Laurel Canyon, where he suddenly stopped. I got out of my car and demanded that she get into mine. She did after some long moments, and I took her and her sister, in total silence, back to their home.

I refused to talk to the both of them. It was the first time in my life I had an issue with a friend or associate in which I chose not to talk or communicate with them; I pretty much ignored them for several months, which is a lifetime for a teenager. Afterward, my feelings changed, and I let bygones be bygones. That night chasing her around killed any romantic feelings I had for her. I became entirely neutral, and without my passion for her, the relationship became unimportant to me. I realized that I had an ideal view of love, more literary or cinematic than real life. I'm not one of those guys who likes to hang out with his girlfriend and go to the mall. I crave solitude, and to surround myself with my thoughts and occasional misery. In many ways, I am so egotistical.

Sadly, few girls were into what I was into, concerning music, art, and culture, except for Patti Clementi, who had a thing for anything to do with gay NYC life and, in fact, knew actual gay people. I never had any gay friends myself as a teenager. Through

Patti, I lived that side of life with her as my guide. Her favorite artist, no surprise, was Andy Warhol, so she had a profound knowledge of him and his world. Since I'd been in a Warhol film, she must have been (ever so slightly) interested in yours truly. She was one of my best friends at Taft High School. What I liked about Patti was that she was nonjudgmental regarding how people led their lives. She was one of the few people at school who accepted the gay world for what it was, and was curious about the world outside the school gates. Unlike the others, who acquired their tastes through their peers at school, Patti obtained her knowledge through the arts, and she had a real appreciation for artists and their craft. Others, I feel were into the social scene and just wanted to get noticed, nothing deeper than that.

When I talked to Patti, I got the impression I was chatting with someone who genuinely appreciated outsiders, those who dared to go beyond their world to do something quite wonderful. I liked spending time with her more than with the girls I had romantic feelings for, who could be dull when they weren't nasty. It was many years later I realized I had a thing for girls who were not that interesting. Cute, yes, beautiful even, but they didn't have the passion that could make them into really fascinating characters. Like most young people, they didn't have a clue, and I can see that, in actuality, I was on the same lollipop ship. I enjoyed the voyage, but I, too, was floating between subject matters. Girlfriends I did have—I was lucky to be surrounded by such wise, wonderful women and girls. I didn't deserve their attention but I craved it, from the bad ones as well as the good ones. The pain I went through made me a better person.

Gary / chapter 48

I didn't have many male friends, but frankly, throughout my life, I never liked guys. I honestly didn't understand that gender. They mostly bored me, except for one exceptional male friend, Gary, who I got to know right after high school. We became friends due to our love for the same music. During school, I'd known him slightly, because he used to hang out with Holly Vincent, who later became known as a musician during the New Wave era with her band Holly and the Italians. At that time, she was a tomboy, but one who was (and is) a vision of elegant beauty. She was reminiscent of Audrey Hepburn, in that her attractiveness never got in the way of her personality. She was a mixture of shyness and boldness, which are a dynamic chemistry in a person. At the time, I thought Gary and her were a couple, but I never asked; I don't like to define other people's relationships. I had male friends, but only rarely did I hang out with them. With Gary, I pretty much lived in his many households or, at the very least, he was very polite for not kicking me out. Without a doubt, Gary is a genius. He is one of those people who can just pick up on something and master it, whatever it may be. I love the music he wrote in our early adult years, and I even attempted to write lyrics to his melodies. They're good—not the words, mind you, but if you take in the whole picture without separating the lyrics from the music, the songs are excellent.

Gary introduced me to incredible music throughout our friendship. Not everything was to my liking, but I knew the quality was superb. If Gary liked it, then it must be either important or of some value. If I didn't like a piece he played for me, I would question myself why. Sometimes it took years for me to appreciate a given piece of music Gary brought to my ears but eventually I always had that "ah ha" moment. During countless hours in front of his hi-fi, he introduced me to the music of Kevin Ayers, Robert Wyatt, Soft Machine, Gong, and others from the Canterbury music scene. Both of us were into Roxy Music, and I remember we went to the local record store, most likely Moby Disc, to purchase the British editions of various Roxy titles on the day they arrived at the shop. We would hang out in his bedroom and make daily phone calls to ask if so-and-so's album came out yet. If we read about a record in *Melody Maker* and noticed it was on the British charts, then we called twice a day. Our anxiety about missing the release date was quite high in those days. When the poor record store clerk answered the phone and said, "Yes, it's in stock now, " we would rush off together to pick up the album or albums. We then went back to his house to listen to it. Both of us enjoyed looking at the cover in depth, with my head over his shoulder or vice-versa. Or we passed the cover to each other like it was a coded message from another part of the world. We glanced at each other to see how we were responding to the new sounds. It was just an amazing time for me. It was the only time I have ever felt close to a male friend. Perhaps it wasn't him, just the music! But I suspect he had a lot to do with it, and when I play Roxy Music *Stranded* (1973) I tend to think of him.

Due to life and all its circumstances, Gary and I drifted apart, but I still think of him highly. As he got older, Gary got really into computers, which like everything else he mastered with great talent and skill, and therefore he became the best in that field. Gary never talked about the job, or what he was doing, or even who he worked for. The thing with him is he hated to work even more than I. Gary's technique of "work" is to work straight through every day for two or three weeks to finish off a job—so he doesn't have to return to it. I could never work in such a manner, but he can do something day and night. The best thing about friendship is learning from each other. Through Gary, I learned how to be social and also how to argue for an aesthetic or issue. We didn't disagree that much, but still we were both opinionated young guys.

The other odd thing is that people would confuse us for one another on a consistent basis. In my opinion, we don't even look alike, yet I've been approached by people thinking I was Gary, and he had people come to him, thinking he was I. As I mentioned, Phil Spector mistook us for the other, the result of which was very awkward, at the very least. Even people we knew would mistake us or get confused who is who. I'm not sure why this happened, but I suspect that we may have conveyed a particular "spirit" or identity that others just believed or wanted to believe. When you get down to it, friends are not that observant, which is a pretty scary commentary on people and human behavior.

Hairdressing / chapter 49

When I graduated from high school, with no particular merits or honors, I became an adult in size and age, but mentally I was still 15. Since I'd failed kindergarten, I was at least a year older than anyone in my class, which made me feel weird. Also, the draft was right around the corner, and when I turned 18, I had to register with the draft board. To my incredible relief, they stopped the draft. I don't think I could have taken Vietnam; if nothing else, humid weather would have destroyed me. And without a doubt, I would have been murdered either by the Viet Cong or, more likely, by my fellow American soldiers. So for about a year after graduating, I did nothing. I never had a job, and I was terrified to ask someone for work. It wasn't because I felt I was above the nine-to-five working life, but rather because I felt totally worthless, and I knew I would be terrible at anything that would force me to work. I would have felt guilty for my employer. I couldn't get the courage up to go up to a stranger or even someone I knew to ask for a job. To me, it was a sign of my weakness, and I dreaded the moment I would leave school and come upon a world of total rejection.

My father persuaded me that I should learn a trade, and in a moment of logical thinking, we agreed I should go to beauty school. The sole reason was that my Uncle Donald was a famous hairdresser, and it would make perfect sense that, when I graduated from beauty school, he would hire me as his assistant. Then eventually I would get my own chair at the Beverly Hills salon that he worked at. I suspect that my uncle thought this was impossible but he never let me or my dad in on his true feelings about the matter. I signed up and went to a beauty school that was situated on the bottom floor of the Topanga Plaza. I bought a white smock, a mannequin head, and combs, brushes, and hairclips from a beauty supply store. With the tools of the trade, I was prepared to be a beauty school student.

Beauty schools are strange. They feel more like businesses than schools, as they have a clientele that pays for cheap haircuts by the students. The students were trained in the back room and then were forwarded to the frontlines. I never made it to the frontlines, because I lacked talent in making pin curls and giving a proper shampoo. In other words, I was back in junior high woodshop, working on my sanding block for the entire semester. In the back of the school, where the customers couldn't see me, I practiced on my mannequin head over and over again. Occasionally, students could practice with fellow students. In fact, most of the students would volunteer for haircuts, facials, or shampoo jobs. But when I needed a volunteer, it seemed all the other students weren't around or, all of a sudden, were too busy to help me out.

As in kindergarten, I met a whole new series of students who came in after the ones that I was first introduced to. Those eventually went out front to work with customers. I stayed in the back, but I did give advice to the brand-new students, due to my time there. The art of shampooing was something I could never master for some reason. You have to hold the nape of the person's neck to wash out all of the soap. Whenever I did that, I got the person's back soaking wet. It happened with all the instructors there because the other students refused to allow me to practice on them. Eventually, after two or three months, all the teachers there called me aside and told me that they couldn't do anything more for me. In gentle terms, they said that some are made for the occupation, and some can be taught on the job, but it seemed that I couldn't be taught and for sure I wasn't made to be a hairdresser or even a shampoo boy. I very rarely cry, but I cried all the way home from the school. It was a mixture of shame and fear for the future, and just being overwhelmed with the feeling I was an out-and-out failure.

With my self-esteem down to zero, I just stayed at home and focused on writing poetry. I used the family typewriter and loved to spend time looking at the blank page and then sending out my poetry to as many magazines and publications as possible. I started from the top, of course: *The Paris Review*. That was the first of many rejection letters that came in the mail to me. It became a depressing trip from the inside of my garage apartment to the mailbox, about seven feet from the entrance, seven feet of absolute despair and shame. By this time, I had a very thick skin, and the rejection didn't make me angry or anxious. I enjoyed the act of writing, especially poetry. Being rejected fit my personality quite well. The good thing about my poetry—now lost to history—was that it wasn't about me or my failures. It was about language and the sense of time passing by. It was very much the work of someone who was 19 and struggling to get to the age of 20. At the time, I was very much influenced by the dada poets, specifically Tristan Tzara. I was fascinated by Tzara's method of composition by selecting words or phrases out of a hat filled with text cut out of a newspaper. I was aware of the fact that Burroughs had done the same, and others as well, but Tzara, I thought, was the best at it. I looked up to him as a sort of role model. It may have had to do with his appearance. I liked his dress sense and the way he wore his monocle.

My father told me to never be concerned with what I was writing about because somehow it would turn out OK on the page. This was not entirely accurate. But what he was really telling me is not to be afraid and to go with instinct. Wallace only gave me advice on two occasions. One was on the writing, and the second was a tad strange: he told me that, if I was in a car and I hit someone, and that person died from the injury that I caused, I should never feel any guilt about it. Guilt, in his opinion, was an entirely wasted emotion. That stayed with me because I realized over time that people use guilt as a weapon or, at the very least, as a hustle to make you change your opinion or stance on something. It's best to be faithful to your real nature and not submit to such an emotion.

Death / chapter 50

February 17, 1976, was a strange day. The next day was my father's 50th birthday. I remember he bought himself a tweed jacket with leather patches at the elbows. That was a weird choice for him. To get a jacket like that was like him in old-man drag; it was very much a middle-aged man's jacket. A new jacket like that probably cost a couple of hundred dollars, so it was an investment of sorts, though it also served my dad's sense of being a dandy. Wallace had very long hair at that time, which sometimes he tied up in a ponytail, or even pigtails, which I had always considered very feminine of him. With his hair like that and with his new tweed jacket with leather patches—well, it was eccentric to me and, believe me, I wasn't fazed by odd dress or behavior at this point in my life. It had always surrounded me. But the jacket didn't make sense to me at the time, though I could imagine turning 50 was a leap into another world for him. He had told numerous people, including my mom and me, that he wouldn't live past 50, but I think most of us thought it was him being James Dean-like, even a tad bit drama queen. But that whole day was not one of laughs, and I had a weird sense of time going by slowly. It was a very long day that day.

We visited his mother Anna in the afternoon. As I was daydreaming in the car on the way to my grandmother's house, I became conscious of a small graveyard. I thought to myself that

I'd never noticed that cemetery before; as I write now, I realize it didn't exist. We had the usual grandmother visit, where Wallace was in his world, there to be seen by the family. He also wanted to show off his new jacket to Anna, who I think offered to pay for half of it as a birthday present. I don't recall if Wallace accepted the gift from her, but most likely yes. In the late afternoon, my parents and I went out shopping to the dreaded Topanga Mall, where I bought Wallace for his birthday two 45 rpm singles: Paul Simon's "50 Ways to Leave Your Lover" (1975) and Dr. John's "Right Place, Wrong Time" (1973). He loved both songs, and that fit my budget perfectly. My dad waited for us while we shopped, and when we came back from the department store, we found him asleep on the bench in the waiting area of the mall. It was very unusual for my father to fall asleep in a public space like that. A couple of days before all this took place, Wallace bought my mom a book about how to take care of the household, stuff like what to do when you smell smoke, what to turn off, and so forth. Not an odd book by any means, but it seemed strange that he bought it for my mom out of the blue. It was like he knew he was going to leave, but didn't know why. It struck both of us as being peculiar.

There was a very popular late-night TV show called *Mary Hartman, Mary Hartman* (1976–77). My parents and I would watch it every night. The show was a parody of an afternoon soap opera, very much a pre-*Twin Peaks* (1990–91) look on life in Middle America. The writing on the show was super sharp, and the acting was faultless. For many people around us, as for us, it became a nightly addiction, and often we talked about it the next day around the breakfast table. That particular night I took a late bath around 10:00 p.m., and through the bathroom door my father said he'd be back shortly. He was very much a disciplinarian with respect to his schedule for work and fun. A little bit of TV in the evening, a quick glass of beer at the local, and then back

Tosh Berman, 1976

home for the show and some work in his studio before going to bed around two in the morning.

Mary Hartman, Mary Hartman was on, and my father didn't show up. We heard his truck pull up in front of the house. My mom and I were puzzled why he didn't come in, so I went outside. I saw his truck, but I didn't see my car. I thought, well, OK, he took my car. The thing is that he wouldn't exchange the truck for the car during the show; he would stay home and watch the show. As I went back in, I heard a siren.

A few hours later, I woke up in my garage apartment below the house, with red and blue lights hitting the wall and the floor-to-ceiling mirror, covering the entire room in a rhythmic fashion. There was a knock on my door, and I got up to put my pants on. I opened the door, and a police officer asked if I was Tosh Berman and if I was the son of Wallace Berman. I could see mom in the backseat of the squad car, and she wasn't saying anything—frozen in time. Once my identity was clear to the officers, they asked me to go with them. After I got in their car, they told me that my father had been in a car accident, and they were taking us to the hospital.

They had no detailed information at that point. It was the first time I had ever been in a cop car, and I was struck by their conversation in the front: they weren't really concerned about us in the back, but talking about their day, what they had for dinner, that sort of thing. Mom and I didn't say a word between us. Our thoughts were blank, wishing it was all some mistake, but mostly I think we felt cold fear.

When we arrived at the emergency room, we were told Wallace had died at the scene of the accident. He'd been revived and sent to the emergency room. They said it looked bad. They stated that amazingly enough, his body on the outside looked good, but his interior was messed up; perhaps every bone in his body had broken due to the impact of the crash, and he had head injuries as well. At the time, I remember thinking, "How is it possible that someone died, and yet they brought him back to life?" We were told that, if he lived, he would be in a vegetative state. My mother called Russ, as well as her parents, who also lived in Topanga, from a payphone in the waiting room. Dean was out of town doing a dinner theater show.

My grandparents arrived at the hospital. Anyone there who saw me would think I was under control, but I wasn't by any means. I excused myself to go to the bathroom. Sitting on the toilet and feeling very alone, I knew that once I left the bathroom, my whole life would be changed. There would be a new world, and that world would either be horrible or . . . maybe OK. I also realized that nothing in my life had ever been as bad as this moment. The worst was now, and I just had to accept whatever would happen. I could feel my body changing from what I was to what I am now. One moment I was Billy Batson, the boy, and then the next I become Captain Marvel—but a Captain Marvel with feeble knees. I was crying, but no tears came from my eyes. I felt an enormous pressure in my chest and my head. I started doing this shadow-conducting, as if I was leading an orchestra for a theater piece. For whatever reason, it calmed me down.

As I finally left the bathroom, I ran into a hospital employee. He asked me to follow him. As we all gathered in the waiting room, he told us that my father died. I have no memory of dialogue or tears at this particular point and time and, in that waiting room, I don't remember anything emotional. The only thing I remember was my grandparents drove us back to the house. At dawn, we reached the front door. My father died on his 50th birthday.

/ epilogue

My dad died, and I lived. My mom lived, and my uncle lived. As of this writing, we're all alive. This memoir stops on February 18, 1976. But my life as an adult (mentally and emotionally) started on February 19, and I had a lot to do.

Wallace wasn't responsible for the car accident. It seems he'd come back from the bar and taken my car—without permission; I was in the bath—because his truck was low on gas. A moving truck was in the middle of the street around a bend in the canyon road, and my dad hit the truck and was killed. The driver of the truck was drunk and stoned. The irony of the story is that the next person driving behind my dad was an actor named Randy Mantooth, who at the time was on a TV show called *Emergency* (1972–77). It was a hit show, and he was a kind of pin-up idol. He played a paramedic/fireman responding to emergencies. So, in a sense, his role came to real life. He held the driver there till the police showed up. I'm not sure how the police were contacted, or if neighbors heard something from their home and called, but if it hadn't been for Mantooth, the driver would've gotten away. And if my dad hadn't been driving the car in front of him, Mantooth probably would have hit the truck. In a way, my dad may have saved Mantooth's life.

Right after my father's death, there was a lot of trauma. The driver who killed my father, "Spike," was a local Topanga drug dealer. He had friends in both the low end and the high end of Canyon society. And I suspect in the courtroom as well. He was represented by Robert Shapiro, who later became famous as one of O.J. Simpson's lawyers, the so-called "Dream Team." Back then, Shapiro specialized in getting actors out of drunk driving charges. He easily got my father's killer off with a six-month jail sentence, and then for whatever reasons, Spike was let out of prison within three months. After the sentencing, the district attorney approached me in the hallway, furious, and told me I should arrange for something to happen to Spike. The Highway Patrol deputy or sheriff totally agreed. That seems unbelievable, but life at that time was odd.

For a while, I continued to live in the apartment Wallace had set up for me in the garage. By 1977, my mom had remarried, to a Canadian former hockey player who was working in the film industry. The marriage only lasted 10 years, maybe less. Meanwhile, that same year, I became an active punk rock club-goer. And I fell in love, with a struggling ballet dancer. We met when I was attending Pierce Junior College in Woodland Hills. I was in the school's cafeteria, and this exquisite woman approached me from behind and asked me about my shoes. (I was wearing green plastic T-strap sandals, then known as "jelly shoes," from a shop in Beverly Hills called Fiorucci.) To be addressed by such a stunning woman was highly unusual for me. As we talked, I learned she was a fan of Robert Wyatt, who at that time was an obscure music artist, known only in certain circles. I couldn't get her love of Wyatt out of my head. That first meeting was like a daydream, where you're fantasizing a series of perfect moments. Surely it couldn't be real?

It's funny how one can meet someone and know that person will be important to you. It wasn't even the sexual angle, but more the feeling of two souls meeting up and finding themselves a match. I felt like she was my gift for all the suffering of the previous year dealing with my father's death. In reality, I think I was shellshocked. I was so numb with pain that I couldn't even tell if what I was feeling was rational or not. Traumatized by the experience of Wallace's death, having had my world change so drastically due to it, I now thought I was heading toward the light, where I could bathe in the sunshine that was this beautiful girl.

When we met, she was living with her mother. When her mother asked her to move out, I, being the gentleman and also madly in love, asked her to move in with me. Not to a new apartment mind you, but into my garage bachelor pad, in the house where I lived with my mother and her new husband. I don't think I even asked them; we just piled her clothing and belongings into my car and I took her up to Topanga. This was a big difference between my life before my father's passing and after. After Wallace died, I found myself making fast decisions and jumping into the fire with both feet. Rarely do I lose sleep over an important decision. Before, with my parents, I would never do anything in a hasty manner. But not only was I comfortable in having my girlfriend living with us, but I was also high from making such an important decision. For her, I don't think she had much choice.

We lived in the family garage for a while until we decided we needed more space. I'd also finally found a job. I'd applied to a record store chain called Licorice Pizza on Sherman Way in Reseda and was hired. I couldn't have been happier, with a girlfriend and a secure, if a low-paying job, much of which consisted of playing records for strippers trying to locate music for their act. I made friends with people who worked in the store and over time got myself transferred to Licorice Pizza in West Los Angeles, where my girlfriend and I found a studio apartment. As at the Reseda store, I made lasting friends at the West L.A. one. I still keep up with friends from that store, but never do we talk about "the good old days." I do remember REM becoming very important in those years, and my revenge against my co-workers for playing that band was playing ABBA really loud during shop hours. They eventually forgave me.

My girlfriend had a habit of leaving me for various musicians, including a musician from Devo whom I was friends with, though I don't recall talking with him after this. I showed up at a show at the Whisky a Go Go and it was obvious they were a couple, not in the sense of living together, but clearly a loving, going-out couple. It was like watching another couple, but the girl was my girlfriend, who I lived with. She came back to me, but a few years later ran off on a European tour with the bass player for The Tubes. Eventually, she came back to me again. At this point in my life, I started having panic attacks where I was convinced I was going to die. I wasn't going to die, but I felt like I was dying. I would have trouble breathing or feel my heart rate double. I thought my body would explode. I believe the problem was the combination of having a girlfriend that wasn't that comfortable being my girlfriend and still dealing with Wallace's passing.

My girlfriend's friend, by chance, was dating a friend of mine, so we often went out on double dates. And their relationship was up and down, like our relationship. I was having dinner with my girlfriend and her friend at her friend's apartment, and for some reason, I refused to leave. I couldn't go back home to a single room with two people in it. At the very least, her friend's apartment was a one-bedroom apartment in the middle of Westwood. I stayed a whole week. Looking back I see this as a nervous breakdown. I wasn't depressed. I wasn't feeling anything. I have to say my hostess was superb for allowing me to stay. And my girlfriend must have figured that I was going through something, because she never discussed or seemed put off by my refusal to leave that apartment. After a week, I decided, "OK, it's time to go back home." To this day, I don't know why I acted in such a manner.

My girlfriend and I finally split up one night when I came home from work and the door was locked. She was there with her lover, who was older, a "producer," though as far as I know he never actually made a film. I remember walking to Canters in the pouring rain, calling her up and telling her to let me in. I came back; she let me in, and he was there lying in our bed. I undressed in front of both of them and went directly to bed. This really upset him. After that, she and I split up for good. We were together for five years. The up parts were incredible, but the downs were so low, they make the up parts unimportant looking back.

I left Licorice Pizza to travel in Europe. My friend Kimley, who worked there and remains one of my best friends, and I decided we should go on a grand European tour. Financially it made no sense, but then again nothing in that world ever did, so we got passports and left. We spent four months crisscrossing Europe, pretending we were in a Midge Ure-era Ultravox video. At the time, Kraftwerk was on top, and Bowie's "Absolute Beginners" (1986) was playing everywhere from Rome to London. It was my first adventure without my parents. I was 32 at the time.

When I got back, I started to work at Book Soup, an independent bookstore on Sunset Boulevard. While working there, I ran a 16mm film club at Beyond Baroque Literary Arts Center in Venice. I showed only films that weren't available on VHS and rarely (if ever) shown in theaters. I always felt literature and cinema had a relationship, and I wanted to explore that within a literary arts organization. I was very much inspired by the Cinémathèque Française in Paris, mostly due to its romantic image of showing obscure films to an audience. Very much part of the show-and-tell aspect of my personality. Also, I was a fan of the reading series put together by Dennis Cooper, and later Benjamin Weissman. Eventually, without ever officially leaving Book Soup, I became the director and head curator at Beyond Baroque. It was a full-time job, and I served in that role from 1993 to 1996. It was a fascinating job, but extremely difficult due to the politics of running an arts nonprofit at the time.

After I came back from Europe with Kimley, I was approached by Gary Calamar, who is now a DJ at KCRW, to do a cable access talk show. Cable companies by law had to have an open station for the local community, in exchange for the ability to broadcast 99 channels (and nothing worth watching) in that city. The only thing you needed to do was purchase the master 3/4" videotape for the recording, and the cable company would supply the tech crew, including two camera set-ups. I agreed to do this primarily out of friendship and the need to work on a project with a group of people. Once we decided to do the show, I came up with the concept of it being *Tea with Tosh*. I projected myself as a combination of Dick Cavett and William F. Buckley Jr., a conservative author and publisher who had a weekly show on PBS, *Firing Line* (1966–99), where he interviewed interesting people. I detested his politics, but he would have Black Panthers, beats, and alternative types on his show, mostly to put them down, but it was always a good discussion. Cavett represented the East Coast Manhattanite with connections to the theater as well as film and comedy. I enjoyed him because he always came off a bit square, especially when he interviewed a rock 'n' roll person, but still, he had great charm. I also had in mind Marcello Mastroianni, if he were an interviewer for Italian TV. In my head, the persona I used while taping shows was a combination of all three, but while I clearly didn't have the talent to channel them, I was pretty good at being "Tosh." In all honesty, I'm not that great of a conversationalist or interviewer, but something about my performance turned out a few good episodes.

The premise of the show was an afternoon chat show for, I imagined, housewives on a coffee/tea break and the unemployed.

In keeping with the Italian aesthetic, I had a painting of the Mona Lisa behind me, and my friend Deborah Hunter made all the furniture for the show, which consisted of three chairs, one table, and me, wearing a suit for all 20 episodes. The exciting aspect of the show was that I prepared as much as possible by researching the artists who came on the show. Sometimes I just had a day or less to think up questions. When you do public access, you only have an hour, a half-hour to get the set-up and try out the camera angles, and then you're on for a half-hour. There's no looking back, only focusing on the present, and worrying about the future after the taping. The most worrying part was getting the guest to commit to coming on the show and hoping that they actually showed up. But all of them did. Our guests were fantastic: Bruce Conner, George Herms, Phranc, Philip Glass, Russ Tamblyn, The Dark Bob, Amy Gerstler, Peter Case, Benjamin Weissman, and others. The focus was always on the arts, and the basis of the show was my interest in show-and-tell. I wanted to expose artists I was interested in but placed in a chat show format. Also since I was (and still am) shy, it was a good excuse to ask my friends and soon-to-be friends why and how they do their art.

I met my wife Lun*na Menoh in 1987, at her exhibition at Cafe Onyx, right next door to the Vista Movie Theater, where Sunset meets Hollywood Blvd. Oddly enough, it was an ex-girlfriend who brought me to the cafe, where Lun*na had her artwork up on the walls. I was intrigued because the work was original; it was like walking into another world. She and her partner-in-crime Rosa worked as a team at the time. Lun*na made the art and costumes, and Rosa was the performance artist. They came from Japan, and this was their first time in L.A. Rosa played a song on the accordion while wearing Lun*na's costume. Lun*na's work at the time looked European, and was, in fact, inspired by 18th-century Italian and French theatrical costume. Her art wasn't just decorative but had powerful contemporary values with respect to feminism and art for art's sake, which I found exceedingly pleasing.

That night I asked her to be on *Tea with Tosh*. Lun*na would end up being the 20th and the last guest of the show. After a year I wanted to do something different. When I asked her to appear on the show, she thought I was a big TV producer. The disappointment must have been crushing. But she did the show, and a week later, I asked her to marry me. As I mentioned, I have no problem making serious decisions in my life. She thought I was joking. Lun*na went back to Japan, and once she was there, I wrote to her every day. After getting letter after letter from me, she agreed to become my wife.

A series of incidents happened after she returned from Japan to move in with me. A block away from our apartment she got mugged; they took her purse, which had a significant amount of cash, her passport, and other papers for travel. When we called the police to report the mugging, she was obviously upset. I remember the cops asking me about my relationship with her, and I told them we were planning to get married shortly. When they asked me her name, I said Lun*na Menoh. She then started crying and told them her name was Atsuko Shimizu. I'd only known her by her professional name. The cops looked at me in a very suspicious manner.

We got married at my family home in Topanga. Lun*na's family from Japan was there, and it was their first time in Los Angeles. The feeling at the wedding was one of great happiness. The original plan was to have the ceremony outside in the yard because my mom had a beautiful garden, but it rained that day like the gods were furious. Our many guests had to pile into the house, which is tiny, along with the live string quartet we'd hired. The wedding was carefully planned out, yet it became chaos. Wet and very much in love, I felt it was the happiest day in my life. I've never asked Lun*na if she felt that way, just in case she may have a different opinion. For our honeymoon, we went to visit her family in Japan, which was an incredibly eye-opening experience. After we returned from Tokyo, we got word that Lun*na's mom was ill with cancer. Lun*na had to go back to Japan to take care of her mom, causing problems with her visa, since she had lost all her paperwork at the time. Once there, she found it would take up to a year to clear up her visa issue, even though she was married to an American, so at that point, I left the apartment to a friend of ours and went to live in Japan with my wife.

As Lun*na took care of her mom in the small port town of Moji-Ko (on the island of Kyushu), I had nothing better to do except work on a book of poems, *The Plum in Mr. Blum's Pudding* (1990). Lun*na's father got me an English-made typewriter and I pretty much wrote the book in Moji-Ko. Working on the poetry while living in Japan that year was an interesting experience because I had no access to English. It was before the Internet, and the only English newspaper I could get in Kyushu was the *Japan Times*, two days after it was printed. It was the tail end of the Reagan years; I remember the Berlin Wall came down, but I didn't know about it until two days later. Everything in the news was two days later. So I was entirely focused on my poems for the book. Wanting to have some independence and money there, I eventually found work teaching English to various students, from children and teenagers to housewives and professors. I was the only native English speaker in the town, so there was a demand for my talents, which I'd obviously acquired merely from birth.

In the early '90s, after our return from Japan, my mom sold the Topanga house. She left Topanga because it's hard to live in a canyon area by yourself, due to the natural disasters that happen, and Topanga was also a very reclusive place to live. She moved into a small apartment by our home in Silver Lake; there was a guesthouse and she moved in. Lun*na and I eventually bought a home in Silver Lake, and Shirley moved out to another apartment in the area. I was working at Book Soup full-time after leaving Beyond Baroque, but I also started a press. Again, international traveling inspired a new adventure in my life. When I was in Japan with my wife, she told me about Boris Vian. The more she talked about Vian, the more I felt like I was Vian. I was writing short stories, which she told me reminded her of Vian's work. I never read Vian till I got back to Los Angeles, when I went to the library and read his novel *I Spit on Your Graves* (1946). I also tracked down the two translations of *L'Écume des jours* (1947) (UK title: *Froth on the Daydream*; U.S. title: *Mood Indigo*). These two books were going to be the foundation of my press. *I Spit on Your Graves* is Vian as a noir writer (pretending to be a Black American, no less, named Vernon Sullivan) while the other is true to the serious side of his literature.

I decided to name the press TamTam Books, after *Princess Tam Tam* (1935), a film starring Josephine Baker, a black American dancer who became an icon in France. For me, she was the perfect symbol of what the press was doing with respect to me being an American and going ga-ga over French literature. Also, Vian was a massive fan of American jazz and culture; that bridge between the pop culture of Paris and America had a strong pull for me. In the back of my mind, as I was working on the Vian titles, I thought about my dad and his *Semina* circle of friends. Vian was the focal point in Saint Germain des Prés, and I feel that my father was the same in Los Angeles. As far as I know, Wallace wasn't aware of Vian's life or work, but I still imagine them together in some fashion. I did 12 books for my press, mostly French writers like Vian, Serge Gainsbourg, Guy Debord, and Jacques Mesrine. On top of that I published an art book by my wife, as well as *In the Words of Sparks . . . Selected Lyrics* (2013) by Sparks (Ron Mael & Russell Mael) with an introduction by Morrissey. After that, I decided to focus on my writing. I wrote *Sparks-Tastic:*

21 Nights with Sparks in London (2013), documenting my 2008 trip to London to see Sparks perform all 21 of their albums, and I reissued my first book of poetry, *The Plum in Mr. Blum's Pudding* (Penny-Ante Press, 2014). For the last ten years, I've been working on the book you've just finished reading.

When someone close to you dies, you find the social world will change. It's like being in a landscape of sand; once the wind comes up, it transforms the land into another shape. That's what death is like for the living; the entire culture around you changes into something different. Friends who were once close to you and part of the family disappear quickly, and a lot of people want or demand a particular aspect of the individual who died, for his memory, or because they know in their hearts "he" would want it that way. My job as the son of Wallace Berman was to say "no" a lot, which tends to piss people off. But in a nutshell, my life, at present, is excellent. At age 63, yet still feeling like the child in this book, I've witnessed so many changes in the world that are both awesome and horrible at the same time. I honestly believe that it is a blessing to be a writer or artist in our age now. It's an honor to be in the presence of those we love, and equally fascinating to be with those we despise as well.

Los Angeles, Tokyo, New York,
Detroit, Paris, & of course,
Moji-Ku, Japan

Acknowledgments

Tosh would not exist if not for my parents Wallace Berman and Shirley Berman. Also a sincere thank you to those who looked at my manuscript over the years: Bethany Handler, Fawn Hall, Josephine Tran, Elizabeth Yoo, Manuel Chavarria, and Cary Loren, who put the thought in my head to write this book.

Also a special thank-you to the Kohn Gallery, specifically Michael Kohn, Karl Puchlik, Courtney Brown, Karys Judd, Samantha Glaser-Weiss, Matt Groce, and Joshua Friedman.

A special thank-you with respect to the Japanese side of the world: The Shimada and Shimizu family. I wrote bits and pieces of the book in Japan while staying with my Japanese side of the family. Thank you for putting up with me.

Also, I have to note that Sandra Starr, Kristine McKenna, Claudia Bohn-Spector/Sam Mellon, and Sophie Dannenmuller have done a series of interviews with me and my mom Shirley over the years. I realize through their remarkable work that I have to treat my memory of my parents and time very carefully and honor that heritage. There is no guidebook to learn these things, so with my chin up and pen on paper/computer screen, I kept working.

Also, my partners-in-crime at City Lights: My editor Garrett Caples, Stacey Lewis, and Elaine Katzenberger—a very strong thank-you!

The book is dedicated to Shirley Berman, Lun*na Menoh, and Donald Morand. And with great affection for his memory, my dad Wallace.

—Tosh

Photo Credits